MUSIC OF HATE
MUSIC FOR HEALING

MUSIC
of Hate

MUSIC
for Healing

TED FICKEN, PhD

LUMINARE PRESS
WWW.LUMINAREPRESS.COM

This book is dedicated to

*My wife, Candi, for her ongoing support,
patience, and love.*

*My parents, Jim and Cassy, for their inspiration,
role modeling, and tolerance.*

*My third-grade church choir director, Robert Quade,
who gave me my first exposure to the
healing world of music.*

All victims of hatred and hate music.

CONTENTS

PREFACE

During my college years, the main music therapy textbook was titled *Music in Therapy* (The Macmillan Company, 1968), edited by E. Thayer Gaston, PhD, a psychologist and musician. In an opening chapter of the book, Dr. Gaston presented his theories and philosophy, to justify the use of music in therapeutic settings. I remember the passage:

> "Music is derived from the tender emotions. The vast majority of all music is concerned with the positive relationships that draw man closer to his fellow men—love, loyalty, patriotism, and religion, to name a few."

In stark contrast, in 2014 I read an article titled, "Music, Money, and Hate," written by Keegan Hankes and published in the *Intelligence Report* of the Southern Poverty Law Center (SPLC). It described the uses of music to spread hate. The concept of hate music was new to me. Hatred is not a tender emotion. What would Dr. Gaston think? I had either not been paying attention, or hate music was a new phenomenon. Through the research for this book, I discovered the former was true, and the latter was false.

As a young boy in the 1950s, I joined the boys' choir at the Menlo Park Presbyterian Church in California where Robert Quade served as our director. During the Christmas season, he took us caroling at local nursing homes. That was where and when I first observed the power of music to influence behavior, improve the quality of people's lives, and help heal.

Since those early experiences, I continued to sing in choirs at my church, grade school, junior high school, high school, and two colleges. I played for a short time in a bluegrass band and sang in a quartet that performed the national anthem at the local minor-league baseball stadium. Recently, I joined a community chorus. I love music. All kinds of music, but some more than others. I gained musical knowledge and some skills. I may not be the most talented musician around, but I learned how to use music to help others.

After completing a bachelor's degree in music education and music therapy from the University of Kansas (KU) in 1974, I became a professional, credentialed Registered Music Therapist (RMT). In 1977, I completed a master's degree in music education and music therapy, also at KU. Eventually, I became a Music Therapist—Board Certified (MT-BC) and licensed in Oregon. My studies included such courses as Psychology of Music, Influences of Music on Behavior, Music in Therapy, Music in Special Education, and others. Those courses trained me to view music as a potent tool, for both good and bad.

My forty-five-year music therapy career, including volunteer work and an internship, took me to ten healthcare facilities in five states. I have worked with children, adolescents, adults, and seniors, almost exclusively in behavioral health and substance-abuse settings. Some of my clients were in institutions due to mental illness and criminal activities. Some of them preferred hate music.

I've had a simultaneous career in the field of health-care quality improvement. In 1988, I became a Certified Professional in Healthcare Quality (CPHQ), which I have maintained to this day. In 2003, I completed a PhD in Public Health, with a major in healthcare administration, at Oregon State University. I've remained involved in the profession of music therapy but, at the same time, worked to improve the quality of overall healthcare services at the facilities where I was employed. Where my music therapy background taught me how music could impact a person's life, my experience in healthcare quality improvement taught me that there are always opportunities to identify root causes of problems and to take actions leading to improvements.

Based on my education, training, and experience, I decided to look at hate music from three angles: as a public health problem, as a situation that could be improved, and through the lens of a professional music therapist.

I decided to begin investigating hate music but also saw how that industry intersected with, affected, related to, or contrasted with stories of music therapists. My journey taught me how hate music attacks various demographic groups: Jews, blacks, gays, disabled, women, immigrants, whites, police, and others. My thinking was that stories of music therapists from those same groups could present interesting juxtapositions when presented alongside stories of the individuals and organizations involved with hate music.

This book shares my investigation, some of the stories I found, lessons learned, and recommendations.

Ted Ficken, PhD
Certified Professional in Healthcare Quality (CPHQ)
Music Therapist—Board Certified / Licensed
(MT-BC/L)
March 2020

ACKNOWLEDGEMENTS

T his book would not have been possible without the input, feedback, and support of numerous individuals. I want to recognize and thank the following people for their contributions and help:

My own family members and friends offered encouragement and understanding as I researched and worked on this book. My wife, Candi, offered helpful editing comments and understood my many hours of sitting at the computer writing. My children and their spouses offered suggestions for the songs and lyrics that I reviewed. My niece-in-law, Becky Blanchard, told me about soccer chants, and her husband, Dan Tankersley, helped with technical support.

I want to thank the many archivists who shared documents and information with me:

Kristina Wilson at the Curtis Institute; Peter Schmid at the Sisters of Providence Health System; Rachel Fritz at the Wisconsin Conservatory of Music; Christiana Dobrzynski at Bryn Mawr College; Jenny Swadosh at Mannes School; Anna Robinson-Sweet at The New School; Richard Schwegel at Roosevelt University; Margaret Ruddy at Cardinal Stritch University; Fr. Schneibel at the University of Portland; Brett Derbes at the Texas State Historical Association; Terry Baxter at the Multnomah County Historical Society

Archives; Trina Vaux and Michael Joy at Shipley School; Oxana Harlamova and Lisa Lopez-Carickhoff at Baldwin School; Daniel P. Scholzen at Mount Mary University; Caitlyn Reilley and Helena Egbert at Oregon State University; Sally Oh at the Ford Foundation; Renee Pappous at the Rockefeller Archives Center; Meredith Morgan Eliaseen at San Francisco State University; and Maurice Klapwald at New York Public Library. It was always exciting to receive new historical information and documents from all of them.

I appreciate others who helped me with my research or encouraged me: Ann C. Kitchel, JD, at the Willamette University Law Library for helping me find articles about music and the First Amendment; Dr. Randy Blazak at the University of Oregon and the Oregon Coalition Against Hate Crimes for his sharing and emails; Jessica Steinhebel, who told me about Randy Blazak; Allen Henderson at the National Association of Teachers of Singing for his verification of information about Felice Wolmut; Dan Knudsen and Paul Martin for sharing information about recordings of "bigot songs"; and Mary and Richard Sauter, former students of Felice Wolmut, who shared stories of her with me. Daniel Kohler at George Washington University provided some input about his work regarding terrorist groups in Minnesota, and Lorens Helmchen, at George Washington University, helped with translating some German documents. Michael Miller at operettaaar@aol.com provided a copy of Felice Wolmut's favorite song. Angela Vrbanac-Libby and Bonnie Banks provided exciting leads that led to a goldmine of documents and contributed to the story of Vally Weigl. Mark Hochhauser, Dean and Cathy Rebuffoni, and Kate Cannon provided information about hate music in Minneapolis. Petra Kern, past president of the World

Federation of Music Therapists and music therapy faculty at the University of Louisville told me about the racist history of some national anthems. Mathew at Tunecore shared documents about standards of music streaming services, and Michael Viega at State University of New York/New Paltz shared thoughts with me about rap and hip-hop music.

For the stories about Felice Wolmut and Vally Weigl, I am indebted to their grandsons and their partners: Karl Weigl and Julie Brand at the Karl Weigl Foundation in San Rafael, California; and Jonathan Wolmut and Claudia Toth, in Portland, Oregon. They were willing to share documents and photographs with me and tell me stories about their grandparents.

I received distant support and sharing from Vienna for the stories about Felice and Vally. Thanks to Dr. Primavera Gruber; Philipp Wagner at the Theatre an der Wien; Michele Calella, at the Department of Musicology, University of Vienna; Dr. Heinz Lunzer at the International Erich Fried Society; and Dr. Michael Ritter, Praesens Verlag.

I recognize and thank the music therapists who allowed me to interview them and tell their stories: Lisa Jackert, Tina Haynes, Sandi Holten, Alice Parente, Joe Parente, Rick Soshensky, Maegan Morrow, Deforia Lane, Jodi Winn-Walker, Russell Hilliard, Jim Borling, Ron Borczon, Barbara Dunn, Olga Samsonova-Jellison, Celeste Keith, and Spencer Hardy. It was a joy to learn more about their journeys.

There were people at professional organizations who responded to my many requests:

Bill Davis at the American Music Therapy Association (AMTA) archives at Colorado State University; Jane Creagan at AMTA, who verified dates and credentials, as well as membership numbers; and Joy Schneck at the Certification

Board for Music Therapists, who provided important numbers about board certified music therapists. Alan Solomon, former AMTA historian, emailed me about Vally Weigl. Jennifer Geiger, past president of AMTA, provided her notes about Deforia Lane's Lifetime Achievement Award.

I am deeply indebted and thankful to The Southern Poverty Law Center and the Anti-Defamation League for their efforts to track and write about hate groups and hate music. Their work inspired me and taught me. I am also thankful to the many other reporters and authors from both sides (see my reference list), whose publications taught me more and more about both music therapy and hate music. They have supplied me with many different perspectives.

The work at the organization Life After Hate is important and inspiring. Thanks especially to Tony McAleer and the books by Christian Picciolini, TJ Leyden (with M. Bridget Cook), Arno Michaelis, and Frank Meeink (as told to Jody M. Roy, PhD). Their books are listed in my references.

The support from Luminare Press was fantastic. I am especially grateful for the thorough editing feedback from Catherine Rourke.

Chapter 1

INTRODUCTION

———————

I n his song "Gotta Serve Somebody" (Special Rider
Music, ASCAP, 1979), Bob Dylan sings about how we
all have choices to make in life. What path will we go
down? What will our philosophy be? Will we choose to be
good or bad, righteous or evil, hateful or loving?

Having a swastika tattoo removed from your neck and
a Nazi Iron Cross lasered from your back can be painful,
but swearing off your preferred hate music may be difficult
and hurt in other ways.

Hate in the United States was on the rise. Between 1999 and
2018, the number of hate groups tracked by the Southern Poverty Law Center (SPLC) grew from 457 to 1,020—an increase
of 123 percent. Black nationalist hate groups accounted for
a quarter of the racist hate groups in 2018 but were greatly
outnumbered by over seven hundred white nationalist groups.
Reports indicate that hatred has been directed at blacks, whites,
Muslims, Jews, immigrants, women, the LGBTQ+ community,
anti-fascists, the government, the police, the disabled, and
other demographic groups. According to the *Washington Post*
(May 11, 2018), hate crimes increased for the four years from
2014 to 2018. In the ten largest cities in the US, hate crimes
increased by 12 percent in 2018, a ten-year high.

After a four-year growth in the number of hate groups identified by the SPLC, 2019 saw a reduction from a high of 1020 down to 940. Hate Music Groups fell from 19 in 2017 to 15 in early 2020, but were still found from coast-to-coast.

These are just some of the known statistics. More than ninety US cities with populations over one hundred thousand failed to report hate crimes to the FBI. Of the sixteen thousand-plus law enforcement agencies that did report, 67 percent did not document any hate crimes. It appears that some victims of hate crimes do not file reports or press charges, possibly due to fear of reprisal or other negative consequences.

Within some limits, expressing hate is not illegal. There are laws, both federal and local, that place some conditions on freedom of speech guaranteed by the First Amendment. In general, expressing hatred in the United States is legal. However, committing a hate crime is not. A hate crime is like any other crime, except it adds the element of bias—usually based on race, religion, disability, sexual orientation, ethnicity, gender, or gender identity. Having a crime labeled as a hate crime could lead to a stiffer penalty for the perpetrator. Judges and juries must determine if they think bias played a role in the commission of the crime.

Some hate crimes—such as vandalism, graffiti, or other property-related crimes—do not include violent physical attacks on persons or groups. Data indicate those types of hate crimes are decreasing, while violent attacks against individuals are increasing. In a story published in the *New York Times* (November 12, 2019), Adeel Hassan reported that in 2018 aggravated assaults were up 4 percent, simple assaults increased by 15 percent, and cases of intimidation grew by 13 percent over the previous year. According to the

FBI's hate crime statistics, from 2017 to 2018, hate crimes against Jewish citizens rose by 37 percent and hate crimes against Latinos increased from 430 incidents to 485.

Also, despite the FBI statistics indicating that hate crimes against Muslims and Arab Americans decreased in those same years, the Council on American-Islamic Relations data showed that 1,554 hate crimes were committed against Muslims in 2018. Now, in 2020, with the worldwide COVID-19 public health crisis, Asian Americans are experiencing an increase in verbal and physical attacks. Many of these violent hate crimes are committed by white nationalists or other scared individuals. In September 2019, the US Department of Homeland Security added white supremacist violence to its list of terrorist threats. I suspect that white power music was a contributing factor, even a root cause, probably more so than most people think.

As with all societal and political trends, there have been backlashes and countermeasures against hate. On March 7, 2019, the US House of Representatives passed an anti-hate measure. The resolution included language that encouraged "all public officials to confront the reality of anti-Semitism, Islamophobia, racism, and other forms of bigotry, as well as historical struggles against them, to ensure that the United States will live up to the transcendent principles of tolerance, religious freedom, and special protection as embodied in the Declaration of Independence and the 1st and 14th Amendments to the Constitution."

The measure added the following "traditionally persecuted peoples" to its list of those previously protected: African Americans, Native Americans, other people of color, Jews, Muslims, Hindus, Sikhs, immigrants, Latinos, Asian Americans, Pacific Islanders, the LGBTQ+ community, and "others." Individuals with disabilities and women were not directly named on the list, constituting glaring omissions. Ironically, they may be viewed as "others."

The measure was not unanimous. It passed with a vote of 407 in favor, and twenty-three opposed. Some of the opposition was not pro-hate but voted against the measure because of disagreement with some of the measure's final wording or, in some cases, for self-serving political reasons—to prevent offending their bases, which could negatively affect their chances of reelection.

Why are we becoming more hateful?

Fueled by the internet and social media, flyer distribution, conspiracy theories, attacks on the free press, misinformation campaigns, economic pressures, criminal activities, and access to upper levels of the government, hate and violence have become normalized in parts of our society. It is a public health issue, in that it threatens the peace and health of individuals and communities.

Following the occurrence of mass shootings in our environment, we often hear opinions expressed about root causes for the growth in violence. Some say it is a mental health issue; others, that it is a gun control issue. Blame is placed on violent media, including movies, TV shows, and video games. A variety of immigrant groups are identified as root causes. Some politicians have been mentioned as contributors—even President Trump. Less attention has been given to the widespread and growing effects of hate music.

As a music therapist trained to use music as a healing tool, I wanted to find out how music was contributing to the spread of hate. I also wanted to see how music therapy could provide a counterpoint, including helping to heal. I was interested in interactions, intersections, contrasts, relationships between the two fields, effects on each other, and juxtapositions. I found many.

I could have used examples from almost any music-related profession. Or from any profession, period. I chose music therapy because of my background and experience in that field.

Most people prefer a certain type of music, although there are some who claim they either love all music or, incredibly, hate all music. Many would agree that music can have effects on mental, emotional, physical, spiritual, social, cultural, and political domains. Music can cheer us up, scare us, or bring us to tears. It evokes emotions. Research shows that when we are listening to music or making music, more areas of the brain are activated than almost any other behavior.

But, can music be harmful? I began investigating how some music might have negative consequences—both intended and unintended—including its use to spread hate.

To start my research of hate music, I had to define it. Here are some definitions I found in various sources:

- "Music that expresses destructive desires against a demographic." (*Glosbe English-English Dictionary*)

- "Music intended to hurt and intimidate someone because of his or her race, ethnicity, national origin, religion, sexual orientation, or disability. Similar to *hate speech*." (*freemuse.org*)

- "Hateful lyrics combined with angry sounds and the violent acts that often accompany them express deep aversions to racial and other differences." (*Trendy Fascism: White Power Music and the Future of Democracy,* by Nancy S. Love, SUNY Press, 2016)

• Radical music, which includes hate music, was defined as "the dogmatic and purposeful expression of racist, superior, intolerant, absolute, hateful or illegal views and actions in violent or nonviolent forms." (*Radicalism & Music,* by Jonathan Pieslak, Wesleyan University Press, 2015)

The SPLC, which has tracked hate groups, defines them this way:

"All hate groups have beliefs or practices that attack or malign an entire class of people, typically for their immutable characteristics. The SPLC list was compiled using hate group publications and websites, citizen and law enforcement reports, field sources and news reports. Hate group activities can include criminal acts, marches, rallies, speeches, meetings, leafleting, or publishing."

Music can be a hate group activity. As I listened to music that had been labeled hate music, I found it hard to have a singular, limiting definition. Instead, I noticed some reoccurring characteristics. These included:

• A direct and forceful expression of absolute hate, stated clearly

- The encouragement of violence against a specific population or demographic (or individual)

- Use of "taboo" slang (generally deemed unacceptable by parts of society), profanity, or derogatory names in describing another group

- The perpetuation of negative or false stereotypes, direct or subliminal

- Lack of support for following the law, or expression of support for criminal behavior

- Antisocial leanings—lack of empathy for others or remorse for behaviors

I intend to match stories from the hate music industry with stories about music therapists, so I also needed to define music therapy for readers. The AMTA website offers this:

"Music Therapy is the clinical and evidence-based use of music interventions to accomplish individualized goals within a therapeutic relationship by a credentialed professional who has completed an approved music therapy program.

Music Therapy is an established health profession in which music is used within a therapeutic relationship to address physical, emotional, cognitive, and social needs of individuals. After assessing the strengths and needs of each client, the qualified music therapist provides the indicated treatment including creating, singing, moving to, and/

or listening to music. Through musical involvement in the therapeutic context, clients' abilities are strengthened and transferred to other areas of their lives. Music therapy also provides avenues for communication that can be helpful to those who find it difficult to express themselves in words. Research in music therapy supports its effectiveness in many areas such as overall physical rehabilitation and facilitating movement, increasing people's motivation to become engaged in their treatment, providing emotional support for clients and their families, and providing an outlet for expression of feelings (https://www.musictherapy.org)."

When asked, "What is music therapy?" I sometimes use this quick "elevator speech" response. "Music education uses music to reach musical goals. Music therapy uses music to reach nonmusical goals." I add, "Music therapy is provided by a trained, credentialed, professional music therapist." I hope that, by sharing stories about music therapists, readers will gain a deeper understanding about the discipline.

The bulk of this book is a series of stories. I will tell you stories about some of the songs, musicians, record companies, distributors, etc. that are examples from the hate music industry. The label "hate music" is not mine, but I will use it throughout the book. I found it being used in a variety of publications and resources. Hate music is found in almost all genres of music, including jazz, country, rap and hip-hop, blues, folk, rock 'n' roll, and others. Some of the music has taken on new labels, such as white nationalist, Oi!, segregationist, neo-Nazi skinhead, white supremacist, black nationalist, jihadist rap, hate core, pornogrind, murder music, and fashwave. My goal is to understand why this music has been labeled as hateful, and what functions it might have for individuals, our society, and around the world.

The stories in this book will not be all-inclusive. Given the current state of the internet and digital music, it is impossible to identify all hate music groups. They are sometimes hidden in secure websites, invitation-only concert promotions, or private blogs and forums. Some of the information about them can be secretive. New hate music bands pop up every day. Most of the hate music stories that I will tell will feature prominent individuals who have been mentioned in diverse media sources.

While readers may be familiar with some of the people involved in hate music, I hope that I can share new information to increase knowledge of the industry and some of its backstories. I started my research on hate music by investigating some of the groups that the SPLC included on its list of hate music groups in the United States. A contact at SPLC noted that their list consists primarily of record companies and distributors of the music, not individual musicians or bands. Given that, I expanded my storytelling to include some artists and performers who were not found on the SPLC list.

In addition to stories from the hate music industry, I will also share stories about some of my favorite music therapists. I have selected music therapists (MTs) who trained at different schools, interned at different clinical sites, work with different client populations, and use music in different ways. They represent therapists from different stages of their careers. I have chosen music therapists who have lived and worked in different parts of the United States. To inject a sense of history, some of my examples are living, and others are no longer with us. Several of the stories will be what I call "counter-stories," or "contrast stories," to the hate music stories. Others will illustrate how both hate music and music therapy coexist in certain geographic locations. Racist music stories will be paired with examples of music therapists from those very races or ethnic groups. "Anti-any-group" music will be presented side-by-side with the story of a music therapist from that group. Some of the stories will even share ways that hate music can be utilized in treatment.

There is another reason for inclusion of the music therapists in this book. The therapists I have selected include Christians, Jews, Buddhists, agnostics, immigrants, women, a gay man, an African American, an immigrant, and a transgender individual—all persons whose lives, or their music therapy practices, have given them insights into hatred. They have chosen to use music to heal, sometimes despite their own human flaws, problems, and challenges. I know quite a bit about the field of music therapy, but I did not know the rich and inspiring details of some of my music therapy colleagues' life stories. I also discovered relevant stories of some music therapy pioneers who experienced situations of extreme hatred and loss, later to become music therapists.

I am a white, older, heterosexual male, born and raised on the West Coast, so I wanted to challenge my own biases. I reached out to music therapists who didn't fit my profile, to find out how hate music may have personally affected them, their families, their ancestors, or others. At the beginning of my investigation, I didn't know what I didn't know. I was ready to be schooled.

To avoid "scope creep," this book is selective in what it covers. It is not intended as an exhaustive, academic dissertation. Think of it more like an introductory course—Hate

Music and Music Therapy 101. I intend to share my own, preliminary exploration. By putting the stories from both fields side-by-side, I hope that readers will learn more about both approaches, notice contrasts and similarities, and gain understanding. I know I did.

There is a large, growing body of literature about the field of music therapy, yet details of its supportive research and practices can remain unknown to the general public. Unless individuals know a music therapist, have read about music therapy, have seen news stories about music therapists, have watched YouTube videos featuring music therapy professionals, or have experienced music in a therapeutic setting, their understanding of the field is probably limited. Assumptions are made, opinions formed.

Hearing the stories of music therapists will help to better inform those perceptions. The stories of music therapists will share some of their earliest experiences with music, how they heard about music therapy, where they went to school, additional training they received, where they found employment, and how they provide music therapy services to a variety of populations and clients. Again, it is impossible to tell stories about all music therapists. There are too many. I have been selective.

As I have worked on this book and shared portions of it with others, I sometimes received the questions "What's the point?" and "Aren't the contrasts obvious?" As you read each pair of stories, my hope is that you and I will share many "I didn't know that!" moments. The point of individual stories might seem obvious, or it might be subtle. Taken as a whole, the combination of stories will start to familiarize the general public (as it did me!) with more information about both fields—hate music and music therapy.

There are already books—very good ones—about both hate music and music therapy. I am not aware of another book that presents aspects of the two fields side-by-side. As I started to work on this investigation, I chose to place the stories next to each other. By choosing this format, readers will have something to compare and contrast.

I sent an email to the Rose City Antifa group in Portland, Oregon (an anti-fascist organization, with chapters in many parts of the United States and world, which challenges racist organizations, sometimes with violence). I asked if they could identify any hate musicians whom I could interview for this book.

They responded, "We are not interested in giving a platform to white supremacist musicians, and don't feel that we can give you any assistance in doing this. We advise you to rethink your book structure, as it sounds like you are giving a great deal of space to neo-Nazis to explain and justify their white supremacy."

I was surprised that they limited their objections to "white supremacist musicians," because hate music is generated by many other groups. I assured them that I was not seeking to justify the viewpoints of others, but to understand how they came to those viewpoints. I am sure there are parts of this book where my biases will show, but I will try to balance that by considering the perspectives of others.

Readers are warned about some of the language used in the songs referenced in this book. There are derogatory words, crude descriptors, profanity, and calls to violence in some of the examples. Those words are not mine. They are the lyrics written by songwriters, some well-known and some "under the radar" of the general public. I aim to share real, authentic examples, but I realize that some of the lyrics are offensive. I believe that the selections illustrate why some have labeled these songs as hate music.

We need to become better informed, in many ways. The two fields in this book—hate music and music therapy—are constantly evolving. As my list of references at the end of the book documents, I read a substantial amount of information to prepare for this book. I relied on newspaper stories, websites, books, YouTube videos, CDs, interviews, and archives. I did not have access to active hate musicians, but I read many books by recovering haters, and read previous interviews. I continuously updated the book as new events occurred, but the growing incidents of hatred and violence in the daily news forced me to choose an endpoint.

This book provides background information up to early 2020. As we move forward, we must be aware of the past, to avoid repeating our mistakes. I learned from both my music therapy and quality improvement experiences that we can often identify things that require change and implement interventions, but sustaining ongoing progress is always challenging.

Every attempt has been made to present factual information in this book. If there are errors or falsehoods, I am willing to hear about them and make changes to future editions.

My storytelling will be followed by a discussion of what I learned by comparing the two fields. How are hate music and music therapy alike? How are they different? What actions are recommended? Where to, from here? From my music therapy, public health, and quality improvement perspectives, I will offer some suggestions.

I think it is safe to assume that a majority of people think of love as a positive thing and hate as a negative thing. They are both human emotions we have all experienced. I intend to try to understand why some musicians have chosen the expression of hate over the expression of love. I might disagree with some of their lyrics, or not prefer the style of some of their music, but can I gain an understanding of their situation, beliefs, influences, and lives?

Are they horrible, hate-filled monsters? Are there ways to influence their thinking and behavior? Why have they chosen to write, perform, and sell music that is so discriminatory, violent, angry, and frowned upon by others? Is there a place for forgiveness, grace, understanding, compassion, and/or change?

This book is pro-love. My training as a therapist taught me that we all have problem behaviors, which are just a part of who we are. Those behaviors are not our whole selves. People can change. Addicts and alcoholics can recover from their issues and find sobriety. Haters and hate musicians can learn to love others and recover from their hateful pasts.

In today's polarized political climate, I am sure that others have experienced, as I have, the urge to avoid certain discussion topics with family members, friends, and neighbors. When going to visit relatives, we might think or say, "Remember, NO talking about religion, politics, scandals, or other subjects." We are afraid that there will be arguments, fights, disagreements, and damaged relationships. That fear is well-founded. But, I believe that we should talk about these forbidden topics—respectfully.

We need to understand each other. We need to challenge our biases. We need to find areas of agreement, along with disagreements. We need to find the good in each other. We need to discover each other's music. Like good music, we need to accept "dis-chords" and dissonance and seek harmony and acceptable resolutions.

Chapter 2

JEW SLAUGHTER/ INTIMIDATION ONE

FELICE WOLMUT

I was reminded of the Beatles song "We Can Work It Out" by Paul McCartney and John Lennon (BMI, 1965). The song, attributed to a couple's argument, makes the point that people can be wrong when presenting their side of an issue, even when they are sure that they are correct. A friend puts it this way, "I would agree with you, but then we would both be wrong." Some former hate musicians have confessed that their previous hateful beliefs were erroneous.

I started my exploration of hate music close to home, in Portland. I knew that Oregon had a long history of hate, but I didn't know if hate music played a role. The state's original constitution banned blacks from residency. In its early pioneer days, some Native Americans were slaughtered. An entire community of Chinese gold miners, employed by a San Francisco company, was wiped out in eastern Oregon in 1887. In the 1920s, Ku Klux Klan (KKK) members swarmed to the state. Japanese citizens were sent to internment camps in Oregon during World War II. And, like parts of the South, "Whites Only" signs had at one time adorned businesses throughout the state. For some, it had been a fertile garden for planting and growing racist, discriminatory beliefs.

I met a young woman by accident, on a flight to a national music therapy conference in St. Louis. A total stranger, she was assigned the seat next to mine. I asked her if St. Louis was her home, and she said, "No, I'm going to a music therapy conference." We introduced ourselves, and I learned that her name was Jessica Steinhebel. Surprised by the coincidence of sitting next to each other, we chatted about the profession, her current music therapy practicum placement at a facility where I once worked, and eventually, I told her about this book. She understood its premise and told me, "You should talk to Randy Blazak." Jessica explained that she knew him from some work she had done at Portland State University in her role with the Oregon Community Foundation.

When I returned home from the conference, I determined that Blazak had left his tenured sociology professor position at Portland State and was now teaching at the University of Oregon and Portland Community College. I sent him an email about my book and some questions. He responded quickly, showing interest in this book's topic and answering some, but not all, of my questions.

We conducted all of our initial contact through emails. Blazak was willing to share with me, but I did not know anything about his background. I just knew that Jessica thought it would be helpful for me to talk to him. In his first email, Blazak had admitted that at one time he had been a singer in a skinhead band.

I googled him. I learned that he had completed his PhD at Emory University in 1995. He had worked as a sociology professor at the University of Portland from 1995 to 2002 and had received several awards for his work. In 2002, he assumed the role of chair of the Oregon Coalition Against Hate Crimes. His area of research focused on hate, hate crimes, prison gangs, and racial bias. For his research, Blazak had worked with the SPLC and the National Institute of Justice. To continue his research, he founded and served as president of the Jamison Research Institute, an organization devoted to studying issues of hate and civil discourse. Blazak was no novice to studying hate and, incidentally, hate music.

He offered to share more information or possibly get together. In time, we agreed to meet in the Alberta Street neighborhood in Northeast Portland, once riddled with gang violence and now transformed into an arts district for youth culture. I had been reading about Soleilmoon Records, a Portland outfit that had been labeled as a hate music group by the SPLC in 2017. I wanted to find out what Blazak knew about that company, which was still in business. I learned that he knew little about Soleilmoon, so he sent me in a different direction.

I explained more about the book, and he offered me new ideas, leads to explore, books to read, possible interview contacts, and his knowledge. Two important ideas stayed with me after our initial meeting. The first was when he said, "Don't hate the haters." That's hard. When we disagree with the beliefs of others, it's difficult to turn off our displeasure with them and try to understand them. That's why Blazak decided to research haters—first, by singing in the aforementioned band. He cautioned me that many hard-core haters had been traumatized at some point in their lives, and that hating them only served to re-traumatize them and reinforce their anger toward others.

In 1999, Blazak had explained some of the findings of his research into young white supremacists in an issue of *The Intelligence Report,* a publication of the SPLC:

> "An important part of this was seeing them as human beings and not as cartoon figures or caricatures of evil. They were concerned kids who cared about social justice in a weird, warped sort of way.
>
> "On a certain level, I admired these kids because they were 17 years old, politically active and knew all about the changing economy.
>
> "They could just as easily have wound up in the Revolutionary Communist Youth Brigade. But it was the right-wing that had access to them. It was the Klan and [California neo-Nazi] John Metzger who gave them the analysis."

Recently, years after it was released, I watched the movie, *American History X.* The movie is fictional but portrays some of what Blazak had written about. As I looked for an understanding of what drives hate music, it was hard for me to look for the positive side of people who are violent, discriminate against others, and consider themselves to be superior. In many of the articles I read about them, there was an overabundance of alcohol use, some drug use, and criminality.

In others, the justification for those behaviors was based on false information, lack of information, or absence of analytical thought. Propaganda was accepted as fact, without study. There were beliefs that random violence against innocent people—due almost entirely to their skin color or perceived race or religion—did, in fact, represent self-defense. These "others" were to blame for a weakened economy, loss of good jobs, destruction of white culture, and the abuse of benefits of American life. They used up resources that should have gone to white people. In the eyes of white supremacists, the Zionist Occupation Government (ZOG), financial systems, and media—all controlled by Jews—allowed this to happen.

The second idea that stuck with me in our discussion about hate music came when Randy said, "It all starts with anti-Semitism."

Jew Slaughter/Intimidation One

BLAZAK RECOMMENDED THAT I LEARN ABOUT TWO Portland-area bands: Jew Slaughter and Intimidation One. I listened to some of the bands' music on YouTube, but then purchased a couple of available recordings to allow for a more thorough review. I don't recommend buying CDs of neo-Nazi skinhead bands, unless for research purposes. After all, you can hear most of them on YouTube. Revenues from record sales are often used to support other haters or hate organizations and to recruit vulnerable youth. Buying the CDs was not difficult, and delivery was fast. After receiving my CDs, I was told by a relative that I would probably be placed on an FBI Watch List for ordering the CDs.

In the liner notes found in the packaging of the Jew Slaughter CD *Alcoholocaust* the group describes itself in unflattering terms, including overindulging in the consumption of alcohol, as devotees of Adolf Hitler, at times incarcerated for criminal activities, and producing music that is hateful excrement.

Jew Slaughter released two albums: *Alcoholocaust* (Holocaust Records, 2002) and *Nazification of America* (Antipathy Records, 2013). I purchased *Alcoholocaust*. Song titles included: "Jew Slaughter," "F**k Morris Dees" (Dees was the director of the SPLC), "Mengele's Rig," "Adolf Hitler," "Again As It Was," "Destroy the Jews," "N****r Loving Slut," "Jew Slaughter Rocks," and others. One song, "S.H.A.R.P. Shooter," includes lyrics about killing a member of an opposing group of skinheads called SHARPs, short for Skinheads Against Racial Prejudice.

Band members of Jew Slaughter were listed as Dean-Oi on bass and vocals, Moosedick providing drums and background vocals, The Kid playing guitar and singing background vocals, and Joey Liver singing lead. But I discovered that there was another notorious member of Jew Slaughter: Wade Michael Page. Better known as the Sikh temple mass-murderer, Page killed six people at a temple in Wisconsin on August 5, 2012. During the incident, after being wounded by responding police, he committed suicide by shooting himself in the head.

Page had been active in white power bands for over ten years, including the bands End Apathy, Youngland, Definite Hate, Max Resist, Aggressive Force, Blue Eyed Devils, and, as mentioned above, Jew Slaughter. Songs by the bands espoused white supremacist ideas and focused racist lyrics on attacking blacks, Jews, and other nonwhites. Reportedly, Page also played or sang for several other bands that performed at a "neo-Nazi friendly" bar in Anaheim, California, called The Shack. Page had sufficient musical skills to be welcomed into many bands.

The second band that Blazak told me to investigate was Intimidation One, whose lineup also once included Page. The band's name refers to a state law, Oregon Revised Statute 166.165, which makes it illegal for one or more individuals to intimidate others because of their skin color, religion, ethnicity, or sexual orientation. Violation of the law is considered a hate crime.

Intimidation One, which included some band members from Jew Slaughter, had a longer list of releases. CD titles included: *Frontline Soldiers* (MC and Frontline Records, 1995), *Call to Warriors* (Imperium Records, 1998), *Falling Heroes* (Imperium Records, 2000), *Brothers Through Blood Vol.2* (Panzerfaust Records, 2003), *Landser* (Panzerfaust Records, 2003), and *10 Years on the Frontline* (Fetch the Rope Records, 2013).

I purchased their *10 Years on the Frontline,* a compilation album, thinking that it would expose me to the most examples of their music. The CD cover art included a photo of a KKK gathering and the fourteen words of the White Supremacy movement: "We must secure the existence of our people and a future for white children," a Confederate flag, the words "fetch the rope" and, in large letters, "White Pride Worldwide." There was nothing subtle about the message and "the cause" of the band. I was struck by the CD cover showing a KKK meeting, similar to the cover of sheet music from "The Bright Fiery Cross," a song about the KKK published in 1913. Some images haven't changed.

Several of Intimidation One's albums have been "indexed" in Germany, which means that the German government's Federal Department for Media Harmful to Young Persons has placed the recordings on an index or list, because the music was found to be objectionable—it was censored. Once "indexed," the recordings could not be advertised, sold, rented, broadcast, or presented to the public, without legal penalties. But in the United States, I was able to locate the albums I purchased and order them without any apparent consequences. Unless law enforcement now had me under surveillance.

The two Portland-based bands have long been associated with Volksfront, a neo-Nazi, white supremacist organization formed by prison inmates in 1994. Volksfront has also hosted an internet radio show and promoted music concerts and festivals. In addition to Jew Slaughter and Intimidation One, other bands that have been connected to Volksfront-related events include Frontline; Red, White, and Black; White Wash; Blood on the Face; Bully Boys; Stormtroop 16; Enforcer; and Criminal Culture. I was discovering that album names, song titles, and band names portrayed some of the common characteristics of hate music: violence, criminality, and discrimination against specific groups.

Over time, Volksfront has formed alliances with other groups including Hammerskin Nation, Christian Guard, Aryan Nations, Women for Aryan Unity, American Front, and other national and international skinhead chapters. It has published and provided literature and propaganda to its followers and to recruit new members. Despite claiming that it is a non-violent organization, several of its members have been found guilty of violent hate crimes. The organization has advocated for a "whites only" community on a property that it has purchased in the Northwest.

Portland has had other hate bands and organizations in its news. Two highly publicized incidents happened in Portland, at least one involving hate music. The first, in 1988, was when three neo-Nazi skinheads attacked a group of Ethiopian students, killing one of them, Mulageta Seraw. One of the attackers was twenty-three-year-old Ken Mieske, who was actively involved in the local death metal music scene. All three of the young men were skinheads, devotees of Tom Metzger and his White Aryan Nation group. Following Seraw's murder, Metzger was sued by Morris Dees and the SPLC for "vicarious liability," due to his sending agents to Portland to distribute literature that encouraged violent and racist ideologies. The trial lasted only six days, and Metzger lost. He was ordered to pay 12.5 million dollars to Seraw's family, effectively bankrupting Metzger's organization.

The second incident happened more recently, in May 2017. Jeremy Christian (the irony of his last name being evident), who appeared to be drunk, began making racist and anti-religious remarks to two black women aboard a MAX train. One of the women was Muslim and wearing a hijab. When three men stepped in to defend the women and attempt to calm Christian, he produced a knife and cut the throats of all three men. Two of the men—Rick John Best and Taliesen Myrddin Nankai-Meche—were killed. The third man, Micah David-Cole Fletcher, sustained non-life-threatening injuries.

Christian was arrested and charged with the crimes. At his trial, he declared, "Death to the enemies of America. You call it terrorism; I call it patriotism. You hear me? Die." An article in *The Oregonian* newspaper reported, "Christian talked about going to black metal shows, as well as being a metal fan in general." The article stated, "While not all black metal is racist, black metal has a porous relationship with a variety of racist movements." On June 24, 2020, Christian was convicted of the two murders, resulting in two consecutive life sentences without the possibility of parole.

On September 11, 2017, a *Washington Post* headline read: "Antifa, far-right protesters clash again in Portland, disrupting peaceful rallies."

Almost a year later, a headline in the *Oregonian* newspaper, on July 1, 2018, read: "Right-wing activist Patriot Prayer, Antifa clash at Portland protests." Permits for the Patriot Prayer rally, which was promoted as a free speech event, were quickly revoked when violence erupted between the two groups. Antifa members reportedly not only attacked the Patriot Prayer group but also clashed with the police. Some law enforcement members were doused by fire extinguishers and struck by thrown objects. Police labeled the situation a "riot" and ordered participants to disperse. Officers sprayed protestors with pepper spray and used "aerial distraction devices" but denied using tear gas. Other groups, including an anti-gay group, also participated.

The conflicts between these groups continued in Portland. *Newsweek* published another story, on October 14, 2018, with the headline: "Antifa and Patriot Prayer Clash with Batons and Pepper spray on the Streets of Portland." Described as "the latest in a series of violent confrontations in recent months between far-right and left-wing groups in cities on the U.S. west coast," the incident reported individuals using hard-knuckled gloves, guns, batons, knives, bear spray, and fists to confront and attack each other.

The police were criticized for not controlling the confrontation between the two groups, which led Portland Mayor Ted Wheeler to put forward an emergency ordinance to allow each group to hold their demonstrations only in designated areas of the city, at a distance from each other. The mayor referred to both sides as "...those who recklessly drain our public safety resources by using our city as a venue for planned street violence." Things haven't changed much in a year. Hate and violence are still around in the Rose City, and hate music and chanting are also present.

Looking beyond Jew Slaughter and Intimidation One, multiple sources confirmed that music played a huge role in the white power, racist movement in the United States. In his book, *Skinhead Confessions: From Hate to Hope* (Cedar Fort Inc., 2008), TJ Leyden, wrote:

> "I continued to use the most effective technique to bring kids in, which was music. I was not the first recruiter to use music to indoctrinate kids about racism and white power, nor was I the last. Huge music labels continue to make tons of money using white power and hate-filled Aryan messages, getting kids as young as grade-schoolers to listen to racist rhetoric. Any time I possibly could, I would get a kid listening to white power music—especially the fast-paced, heart-pounding music that they liked, and soon enough he would be embodying, believing, and spouting all kinds of racist verbiage. Then I could get him to pass out a hundred CDs to all his friends."

Frank Meeink wrote in his book, *Autobiography of a Recovering Skinhead: The Frank Meeink Story as Told to Jody M. Roy, Ph.D.*(Hawthorne Books,2010), "…Joe Morgan was one of the highest-ranked members of the Eastern Nazi Alliance and he was starting to become a legend himself within the white supremacy movement. He was the lead singer of a white power band that was starting to get a lot of notice. Thanks to word of mouth and boot-legged tapes, by the summer of 1991, skinheads all over North America were gushing about Joe Morgan."

Similarly, in his book, *My Life After Hate* (la Prensa, 2012), Arno Michaelis, lead singer for the band *Centurion,* wrote, "A focused soundtrack of white power rock-n-roll inspired our bond to each other and crucial hatred for everyone else. Brutal Attack, a seasoned Oi! band from Britain, had just released their 3rd album, *Tales of Glory,* whose title-track soon became the theme song of The Hall. Night after night was spent immersed in our own Tales of Glory."

A final example comes from the book, *White American Youth: My Descent Into America's Most Violent Hate Movement—And How I Got Out* (Hachette Book Group, Inc., 2017), in which Christian Picciolini, lead singer in the band White American Youth (WAY), shared:

> "Carmine told me Martell had even arranged for Skrewdriver to come to the United States to perform, but the plan was foiled when several members of the band couldn't acquire travel visas because of their criminal records. Martell, with Carmine's help, settled for being the sole conduit to import Skrewdriver and other Rock-O-Rama records into the United States. And so, the Romantic Violence mail-order service became the first to distribute white-power music in America."

Picciolini also shared about his musical involvement. "So I threw myself into WAY, lining up whatever gigs I could. I spent hours writing new lyrics, figuring out beats, piecing together songs from the few guitar chords I knew. Music was a means to an end, the end being more control. Respect."

Music was used to recruit youthful members to the cause, to pump them up with propaganda about white supremacist and other hate-based beliefs, to raise money for organizations, and to provide a music-accompanied social environment to join together with others seeking a place to belong.

In 2012, the ADL estimated that there were between one hundred and one hundred fifty white power bands performing and/or recording in the United States alone. The ADL maintains a list of hate music bands in over thirty countries, a worldwide phenomenon. At that time, the ADL gave the following examples of white power bands: Aggravated Assault, Angry Aryans, Attack, Definite Hate, Final Solution, Force Fed Hate, Fueled by Hate, Hate Crime, and White Terror. The names of the bands reflect the themes of their music: anti-Semitism, anti-immigration (both legal and undocumented), anti-various religions, antigays, and violence. These bands are promoted by small record labels and distribution companies, through mail order, internet downloads, web-based sites, and blogs, or often secretive live concerts.

The music has also perpetuated other genres, such as hatecore and National Socialist Black Metal (NSBM). In 2020, it's possible (probable!) that the number of white power bands has increased. The ADL points out that neo-Nazi hate music serves three important functions: recruiting new members to neo-Nazi white supremacist organizations, raising funds for those organizations, and creating a white nationalist sub-culture in several countries.

White power hate music continued to grow in the 1990s and early twenty-first century. A resurgence of far-right extremist groups, the availability of music on the internet, and the success of small record companies, such as Resistance Records and Panzerfaust Records, contributed to the growth.

Panzerfaust notoriously launched its program "Project Schoolyard" in 2004. The program circulated racist CDs to middle school and high school kids using the catchphrase, "We don't just entertain racist kids. We create them." The owner of the company, Anthony Pierpont, was quoted as saying, "We know the impact that is possible when kids are introduced to white nationalism through the musical medium." The company folded when it came out that Pierpont had a Mexican mother and had slept with non-Aryan prostitutes. At different times in the past, there were also backlashes. In 1980, the punk band Dead Kennedys released the song, "Nazi Punks F**k Off" written by Jello Biafra.

In a poll completed in 2020, the Pew Research Center reported that only 45 percent of thirteen thousand surveyed individuals in the United States knew that six million Jews were slaughtered during the Holocaust. They also lacked knowledge that Hitler had risen to power by way of a democratic political process. The results of the poll came on the heels of the seventy-fifth liberation of the Auschwitz death camp—January 27, 1945.

To me, these are essential facts if we are to prevent a repeat of history, and they amplify the need for ongoing education and the search for truth.

I was just beginning to learn about hate music. Jew Slaughter and Intimidation One gave me my first ideas about possible root causes including alcohol consumption, propaganda, and the influence of outside organizations.

I decided to match the story of those two bands with another Portland resident, Felice Wolmut.

Felice Wolmut

I heard about Felice Wolmut three years before I met her. During my music therapy internship at Fairview State Hospital in Costa Mesa, California, in 1974, both of my intern supervisors served as editors of *The Sounding Board,* a newsletter for members of the Western Region of the National Association for Music Therapy (NAMT). They wrote many of the articles, but they also published reports from officers of the organization, summaries from conferences, notices of continuing education opportunities, general announcements, ads for music therapy supplies and equipment, and job postings. They received submissions from members who lived in the region, which included nine western states.

They found it unusual that a member from Oregon had submitted several items, all partially written in German. Neither they, nor I, recognized the name of the author, Felice Wolmut, but they were pleased that Wolmut was taking the time to submit something about her work. Efforts were successful in finding somebody who could translate German so that the articles could be published for the mostly English-reading recipients of the newsletter.

As I approached the end of my internship, I began sending out letters, my resume, and applications for employment—seeking my first professional job as a music therapist. Several of those packets went to healthcare sites in Oregon. I had visited my grandmother in Portland as a child and had always loved the rain and the rich, green environment of mountains and forests.

For other parts of the United States, I usually tried to contact existing, employed music therapists for job leads, but I could not find any existing music therapists in Oregon with whom to network. I received mostly rejections back from my "cold call" letters seeking employment, but a different kind of letter came from Providence Children's Center in Portland, informing me that they already had a credentialed music therapist—Felice Wolmut.

At that time, my search for employment in Oregon struck out. I headed back to the Midwest to look for that elusive first job. A few short years later, I would again search for a position in Oregon, with better results. I landed a spot at Woodland Park Mental Health Center, a private psychiatric hospital in Portland. That's when I finally met Wolmut, in 1977. She was eighty years old and still working as a music therapist.

Felice Gertrude Landesberger d'Antbourg was born in Vienna, Austria, on January 14, 1897. In the 1970s, one of her voice students asked her how she had learned music. She replied that her parents had a double grand piano in their home, and that she would lie under the piano and "absorb every vibration." She shared that her family also lived down the street from composer Johannes Brahms, who would knock on their door and ask Wolmut's stepmother to sing his latest vocal compositions.

As I began to research Wolmut's story, I discovered that she used several names during her life: Felice Landesberger, Gerty Rheinhardt, Felice Wohlmuth, Felice d'Antbourg, Madame Felice d'Antbourg, Frau d'Antbourg Wolmut, Gertrude Natalia Stafania Wohlmuth, and finally, Felice Wolmut. Birth name, first marriage name, second marriage name, professional name, Austrian name, Americanized name, etc. Researching her story required me to provide the full list of names to several archivists, in the hope that one of those names would show up in their records. As I tell her story, you will notice her name change.

Little could be discovered about her childhood, except that she loved music and singing. One story in a Texas newspaper, later in her life, reported that she admired American music and became more curious about the United States after reading Walt Whitman's *Leaves of Grass* at age fifteen. In the same article, she was reported to be "fascinated" with the word "democracy."

Wolmut married Emil Alphons Rheinhardt, a lyricist, writer, and editor, in 1920. She was his second wife. They collaborated on many projects, and sometimes he took credit for her work. He wrote several large biographies, but his most successful book was a biography of Eleanor Duse, an actress, which has been published in seventy-five editions since 1928. He was also known to have had affairs with many women, and Wolmut divorced him, but kept in touch.

Rheinhardt had served in World War I as a medical officer and then in a propaganda department. As World War II approached, he became politically active and was persecuted several times. He participated in the French Resistance during the years before and during World War II. He was interned at the beginning of the war but released back to France.

Other internees sought emigration visas, mostly to the United States, but his was not granted. He wrote to Wolmut that he felt ambivalent about leaving Europe, with a belief that some of his best works could still be written there. He was eventually rearrested and, after transfers to several camps, transported to the Dachau concentration camp where he died from typhus.

Another prisoner smuggled out his diaries and got them to Rheinhardt's secretary. The secretary tried to sell the documents but, when she could not, she sent them to Wolmut. They included passages written to and about her. According to one source, Wolmut donated the documents to the Viennese Documentation Archive of the Austrian Resistance Movement.

After studying music at the University of Vienna, Wolmut had studied voice in Italy. Recognized as a talented coloratura soprano, she performed throughout Europe. She sang live and on the radio in France, Germany, Belgium, Switzerland, Luxembourg, and Austria. According to a copy of her resume, which I obtained from one of her US employers, she studied with composer Karl Weigl, among others (more about Karl and Vally Weigl later in this book), and sang in operatic standards such as Richard Strauss's "Rosenkavalier" and "Ariadne auf Naxos." However, being labeled Jewish in the 1930s, Wolmut found that growing anti-Semitic sentiments made it more and more difficult, and potentially unsafe, to sing in Germany and other parts of Europe. Songs like "Horst-Wessel-Lied", an anthem of the Nazi party, were spreading German nationalist, anti-Semitic messages.

Following her divorce, she returned to Vienna in 1934, auditioning for the role of Rosina in *The Barber of Seville*. She told the judges that she had sung the part numerous times, when, in fact, she had never sung it before. In private, she confessed the truth to one of the audition judges, Dr. Hans Wohlmuth.

She noticed that he appeared to be very forgiving, friendly, and interested in her. She passed the audition and the actual performances went well. They married five months later and changed their names to English versions when they later moved to America—John and Felice Wolmut.

Anti-Semitism had been growing in Austria in the 1920s and 1930s. Christians attacked Jewish residents, and Hakenkreuzler patrols of thugs wearing swastikas were present. The situation was growing bleaker for the Jewish population in Austria. As World War II approached, Wolmut recognized the danger of Adolf Hitler and the Nazis. She is quoted in a newspaper article as saying:

> "Austria was a paternalistic tyranny in the early 30s, no question about it.
>
> "I opened my mouth about Hitler a little too often. Austrians do open their mouths too much, you know.
>
> "I was quite sure Hitler would come to Austria, even though other people scoffed at the idea. Sometimes pessimism pays off."

On March 12, 1938, Wolmut's prediction came true when Nazi troops invaded Austria, and Hitler announced his Anschluss—the annexation (some say, "invasion") of Austria as a part of Germany. Hitler, who had lived in Austria earlier in his life, aimed to make Austria *judenrein*, or free of Jews. Nazis began persecuting political enemies, including all Jewish citizens.

Jews were forced to wear yellow badges, their freedoms were taken away, they were prohibited from pursuing most professions, their businesses were plundered, their synagogues were destroyed, they were forced to perform demeaning tasks, and they were kicked out of schools and universities. Musicians were fired from choirs, opera companies, orchestras, and other musical organizations, including the Vienna Symphony and the Viennese State Opera.

Later, in 1962, Wolmut applied for benefits under the Austrian Victim Support program, Hilfsfonds. In her application, she described how Hitler's Anschluss affected her (note: any grammar or spelling errors are hers):

> "I was persecuted because my husband was Jewish. I myself was born Catholic, but my grandparents were Jewish. My husband would never have got [*sic*] an employment as stage director and opera coach. The same for me as a concert singer or opera engagement.
>
> "My professional activity on March 13, 1938, was severely restricted because I was five months pregnant, so not fit for public performing. At that time, I earned a living with private lessons, singing, and accompaniment, role study. But after 25 years, I would not be able to name the names of my pupils; I just have forgotten; too much since then has flooded us to be able to remember names of pupils. I have never been on the payroll of the Vienna State Opera. 1934-37 I have sung at Jubals Theatre of 49 (a small cellar Theatre), under Rudolf Nilius at the Volksheim (adult education center).
>
> "I gave my own concerts and collaborated as singer in many productions, for which I was paid. I hope these informations [*sic*] will do: as evidence I have reviews in many papers but would prefer not to part with; they are a part of my past."

In Germany, on November 9 and 10, 1938, over ninety Jews were murdered by members of the Nazi Storm Troopers and Hitler Youth. Jewish-owned businesses and their places of worship were attacked, vandalized, or destroyed in the Anschluss. This became known as *Kristallnacht* or the Night of Broken Glass. *Jew Slaughter.*

Following Anschluss, initial efforts focused on trying to get Jewish people to leave Austria. One hundred and thirty thousand Jews left Vienna by 1941, with thirty thousand coming to the United States. Adolf Eichmann established a Central Office for Jewish Emigration, where Jews were charged a Reich Flight Tax—a way to extort money from them as they left Austria. Those who either chose to stay or were unable to pay the tax were eventually sent to concentration camps. Like Wolmut's first husband, Emil Rheinhardt, more than sixty-five thousand Viennese Jews were taken to concentration camps and, reportedly, only approximately two thousand survived.

In addition to the persecution of the Jewish people, the Nazis also stole or destroyed works of art by Jewish artists, including musical compositions by many well-known composers. A list of composers was created by the Nazis, and all Jewish, or even "half-Jewish" individuals, were crossed off the list. Music written by or performed by Jews became forbidden. Composers were denied their royalties.

In this atmosphere, Felice Wohlmuth decided to immigrate to the United States. Her husband was not so sure and had to be convinced about the danger and the need to leave their home country. One of Wolmut's friends, an American woman, took an aggressive approach to get him to act. As reported in one newspaper article, Wolmut remembered, "She practically got him by the scruff of the neck and marched him down to the consulate."

Despite protests from their families, the couple made plans to leave Austria. They came to the United States in April 1938, sailing from Le Havre, France, aboard the *SS President Roosevelt*. The ship's log listed them as a music teacher and housewife and Hebrew. I found it interesting that women who immigrated to America at that time were often listed on ship's logs as "housewife," even if they had some other occupation or profession. Men's occupations were recognized; women were housewives.

Wolmut was pregnant at the time of their move and, soon after arriving in the United States, gave birth to a son, Peter, in New York. The family settled in Philadelphia, where Dr. John Wolmut, formerly known as Hans Wohlmuth, became director of the opera program at the Curtis Institute. This was at a time, following the Great Depression in the United States, when many professional musicians could not find work, but his experience and skills were welcomed. Records indicate that the Curtis Institute was interested in Dr. Wolmut even before he left Vienna and had already been checking his references. He found work quickly.

While John Wolmut jumped into his work in Philadelphia and New York (and later Milwaukee), Felice Wolmut completed a bachelor's degree at the Philadelphia Conservatory of Music to become a music teacher. Her thesis about "The American Art Song" was completed under the supervision of composer Paul Nordoff, who eventually became a well-known music therapist and founded the Nordoff and Robbins Music Therapy Centers with Clive Robbins.

Wolmut created employment opportunities for herself, teaching voice at Shipley School and Baldwin School in Bryn Mawr, Pennsylvania, and the Mannes School in New

York. A newspaper article from September 1941 announced that Mme. Felice d'Antbourg was opening a voice studio in New Jersey.

She applied to become a naturalized US citizen in 1943, listing her name as Felice Gertrude Wolmut. On her application, in parentheses, there appears to be another version of her name: Gertrude Natalia Stafania Wohlmuth, with the note "changed."

While working at the Curtis Institute, in his spare time, John Wolmut studied to become a machinist and applied for a job in a war plant. He was quoted as saying, "I want to give this country everything, because this country has given me everything. My feeling for this country—I just cannot express it."

After a decade in Philadelphia, the Wolmut family moved to Milwaukee, Wisconsin, where John had worked with the Milwaukee Music College's Opera Workshop, providing direction for its First and Second National Opera Festivals. After moving to Milwaukee, he continued to teach at the Milwaukee Music College and the Chicago Musical College, one of the first colleges to offer a degree in music therapy. Unexpectedly, he died from a heart attack, while attending a concert in Chicago. After his sudden death, a newspaper story in the *Milwaukee Journal* described him as "one of the leading figures in Milwaukee's music world."

Felice followed in his footsteps and became a stage director, supervising productions such as *The Bartered Bride*. She continued to teach music in Milwaukee at Mount Mary College and Cardinal Stritch University, with her voice students winning both local and national competitions.

Her next move was to Amarillo, Texas, in 1956, where her son had started his college career. She was head of the voice department at the Musical Arts Conservatory. Newspaper articles from Amarillo identified her as Madam Felice d'Antbourg Wolmut.

On a website titled Miracles of a Lifetime, a voice student tells a story about studying with Wolmut in Amarillo. Handing her a worn piece of music that appeared to have been torn from a book, Wolmut stated, "Let's try this." The song was titled "War's Auch Nur Ein Traum," from the operetta *Monika*, by Nico Dostal. Wolmut said it was the most beautiful song she had ever heard, but it was in German.

Wolmut explained that Adolf Hitler and the Nazis had destroyed large portions of music and literature in their rise to power, but she had saved this song, at great risk, and had brought it to America hidden in her belongings. She had saved it until she recognized a voice that could sing it well and then gave her only copy to that student. The student sang it at many recitals, never knowing what the words meant in English.

Another newspaper article, from her brief time in Amarillo, documented a trip she took to Mexico to study the culture and music. Wolmut visited the Conservatoro National de Musica in Mexico City. She described being impressed with the "sincere dignity of the Mexican combined with respect for art in all forms." Quite a contrast to how Mexicans have been recently portrayed by some factions in the United States.

Wolmut left Amarillo to come to Oregon in 1957. She taught voice at the University of Portland (U of P). She eventually became chair of the voice department there and led an opera workshop that presented *The Magic Flute*, *Fidelio*, and other operas. While at U of P, she completed another degree, in sociology and psychology, and gained additional experience with the creative music program for special education students in the Philadelphia school system. She had maintained ties in Philadelphia.

A newspaper article confirmed that Wolmut completed a music therapy internship at the Milwaukee County Mental Health Center, so she had also maintained contacts in Wisconsin. In the same year that she retired from the U of P, she became an RMT with the NAMT, at sixty-eight years old—RMT credential Number 525, granted November 1, 1965.

Even though there was a music therapy degree program at Willamette University in Salem, there were only a few music therapists employed in Oregon in 1978. That's when I met Wolmut. Practicing music therapists organized to meet once a month to share about our jobs, swap resources, visit each other's clinical sites, and offer support. Wolmut was invited to those meetings, and I offered to pick her up and drive her to the various locations. She was an active participant, telling us about her work and sometimes encouraging us to improve our music skills. In her eighties, she was still teaching us and learning from those of us who were much younger. I remember her chiding some of us because we could not spontaneously and quickly transpose music from one key to another. I just used a capo on my guitar.

Through her work with Paul Nordoff, Wolmut had perhaps been exposed to music therapy. She may have also heard about developments in the field of music therapy on the West Coast. A pioneer in the West Coast music therapy movement was Wilhelmina K. Harbert.

Harbert had volunteered during World War I to provide music concerts to American forces in France. She performed in a variety of situations and venues, including hospitals, recreation halls, and rest areas. As she provided music for traumatized and sometimes injured or dying soldiers, she observed that music served as more than entertainment. When she returned to the United States, after a year of volunteering overseas, she began to study the psychology of music.

As the Great Depression of the 1930s took place, Harbert took the initiative to establish a private home school for music understanding, The Oaks, just outside Stockton, California. A victim of the economic pressures of the depression, The Oaks only stayed open for three years, but the experience pushed Harbert to learn more about music therapy. She had taught music to both children and adults, but she became aware of the uses of music for nonmusical purposes. Married to a physician and surgeon, she was encouraged by him and others to study physiology, psychology, and problems with human adjustment. As she studied, she began to develop music therapy methods based on information from other disciplines.

Harbert began to offer courses in music therapy to governmental occupational therapy students at Mills College in Oakland, California. She continued to teach there during most of World War II, from 1942 to 1945. While teaching, she continued to do volunteer work in many settings, giving her additional practice in the therapeutic uses of music.

Finally, in 1946, she established the first, West Coast music therapy degree program at College of the Pacific (now University of the Pacific), in Stockton. The program emphasized a multidisciplinary approach to treatment and featured music therapy clinical experiences at Stockton State Hospital and the children's ward of the San Joaquin General Hospital.

Later, in 1974, Harbert published *Opening Doors Through Music: A Practical Guide for Teachers, Therapists, Students, Parents* (O J. G. Ferguson Publishing Company), which summarized the music therapy theory and methods that she had developed over several decades. Not only had she taught numerous music therapy students, but she had also, almost single-handedly, convinced the California State Legislature to create a Civil Service classification for trained music therapists to work in state hospitals and other state-funded facilities.

Felice Wolmut was a short, slight woman but she had a powerful, strong personality—similar to Harbert. She is described in some documents as being feisty. Her grandson, whom I located in Portland, told me that each spring he would be dropped off at her home to replant her flower bulbs, sometimes rearranging them several times to meet her satisfaction.

When I drove her home, following one of the monthly meetings, she invited me into her home for tea. She referred to her neighborhood as "the ghetto," a holdover from an earlier chapter of her life. It was in a northeast Portland area, populated with many of the city's minority groups. The particular area had a reputation for more crime than other sections of Portland, but that did not seem to bother her. She felt safe there in the Alberta Street area. Funny that almost forty years later, that neighborhood is where I had met with Randy Blazak.

As I entered her home for the first time, I was amazed to see stacks of sheet music, wall-to-wall in some rooms. We shared tea and chatted, but I don't remember Wolmut opening up about her story. She was more interested in what I was doing. It wasn't until years later, after moving away for other job opportunities and then returning to Oregon, that I decided to learn more about Wolmut. I found print stories, and even photos of Wolmut working with some of her clients. Her story grabbed me.

For the remainder of her career and life, she used music less like a teacher and more like a therapist. Music became a tool to work on nonmusical goals. She worked at the Edgefield Lodge for Disturbed Children, a state-run facility in Troutdale, Oregon; performed at nursing homes in the Portland area; was on the faculty of the Nordoff and Robbins Music Therapy Center in Philadelphia; and worked with "retarded" children (now referred to as individuals with developmental disabilities) for thirteen years at the Emily School of the Sisters of Providence Child Center. Wolmut described her work at the Emily School this way:

> "Music therapy is a matter of love. I've loved them to self-confidence. Music can touch them where nothing else can.
>
> "Many of these kids are nothing to themselves; they have only a name but no sense of who they are. When they do music, they are somebody. Music gives them self-confidence.
>
> "My sort of music therapy is unorthodox. I base it on loving them and improvising to get the best performance out of them."

A talented musician, Wolmut used those talents to help others. She escaped from an anti-Semitic atmosphere and the threat of Adolf Hitler and the Nazis and moved away from her family and home to lead a long, productive life. Some of her relatives and friends, left behind, died in concentration camps. She overcame many hardships and always persevered. She never thought about controlling the government, the media, financial institutions, or other entities. She just wanted to use music to teach and help others.

I reviewed the music therapy newsletters in which I had first heard of Wolmut. They documented that for four summers, during the breaks from teaching at colleges, she returned to Europe to work at a school for "educable" girls in France and a "children's village" in Vienna, where she worked with epileptics, autistics, hyperkinetics, and disturbed children. She represented the NAMT at the European Conference on the Education of the Handicapped Child in Norrköping, Sweden. She also published an article about music therapy in *Caritas*, a publication of *German Catholic Welfare*. She discontinued her 19-year membership in the National Association for Teachers of Singing, refocusing her life as a member of NAMT.

A believer in a lifetime of learning, Wolmut sought out academic opportunities, completing at least two college degrees and other professional training in the United States. She demonstrated that music could have a profound, positive effect on people of all ages. She could have responded to her situation with sadness, grief, and hatred, but, instead, she chose to spread love in the world. She chose another route than that taken by members of Jew Slaughter and Intimidation 1.

Wolmut died in 1989. Jew Slaughter was formed in 1987, growing out of the group from Milwaukee, Oregon, named Youth of Hitler. I don't know if Wolmut ever heard any of their music, but I pray that she did not.

In October 2018, I finally was able to locate a copy of Wolmut's favorite song, "War's Auch Nur Ein Traum," from the operetta *Monika* by Nico Dostal. It was the song that she had smuggled out of Austria. It was the song that one of her students sang, not knowing what the German lyrics meant. Julianne Brand, a musicologist at the Karl Weigl Foundation, referred me to Michael Miller at the Operetta Foundation in Los Angeles. Michael graciously provided a copy of the song, and Julianne translated the German lyrics:

> "Even if it was just a dream
> Flowers bloomed all 'round the valley
> in the beautiful month of May.
> That's when for the first time I felt
> The joy of being two.
> Why must happiness die so fast?
> It was so lovely, so lovely.
> Even if it was just a dream
> brought to me by Love,
> even if it was just a dream,
> it was a dream that made me happy!
> Must I now forget all
> that was so lovely
> and that I once possessed?
> Yes, even if it was just a dream
> I dreamed in the spring,
> it was my entire portion of happiness
> that I lost.
> Everything may pass, but the love
> that made me so happy will survive!
> In bleak, fearful winter
> That dream left me.
> Now holy Lent is far along

in its colorful display,
And May and joy and blooming trees
were just a dream, a dream.
Must I now forget all
that was so lovely
and that I once possessed?
Yes, even if it was just a dream
I dreamed in the spring,
it was my entire portion of happiness
that I lost.
Everything may pass, but the love
that made me so happy will survive!"

(English translation © Julianne Brand, 2019, used with written permission)

Maybe these two stories illustrate the triumph of love over hate. Should Wolmut have been forced to leave her family, friends, and country to come to America? Since she had a long productive life here, should she be thankful for her forced relocation—as some haters might rationalize? Would love have guided her life no matter where she lived? Is it possible that her life laid the foundation for later music therapists in Portland, Oregon? We can only guess the answers to some of these questions.

I was just beginning to learn about hate music. So far, I had heard the music of Jew Slaughter and Intimidation 1. My mind was formulating possible root causes for this neo-Nazi skinhead hate music. I was just starting to hear the musical characteristics of hate songs. Randy Blazak had warned me that "it all starts with anti-Semitism." My next pair of stories taught me that it didn't end there.

Felice Wolmut: An early opera role in Europe, Innsbruck, Austria, 1929. Photo provided by Wolmut family, with permission.

Felice, at the piano, Milwaukee, Wisconsin ca. 1955

Felice working at Sisters of Providence Children's Center,
Portland, Oregon, ca. 1979. Used with permission
from Providence Archives, Seattle

Felice working with children, at age 82, ca. 1979. Photo is the
property of Oregonian Publishing Co. Used with
written "no objection" letter.

Chapter 3

JOHNNY REBEL

DEFORIA LANE

Life has its ups and downs we know,
not always fair, but still we go
From day to day seeking ways to make it better.
So we strive on and on, sometimes sighing or
singing a song
If there's a lesson we have learned,
it's we can cope.

(From the song "We Can Cope" © Deforia Lane, 1985,
used with written permission)

T hese next two stories pair an example of an antiblack, segregationist songwriter, with the story of
a music therapist whose family had to deal with
the beliefs and opinions that he clearly expressed through
some of his songs.

My research was turning up examples of recent antiblack music, and I was growing curious about how long

that type of music had been around. A friend suggested that I visit online historical sheet music archives. I visited the ones at Duke University, the University of Oregon, UCLA, and the Lester Levy collection at Johns Hopkins University. I also searched the historical sheet music collection at the Library of Congress.

Here are examples of song titles I found: "The Original Jim Crow" (1828), "Old Abe has Gone and Did It, Boys" (1862), "N****r Will Be N****r" (1864), "Never Trust a N****r With a Gun" (1886), "When They Straighten All the Colored People's Hair" (1894), "All Coons Look Alike to Me" (1896), "Stay in Your Own Backyard" (1899), "Coon, Coon, Coon" (1901), "N****r Love A Watermelon. Ha! Ha! Ha!" (1916), "That's Why Darkies Were Born" (1931), "There's a Dark Man Coming With a Bundle" (1905), Run, N****r, Run (heard in 1851, re-recorded in 1927 and recently featured in the film *12 Years A Slave*), "The Pickaninny's Paradise" (1918), "If the Man in the Moon Were a Coon" (1907), and "Down in Jungle Town" (1908).

There were two songs about the KKK: "Ku Klux Klan" (1868, used as an anti-KKK song in the presidential campaign of Ulysses S. Grant), and "The Bright Fiery Cross: Our Song" (1913), its sheet music cover showing figures in white hoods and robes standing around a large cross.

"Coon" songs were seen in productions in the late 1700s, continuing into the early 1800s. They returned to popularity after the Civil War, between the 1880s and the first two decades of the twentieth century. These ditties, often referred to as "comic" songs, made fun of African Americans—how they talked, how they acted, how they danced, and how they looked. Many of the lyrics mimicked their dialects. The word "coon" apparently referred to individuals who ate raccoon meat, supposedly part of the diet of some Southern slaves. Some songwriters used the word "possum," but the genre of music is referred to by historians as "coon" music.

A friend loaned me his copy of a CD titled, *Bigot Songs*, sold at Earth Station 1.com. (The site offers many CDs of historic music, including such collections as *World War I: Historic Music and Voices*, *World War II: US Pop and Third Reich Marching Songs*, and *Swing Under the Swastika*.) The *Bigot Songs* CD contained taped examples of an additional seventy-five songs from the early twentieth century.

Whether the songs used the words coon, n****r, darkie, or pickaninny, the effect was the same. Blacks were portrayed in a bad light. They were made fun of. Americans were entertained. White grandmothers sang the songs to their white grandchildren. And negative stereotypes were etched in the minds of audiences. Much later, in 2004, a group named The Bleeding Vaginas released a song titled "The Most Racist Song Ever," which expanded the use of hateful labels to include such words as *jigaboo, spearchucker, bootlip, spook, wetback, spic*, and *Chink*.

Even national anthems have been criticized for being racist. While individuals may believe in putting their country first, nationalist movements have historically favored a single demographic group and discriminated against others. Several countries have revised their national anthems, or eliminated whole verses, due to perceived racism.

For example, "The Star-Spangled Banner," the national anthem of the United States, included a third stanza—no longer used—that put down slaves for fighting on the side of the British during the Revolutionary War. What the verse does not convey is that the British had offered freedom to the slaves. That verse is still controversial and, in today's environment, is perceived by some as supporting slavery. The recent cases of professional athletes kneeling during the national anthem continue to be sources of division.

In Germany, citizens are now forbidden from singing the original, first two verses of its national anthem "Lied der Deutschen (Song of the Germans)", also known as "Deutschlandied (Song of Germany)." The music was composed by Joseph Haydn. Some of the original lyrics, written by the poet August Heinrich Hoffmann von Fallersleben, included "Germany above all/Above all in the world." Viewed as harmless when it was written in 1797, the song was seen as supporting the unification of many independent German principalities.

Today, those words are considered by some as expressing white supremacy, racism, and world domination. Those sentiments were exploited by Hitler and the Nazis around World War II. They also prohibited the music of Gustav Mahler, a Jewish Austrian. The opera, *Die Schweigsame Frau*, by Richard Strauss, was banned because Stefan Zweig, a Jewish librettist, wrote the lyrics. The first two verses of "Deutschlandied" are now prohibited at official events but allowed at nonofficial events.

Australia also has a history of controversy with its national anthem. In 1910, the song "White Australia March" was published, which included the chorus:

"White Australia March Australia, the white man's land, Defended by the white man's guns. Australia, Australia, For Anglo-Saxon race and South'n Cross.

God bless and help us to protect our glorious land Australia."

The sheet music included a heading, "March of the Great White Policy," and the words "Advance Australia." The song was not the national anthem but, years later, the Australian government-sponsored a contest to select one. When none of the submitted songs were deemed suitable, three songs still remained under consideration: "Waltzing Matilda," "God Save the Queen," and "Advance Australia Fair." The latter was selected as the Australian national anthem in 1984. It came to light that some of the words seemed to have been borrowed from the "White Australia March" songbook and were viewed as racist.

I found that the products sold with hate music are sometimes just as offensive as the music itself—the buttons, patches, banners, shirts, posters, tattoo designs, bumper stickers, flags, etc. In the case of coon songs, the art on the cover of the sheet music served the same purpose. African Americans were often portrayed with exaggerated features and as negative stereotypes, common characteristics of hate music.

Some people would excuse these past attitudes and behaviors as "the zeitgeist of the past." The *Oxford Dictionary* defines "zeitgeist" as "the defining spirit or mood of a particular period of history as shown by the ideas and beliefs of the time." We might hear, "Things were different back then," or "Those ideas were not considered offensive at that time." But were they? Shouldn't they have been? When it comes to more recent hate music, is the zeitgeist defense still being used? More recently than I expected.

Johnny Rebel

Johnny Rebel's real name was Clifford Joseph Trahan, but one website said that he used other stage names at different times, including Tommy Todd, Jericho Jones, Johnny "Pee Wee" Blaine, Johnny "Pee Wee" Trayhan, Johnny "Pee Wee" Trahan, and Caleb McNutt.

Trahan was born in Moss Bluff, Louisiana, in 1938—the same year that future music therapists Felice Wolmut and Vally Weigl left Vienna for the United States. When he was about twelve years old, his mother bought him a guitar and he began to learn chords and sing. He learned mostly from other musicians on the television, especially on *The Grand Ole Opry*. His parents divorced, and he moved with his mother to Crowley, Louisiana.

After graduating from high school in 1956, Trahan began frequenting a Crowley recording studio, owned and operated by Joseph Miller, a guitarist, record producer, songwriter, businessman—and a relative.

Miller had been around the music business for a long time, playing guitar in bands since the late 1930s, recording other artists for a variety of small record labels, and riding the popularity of Cajun, swamp pop, blues, rhythm and blues, and rockabilly styles. He wrote the lyrics to the hit, "It Wasn't God Who Made Honky Tonk Angels," which was recorded by Kitty Wells, hitting the top of the charts for several weeks and earning a gold record.

Miller claimed to be a segregationist but also used black musicians and interracial bands in his recording studio. He claimed that African American blues was his favorite musical genre. He even recorded some blues songs under a fake name, apparently to hide his race. Miller worked with a long list of musicians, some with minor successes, but not many with commercial breakthroughs on a grand scale. John Fogerty, of Creedence Clearwater Revival fame, recorded a cover of Rockin' Sidney's "My Toot Toot" there. One of the best-known artists to use Miller's recording studio was Paul Simon, who visited there to record a song for his Grammy-winning *Graceland* album.

Trahan started his musical career like others, playing songs of the day wherever they could. YouTube has a variety of Trahan songs and recordings, in the hillbilly style, including "Thanks A Lot," "Lonely Street to Hell," and "Play That Song One More Time" on the Viking label; "Tag Along" on the Zynn label; "Black Magic" on the Todd label; "I Can't Walk the Line" and "King Sized Bed" on the Wildwood label; and "I'll Be Living It Up, While You're Living It Down" and "Just Hang Around" on the Ringo label.

Trahan also wrote special songs for Notre Dame High School and Crowley High School. Many of those recordings are listed as very rare and no longer readily available. Trahan later shared, on the *Howard Stern Show*, that at points in his career, he had a day job but was performing seven nights a week. He went to Nashville, to try his luck at making connections and performing, but not much happened. When Todd Records folded, he got married and worked for a time in Mississippi as a shipyard inspector. He eventually returned to Crowley.

Miller had started a new label, Reb Rebel Records, and asked Trahan if he could write some segregationist songs. In an interview published in the New Orleans' *Gambit Weekly*, Trahan admitted, "...he didn't entice me in any way, and he didn't try to influence me in any way. All the songs I wrote were my complete ideas. My ideas. When I got them done, I brought them to him, and he said, 'Let's put them down.'"

They recorded twelve songs, approximately between 1966 and 1967. Miller gave Trahan a new name for the releases: Johnny Rebel.

Consider the titles of the songs he either wrote, recorded, or both: "N****r Hatin' Me," "Who Likes a N****r?" "Kajun Ku Klux Klan," "N****r, N****r," "Move Them N****rs North," "In Coon Town," and one of the most offensive (if that's possible), "Some N****rs Never Die (They Just Smell That Way)."

One of Trahan's songs, "Lâche pas la Patate," or "the potato song," was performed by Jimmy C. Newman and won a gold record in Canada in 1976. The song "Some N****rs Never Die (They Just Smell That Way)" was used in the film *What Is It?* directed by Crispin Glover in 2005. Some might remember Crispin Glover as Marty McFly's dad in the film *Back to the Future*.

In the *What Is It?* film, the song plays over a scene where an African American woman in an ape mask performs a sex act on a white, disabled man. More recently, in 1998, twenty-one seconds of one of Johnny Rebel's songs were used in the film *American History X*.

Only two of Trahan's released songs as Johnny Rebel did not deal with race. Still, he maintained that he was not a racist. He said that he had many black friends, and that he would do anything for them, but that there was a different mindset in the 1960s. Zeitgeist? He claimed that his attitudes had changed since then, "up to a point."

Trahan told radio show host Howard Stern that he would not let his daughter marry a black man. In another interview, he expressed his distaste for race-mixing, saying,

"...they wanna marry f**kin' white people... that irritates the livin' s**t outta me. When I see a black guy with a white girl, that turns my stomach."

He admitted that his songs might be "a little racist" and that they could "hurt feelings," but that the songs reflected how he and others felt at the time. Notes for a later compilation album, *For Segregationists Only*, described Johnny Rebel's songs in this way: they "express the feeling, anxiety, confusion and problems of many of our people during the political transformation of our way of life." The songs did not demand much radio play but sold in parts of the United States and could be heard on jukeboxes in some establishments. Many of those restaurants, bars, and honky-tonks stocked extra copies to sell to patrons who liked the racist songs. In retrospect, they were not well accepted and seldom heard by the general public, especially by African Americans. But they were popular with segregationists, racists, and white supremacists. And still are.

At the start of the twenty-first century, Trahan was surprised to learn that his Johnny Rebel songs had gained new popularity worldwide, due to bootleg re-issues of the recordings, and the internet. He hired a new manager to try to cash in on the growing interest. The new manager arranged for the interview on the *Howard Stern Show*, and he and Trahan established an official website.

Johnny Rebel wrote, recorded, and performed his "segregationist" songs mostly in the 1960s. It was only one hundred years since the Civil War. There were still strong feelings on both sides of the racial divide. Civil Rights struggles continued then and still remain. Trahan shared that he wrote the songs to make money, and he told Howard Stern that he made around four-to-five thousand dollars. He still maintained that he was not a racist, but the attitude of some blacks irritated him.

He is quoted as saying, "I don't care about black. Black don't rub off. There's not a black in this country that has to be black. There's not a white that has to be white. They just came here like that. They were born that way, but they didn't develop the damn attitude. Whites didn't develop the attitude. Blacks develop an attitude toward whites, and they won't let it go. They won't let go of what happened," and "Why should we pay reparations for things that happened two hundred years ago? I was run out of my country…my ancestors were run out of Nova Scotia." (both quotes from "Johnny Rebel Speaks" by Nick Pittman, *The Gambit,* June 10, 2003)

I wondered why. Shouldn't that have developed empathy for others? And didn't his statements indicate that he, too, had developed an attitude toward blacks?

In her book, *Post Traumatic Slave Syndrome: America's Legacy of Enduring Injury and Healing* (Joy Degruy Publications Inc, 2005), Joy DeGruy, PhD, describes and discusses the ramifications of slavery in America and the lasting effects on the thoughts, feelings, behaviors, and attitudes of black Americans.

Attitudes. One of Johnny Rebel's albums was titled *It's the Attitude, Stupid.* He may not have understood or appreciated the attitudes of some blacks around him. He did not try to walk a mile in their shoes. He may not have understood how it felt to be discriminated against on a daily basis. To be denied a level playing field. To be denied the same opportunities as white Americans.

Clifford Trahan, a.k.a. Johnny Rebel, was not alone. Many of the feelings expressed through his songs were shared by others and, unfortunately, are still felt today.

Around 2001, the catalog of Johnny Rebel songs became valuable, and there were legal challenges to copyrights. One company claimed that Trahan's wife signed over the rights to the songs but could not provide proof. Another distributor challenged the idea that Trahan was really Johnny Rebel. Copies of the recordings are available on a variety of websites, but the largest distributor was Resistance Records, which estimated at one point that the Johnny Rebel compilation recording, *Klassic Klan Kompositions,* was its second largest seller, behind the videogame *Ethnic Cleansing.*

Victor Gephard, an attorney involved with one company that sells bootlegged Johnny Rebel recordings—whitepowerrecords.com—stated, "…if managed and properly represented by attorneys, the real Johnny Rebel should be worth millions."

Trahan eventually faded from public view and retreated to a private life and ran a driving school in Crowley. At the time of his death in 2016, he had been married to the same woman for fifty-six years and had four children and several grandchildren. He must have had love in his life. Unconditional love. Did he extend that kind of love to his friends of color?

Except on rare occasions, he did not perform or grant interviews. He did not like to be photographed but admitted that there were accurate photos of him on the internet. He claimed that he only performed one time in public as Johnny Rebel. Was he embarrassed by the Johnny Rebel song catalog? Was he concerned for the safety of himself and his family? Did he tire of the negative backlash? Did he just do it for the money? Or did he really change his mind about some things?

Trahan died on Saturday, September 3, 2016. Though he started as a simple singer of country, rockabilly-style songs, he has inspired new waves of racist hate music around the globe. He is considered a legend among white supremacists and white power musicians.

Deforia Lane

WHETHER DEFORIA LANE EVER PREVIOUSLY HEARD THE songs of Johnny Rebel is immaterial. She and other members of her family lived with, and reacted to, the same type of racist thinking and behaviors, through several generations. Lane's story, and that of her family, illustrates the effects of extreme racism and the ways that they were forced, either through actual violence or threats of violence, to make changes in their lives to survive and thrive.

Lane told me about an incident at the hospital where she works. It involved taking well-known trumpeter Wynton Marsalis and his friend, saxophonist Walter Blanding, a Jazz at Lincoln Center Orchestra member, on rounds with her. Together, the three had entered the room of a woman who was nearing the end of her life. A group of hospital administrators, nursing executives, and others accompanied Lane, Marsalis, and Blanding on rounds, anxious to interact with the two special guests. They stood just outside the door to the patient's room, peering in.

The woman's breathing remained shallow as she lay still and alone, with no family members by her bedside. She appeared ghostly white but comfortable, possibly close to death—a somber and private scene.

At Marsalis's beckoning, Lane gently closed the door. This part of the rounds was not meant for casual observation or exhibition. The end of a person's life deserves privacy, respect, and care.

Marsalis and Blanding were strangers to this woman, but not Lane. With her permission, they began to play their instruments. At first, the woman showed no reaction, recognition, or response. As the soft music filled the room, slow changes were observable. The woman's breathing became more regular and relaxed, but her affect showed few discernable signs of appreciation or response. As the music concluded, the woman opened her eyes slightly but seemed confused. Lane bent down and quietly explained what was going on and asked her, "What were you thinking?" The woman hadn't spoken for some time, but she softly replied, "Now I know what heaven sounds like."

Lane is full of stories from her years as a music therapist. Hospital leaders encouraged her to take guests on rounds and provide demonstrations to celebrities or those interested in starting music therapy programs in their institutions. She excelled at it. Her warmth, knowledge, and ability to influence were well respected. Her involvement never hurt public relations.

During her career, Lane considered it a privilege to take several notable people on patient rounds with her: Audrey Hepburn, Al Gore, Mary Wells, Johnny Johnson, and Maureen McGovern. She fondly remembers touring General Colin Powell and Harry Belafonte. Opera legend Renee Fleming and National Institute of Health Director Dr. Francis Collins were among those whom she informed and educated about the impact of music therapy.

Those opportunities are dear to her heart and remembered with fondness—chances to spread the word, ignite the flame of music therapy, and demonstrate its power. But the rich stories of the patients carry special meaning for Lane.

Now we were meeting over dinner in a restaurant in the Union Station Hotel in St. Louis. The night before—November 16, 2017—Lane had received a Lifetime Achievement Award from the AMTA. Earlier in the day, I had met Lane's husband, Ernest, who was proud of his wife's honor.

Other people wanted her attention, for good reason, and congratulations were in order. It was her time in the spotlight—and her time to let her light shine. She had previously and graciously—via email—accepted my invitation for dinner and what was supposed to be an hour-long interview. I had communicated with her about the book I was working on, and she permitted me to tell her story. Almost three hours after we had sat down, we eventually got up to approach the dessert bar. My so-called interview had turned into an entire evening of sharing and discussion. A delicious feast of nourishment and sweetness, both the food and the conversation.

I had met Lane many years earlier, in Portland, Oregon, when she was the featured speaker at a catered dinner, sponsored by the American Cancer Society. Invitations to the dinner had been sent to physicians and registered nurses from the Oregon Health and Science University Hospital, as well as the growing group of music therapists working locally. Not one of those MTs worked at OHSU, so it offered a chance to stimulate interest in music therapy and share success stories, with the possibility of creating new employment opportunities for somebody, in a major medical setting. The invited guests created an interesting mix. Lane was in top form that evening—sharing her story, entertaining, teaching, and demonstrating.

Before the dinner in Portland, I had read some of Deforia's publications and heard about her prior research. After that dinner, I purchased a copy of her autobiographical book, *Music as Medicine.* Now I was eager to interview her in St. Louis, twenty years later, to obtain an update on her life and career, ask additional questions, and seek her thoughts about hate music

We asked for a private table, in a corner of the restaurant, so that we could talk freely. Since I had read her book and knew a great deal about her life, I jumped right into questions about race and hate. If you haven't guessed, Dr. Deforia Lane is African American.

"Yes," she said, "my ancestors were slaves." At first, Lane shared that her family did not talk much about slavery or other negative past events. She noted, "Thinking about those things stirs up the hate in me. I see what it does to you." However, she shared some stories with me and, in 2018, she addressed issues of race in a joint keynote speech at the national conference of the AMTA in Dallas, Texas.

She told me that her mother remembered four lynchings in her neighborhood in a southern state when she was growing up. Lane's mother had also suffered a fractured skull when a white boy threw a rock at her as she walked home from school. Lane shared that her maternal grandfather and his younger brother, while walking home on a back road, were offered candy by several white adolescent boys in a pickup truck. When the younger brother, only four or five years old, stretched out his hand to accept the candy, he was grabbed by the wrist, yanked into the truck, abducted, and never seen again. This crime was never solved.

Lane's father, as a young man, worked as a chauffeur for a banker in a small town in Louisiana. The banker's daughter flirted with him, and when the girl's brothers overheard her confide to a friend that she thought Lane's dad was hot and handsome, they organized a gang to "cut it off." They even broadcasted when and where they would commit the assault. Upon hearing of the plan, the family arranged for her dad to be secreted away on a bus in the dead of night to the North or, as one of Johnny Rebel's songs put it, "Move Them N****rs North." Unfortunately, her father's cousin was not so lucky. He stayed in the South, married a white woman, and was castrated by a group of white supremacists.

These things happened to past generations, but Lane has tried to rise above any anger or hatred. It hasn't been easy. She told me that she has never seen the movies *Selma* or *Mississippi Burning*.

"Why would I want to drink that in?" she explained.

However, she could not isolate herself from the nightly news—witnessing the bombing of churches; African Americans beaten and attacked by dogs and fire hoses at protests; segregation policies; and the refusal of services and education to members of her race. She saw efforts of voter suppression against blacks. When she eventually went on speaking tours, her husband would not allow her to visit certain places, fearful for her safety.

In her words, she shared, "I made up my mind to work twice as hard to prove myself in school, in my church, and in my community, to set the record straight that we as people are intellectually astute, physically and emotionally resilient, and have the blood of kings and queens pulsing through our veins."

Throughout Lane's life and career, she has frequently been the only person of color in many situations. She has spoken at medical and academic conferences, gone on national speaking tours, treated patients from many races and ethnic groups, worked with diverse colleagues, and sung in front of "audiences full of white women wearing white gloves." She has experienced direct and subtle racism.

She has had patients assume that she was there to wait on them, demanding, "Get my food tray," not realizing that Dr. Lane was there as a part of their treatment team.

Still, she claims, "I've been given generous support, encouragement, and opportunities greater than I could imagine from more Jewish, Caucasian, Muslim, Latino, African American and Arabic people than I can name or number. They've nominated me for awards, created a job for me where there was none, bountifully increased my salary, fought for me to have a seat at the table, opened doors that I could never have opened on my own, mentored me, and yes, kept me from walking into unseen trouble. It's those acts of kindness for which I am grateful, choose to focus upon and want to extend to others."

So, how did her life lead her to this philosophy—or in Johnny Rebel's words, "Attitude" —of grace, forgiveness, acceptance, and self-determination? Her family moving north had not removed them, or her, from racism.

Lane was born March 16, 1948, in Ohio, after both of her parents had moved to the North from the Deep South. Her father worked for General Motors and also washed cars part-time on the weekends, to earn extra money to buy his family a piano. Both parents filled their home with music—Lane's mother played piano, and her father sang baritone. Lane started piano lessons at age five and voice lessons at sixteen.

Based on her musical talents and singing skills, she received a scholarship, right out of high school, to pursue dual degrees in vocal performance and music education at the University of Cincinnati College Conservatory of Music. She and her college roommate were the only African American students in the program.

Challenged by the high standards and competition, Lane excelled. She sang major roles in operas at the conservatory, auditioned for the Metropolitan Opera, worked summers at the Cincinnati Opera Company, and when she graduated, she was awarded a full-ride scholarship to attend the Curtis Institute of Music in Philadelphia (where Dr. John Wolmut had once worked). It was a dream come true and seemed to be part of God's plan for her.

But after experiencing difficult classes and a disappointing recital at the end of the first year, she was told that she could not continue in the program. It was a major setback in her life, and she was not sure what her future held. She felt humiliated, embarrassed, defeated, and unwanted.

With little delay, she decided to return to the University of Cincinnati and pursue a master's degree. After all, she thought, more education might help clarify what to do with her life. However, early in her program, she also met her future husband and got engaged. Once again, her life and education were interrupted by moves, marriage, the approaching birth of her first child, and other events. She and her new husband moved to West Point, Germany, Boston, and finally back to Cleveland—glad to be much closer to their families. With some stability established in their new city, Lane enrolled at Cleveland State University to take one more stab at completing a master's degree in music.

She noticed an elective course, "Introduction to Music Therapy." Like others, the combination of the words "music" and "therapy" struck a pleasing chord in her. She took the course and immediately saw the career possibilities. She already had a bachelor's degree, so between 1976 and 1979, she completed a post-graduate music therapy equivalency program, which led to a required six-month internship and a master's degree in music. She completed her internship at the Cleveland Music School Settlement, under the supervision of Louise Steele. The internship involved her in providing music therapy services at five different locations, helping clients with a variety of labels: developmental/cognitive disabilities, geriatric, psychiatric, and behaviorally disordered.

Lane's first job as a music therapist, post-internship, was at a developmental center in Cuyahoga County, Ohio, serving over two hundred thirty children with a multitude of issues and disabilities. She worked there for over six years, writing treatment care plans, providing interventions, graphing results, and learning to become more evidence-based as a credentialed, professional music therapist. She felt gratified, challenged, appreciated, and exhausted. The work proved rewarding, but her personal life was also full and fulfilling. In her roles as wife, mother, church choir director, Sunday school teacher, scout troop leader, and Parent-Teacher Association member, her life left little time for rest. And another baby was on the way.

Just when life seemed abundant and gratifying, Lane encountered another speed bump: she was diagnosed with breast cancer. She was treated at the Ireland Cancer Center (now Seidman Cancer Center), where she had a total mastectomy, followed by the return of cancer ten months later. At Seidman, she received radiation therapy and a long course of oral medications. She still raves about the excellent care she received from the medical staff at Seidman.

Upon completion of treatment, she provided educational training about music therapy, to thank them. She shared personally, and from the literature, how music could address the physical and emotional needs of the patients whom the staff served every day. She knew this, now, from the receiving side. Soon, she volunteered twice each week after her work at the developmental center to provide music therapy services for the oncology unit. She showed the medical staff how music therapy could be incorporated into their program, helping other patients who were experiencing medical challenges similar to her own.

Six months later, the director of the Seidman Cancer Center heard about her and summoned her to his office. Lane was nervous. He explained that he had been informed of parts of her volunteer work with patients.

He said, "I hear that my patients are taking off their oxygen masks and singing with you; nurses are bringing in instruments and playing for patients in the middle of the night; and I have letters from families telling me what you are doing with their loved ones."

Lane was afraid that her volunteer involvement was about to be terminated, due to her interference with normal processes. But the director surprised her with two questions: "When can you come to work for us?" and "How much money do you want?"

Starting with little knowledge of the processes and routines in a full-blown medical facility, Lane instituted an ongoing course of self-directed study. She called other music therapists working in hospitals, read journal articles and books, and began experimenting with intuitive interventions. In some cases, she did not even use music. She did not want to use music just to say that she was a music therapist. She also wanted to reflect that she was a therapist and that music was one of her tools. She focused on developing relationships with patients and staff members and on increasing her counseling skills.

Still, when she did use music, she did not want to be perceived as just providing entertainment. She always had nonmusical treatment goals in mind: pain reduction, end-of-life care, the expression of thoughts and feelings, physical rehabilitation, and others. She has consistently used another tool: humor.

Over thirty years have passed since Lane accepted the job at University Hospitals of Cleveland (now called University Hospitals Cleveland Medical Center). Her title, Director of Art and Music Therapy, was augmented with Assistant Clinical Professor of Medicine at Case Western Reserve School of Medicine and adjunct professor at the Frances Payne Bolton School of Nursing. She has treated thousands of patients and trained over seventy music therapy interns.

Today, the University Hospitals Cleveland Medical Center that first hired Dr. Lane employs multiple music therapists at its main campus and in its community hospitals.

Due to her personal experiences with cancer, and her demonstrated clinical experience and expertise, she was asked to be a spokesperson for the American Cancer Society (ACC), resulting in multiple speaking engagements in the United States and abroad. She composed the song, "We Can Cope," which was recorded and used extensively by the ACC.

FINALLY, IN 1991, LANE COMPLETED A PhD IN MUSIC education at Case Western University in Cleveland. Her doctoral research showed that music therapy could be used to boost the immune systems of pediatric patients, as measured by the levels of Immunoglobulin A in their saliva. Since then, she has published numerous articles in professional journals, taught college courses, and consulted with several health care organizations and associations.

Lane has received widespread media attention and awards for her work. Examples include coverage in *Reader's Digest, Coping Magazine, National Public Radio, CBS This Morning*, the *Wall Street Journal, ABC World News*, the Oncology Nursing Society's Mara Morgensen Flaherty Lectureship Award, the Cleveland Negro Business and Professional Women Award, and, in 2009, the Ohio Hospital Association's Health Care Worker of the Year Award. A search on YouTube revealed over twenty videos about her work.

Her residency in Cleveland also resulted in a surprise involvement at the Rock 'n' roll Hall of Fame and Museum. The AMTA gave the museum Lane's contact information and in 1999 she was invited to start a program for underserved preschoolers. The program, *Toddler Rock,* uses music to increase literacy skills and improve school readiness for over four hundred Head Start children each week. It is still active today, twenty years later. It utilizes the services of eighteen music therapists and has provided music therapy to over four thousand children.

When we talked more about hate music, Lane told me that she could not remember a single client who stated a preference for hate music or requested that type of music during their time together. She had encountered patients who liked gangsta rap, including some songs that expressed extremely lurid, derogatory views about women and vilified police, or used "gutter language."

With one patient, she offered to listen to a song, in return for the patient agreeing to listen to a song of her choosing. The patient "backed down." In retrospect, she now thinks a better approach would have been to listen to the patient's song with no conditions and then process the elicited feelings and thoughts. She does not believe that hate music should be censored, but that it must be dealt with wisely, preferably with a therapist who has excellent counseling skills.

Lane retired from University Hospitals in 2018 and is considering her plans. She knows that she will continue to advocate for uses of music as a therapeutic tool and to support AMTA. She will continue to mentor and teach the next generation of music healers. She tells me that previously she had never heard the music of Johnny Rebel, but she has experienced clients whose musical preferences were unfamiliar and required her to learn. Through many challenges, including both overt and covert racism, she has provided a compelling counterpoint to hate music.

I finally asked her if she has now heard any of the music of Johnny Rebel. Here is part of her response:

> "I made myself listen with a purpose, that is, with an ear to determine what kind of person he was. What was in his background that led him to think like this? What message was he trying to send? Did he have a specific ax to grind or did he hate for the sake of hate? Was he looking to shame, humiliate, denigrate, antagonize? Was he angry? Vying for attention, had a specific grudge, resentful because of something that had happened to him or his family? Did he enjoy being in the throes of controversy? Did putting others down make him feel like a better/bigger man? I wondered if he'd been hurt. I'm

sure you have heard that saying, 'Hurt people hurt people.' Could this have applied to him? I guess if I thought I could see between the lines that I might see into his heart and get a glimpse into his mind. I asked myself why and how much time to spend seeking to understand a man's thoughts. Could I spend time more wisely?"

<hr />

MY FAMILIARITY WITH HATE MUSIC WAS GROWING. I HAD learned something about anti-Semitic music, as represented by the examples of Jew Slaughter and Intimidation One. Now I had also learned about antiblack music through the "segregationist songs" of Johnny Rebel. In both cases, I had seen how hatred had been a part of the lives of music therapists—Felice Wolmut and Deforia Lane. The hate music used by the Nazis had played a role in Wolmut coming to America. The ideas expressed in Johnny Rebel's music represented attitudes that affected Lane's family and moved "Them N****rs North."

My next pair of stories considered if music therapists ever treated victims of hate crimes.

Dr. Deforia Lane. Used with written permission.

Chapter 4

JARED LEE LOUGHNER

MAEGAN MORROW

*Isn't it crazy how nothing's the same? In just one
moment, everything changed*

*With a little hope, You can make
it through today*

*With a little faith, Someday you'll get
through the pain*

*Just a little love is enough to light the way
through your darkest night. Hope survives!*

(From the song "Hope Survives" © Cristabelle Braden,
2017, used with permission)

I n this pair of stories, I present the intersection of an
individual who was influenced by hate music, leading
to the commitment of a violent crime, and a music
therapist who was involved in treating the crime victim.
This is also one example of how music is used with individuals who experience traumatic brain injury.

Jared Lee Loughner

On Saturday, January 8, 2011, Tucson, Arizona was sunny and clear, a perfect day for an outdoor community event. US Representative Gabrielle ("Gabby") Giffords, a Democrat from Arizona's Eighth Congressional District, was hosting a "Congress on Your Corner" event for her constituents, in the parking lot of a local Safeway grocery store. A table had been set up, and according to security camera videos, a crowd of between twenty or thirty people was assembled to see their congresswoman and hear her speak.

At 10:10 a.m., a twenty-two-year-old named Jared Lee Loughner, produced a 9mm Glock 19 pistol, with a 33-round magazine, and shot Giffords in the head, from point-blank range. There are reports that she remained conscious but required immediate medical attention. One of her interns, Daniel Hernandez Jr. applied pressure to her forehead and was later credited with saving her life.

Loughner shot eighteen other people that day. Six of those died, including Christina-Taylor Green, who was only nine years old, and a federal judge, John Roll. Others who were present, including one person who had been shot, eventually subdued Loughner.

Loughner had one previous arrest for a minor drug offense, had been kicked out of his college due to disruptive behavior, and had been refused in an attempt to enlist in the army due to being found "unqualified" for service. He had used drugs but had no known, previous history of violence. His parents and friends described Jared as needing help and noted that it was difficult to carry on a coherent conversation with him.

Loughner displayed other symptoms of mental illness. It was reported that he had become paranoid about government and had developed a highly negative preoccupation with Giffords. His parents reported that he had become distant and would not talk to them. He made noises and talked to himself. Some of his friends had broken off their relationship with him, becoming alarmed by his personality. When stopped by police before the shooting, he had started crying.

Several agencies started investigations of the shooting, including the Pima County Sheriff's Department, the Tucson Police Department, and the Arizona Department of Public Safety. President Obama ordered the FBI Director at the time, Robert Mueller, to the scene, and the FBI took over the investigation. If that name sounds familiar, he is the same Robert Mueller appointed as Special Counsel to investigate Russia's interference in the 2016 US presidential election.

Following the incident, Loughner was found to be incompetent to stand trial, diagnosed as a paranoid schizophrenic. As reporters and investigators delved into his past, they found a history of serious mental health issues and bizarre behavior. He received treatment, including involuntary medications, and was eventually determined competent to stand trial. Loughner pleaded guilty to nineteen counts, and was sentenced to seven consecutive life terms plus one hundred forty years in prison without parole.

Was hate music a contributing factor?

An article written by Dennis Wagner, published in *USA Today,* mentioned that Loughner "favored satanic music and had begun espousing conspiracy theories about the 9/11 attack and government control of grammar." Another source said that one of Loughner's favorite YouTube videos was from a satanic site and included the song "Bodies (Let the Bodies Hit the Floor)," by rock group Drowning Pool. It was a mainstream song that received radio airplay.

That band's video appears to depict a mental patient in a hoodie (which Loughner had worn at the time of the shooting), in denial of his illness, wanting change, and advocating violence, as reflected in the song's title. A heavy metal song, its lyrics are screamed at the apparent patient. It has also reportedly been used by the US military to energize soldiers going into battle. One of Loughner's former teachers reported that he submitted a test with "Mayhem Fest" written on it—a reference to a rock festival featuring heavy metal bands.

Immediately following the shooting, Congresswoman Giffords was taken to the University Medical Center in Tucson and listed in critical condition. The bullet had torn through the left hemisphere of her brain, traveling from the left rear of her head and exiting at the left front, close to her left eye. It passed through the part of the brain that controls language, movement on the body's right side, and vision. However, doctors reported that it missed several crucial structures and did not enter the right side of her brain. This would prove to be important during the congresswoman's rehabilitation and recovery.

The horrible, violent incident stimulated many debates on important topics. There were political debates about the use of violent images and hateful language in political campaigns. Both major political parties were criticized. Sarah Palin was singled out for using crosshairs on an election map on her website, indicating that Giffords's congressional seat was one targeted by Republicans. The crosshairs were taken down.

There were debates about mental illness and whether or not mentally ill individuals perpetrate more violence than the general population. The cited research concluded that the mentally ill are no more violent than other members of society, that most violent acts are not perpetrated by mentally ill persons, but that people with mental problems are eleven times more likely to become victims of violence, including suicide or other forms of self-harm. Treatment of the mentally ill was discussed. There were renewed debates about gun control, who should have access to guns, and the types of guns that should be allowed under the Second Amendment of the US Constitution. And…intense attention started to be given to a part of Congresswoman Giffords's medical treatment: music therapy.

Maegan Morrow

WITHIN THIRTY-EIGHT MINUTES OF THE SHOOTING, GIFfords received emergency surgery. A piece of her skull was removed to allow for swelling of her brain, and she was placed in a medically induced coma to facilitate brain rest. Improvement was fairly rapid. Within two weeks of the incident, she had begun preliminary physical therapy. She was transferred to Memorial Hermann Medical Center in Houston, and within days she was moved to The Institute for Rehabilitation and Research (TIRR) Memorial Hermann. This is where part of her treatment included music therapy, with a team that included Maegan Morrow.

The confidentiality of individuals' medical records is guaranteed by the federal Health Insurance Portability and Accountability Act of 1996 law, so many details of Giffords's care are unknown and protected. However, Giffords gave permission for some aspects of her care to be shared, as many media accounts indicate.

Giffords was initially unable to speak, which is referred to as nonfluent aphasia. She also lost part of her vision and was having difficulty walking. A team that included Morrow, speech therapy, physical therapy, nursing care, and neuropsychology—all under the direction of physicians—treated her.

I contacted Morrow, and although she had been through years of interviews, and could not reveal protected details of her work with Giffords, she agreed to talk with me about herself and her work. We exchanged emails and talked on the phone.

How did music therapy help Giffords regain speech?

One way of describing it is that music and speech are stored in different areas of the brain. When the speech center is damaged, music centers can be used to develop new pathways in the brain. Magnetic resonance imaging has demonstrated that music activates multiple areas of the brain. Melody goes to one area, timbre to another, lyrics to another, rhythm to another, and so on. Starting with singing familiar melodies and long-ago memorized lyrics, music facilitates new pathways for speech. This phenomenon is called neuroplasticity.

In Giffords's case, the following songs were used: "Maybe" from the musical *Annie*, "I Can't Give You Anything But Love," "Happy Birthday," "American Pie," "Girls Just Wanna Have Fun," "Free Fallin'," and others. Morrow utilized techniques such as music speech stimulation and melodic intonation therapy in her work with the congresswoman.

Morrow shared that if she had a patient who preferred, or was familiar with, hate music, she would use that music. It's hard to imagine that type of music stored in a person's brain. Most people I have talked with, when asked to recall music from earlier times in their lives, remember songs that were more melodic and had strong hooks. Sing-along songs. Not the usual formula for some hate music.

Music also contributed to Giffords's improvements in her ability to walk and in her emotional recovery. Rhythm was used to support gait training, and the use of well-known songs plus her therapeutic relationship with Morrow supported her mental adjustments to her injury. Morrow shared that she has seen a patient's preferred music help them relax, no matter what the genre, even if it is hate music. Prayer also played a major role, as did Giffords's incredible personal motivation.

Morrow told me that she was attracted to the field of music therapy because she wanted to "use my music and artistic talents to help those in need." She shared that she first heard about music therapy when she was ten years old, because her mother had music and art therapy as a part of her own drug rehabilitation program. She went on to tell me more of her story:

> "I was raised in a very conservative and strict school-ing system. It was predominately Christian. There were rules regarding what music was allowed in school and life in general. I had to follow those rules at school. I was taught in a very legalistic way to worship God by following rules of the Bible and, as I see it, added rules. I was told that rock 'n' roll music was "of the devil" and that I could go to hell or connect with a dark power if I listened to it. I knew from the very moment that I was taught these things, that this could not be true.
>
> "Thankfully, my parents did not agree with that part of the school, and I was allowed to listen to

all types of music growing up. I was encouraged to learn the songs on my own instruments. My parents taught me to sing and harmonize and ear-trained me with some of the greatest popular bands of all time. They made sure that I was classically trained on piano for many years and prepared me to be a strong performer and music major by the time I got to college. I give credit to them for raising me up to be a great musician and music therapist."

Talking more about her parents, Morrow said,

"I have all of their record collections from the seventies and eighties. I also like to say that I was raised on MTV as well. It was a babysitter for me. Even though some people may criticize a child watching MTV at five years old, I actually think it shaped me as a person, musician, and now a therapist.

"I learned at a young age that the arts are going to be attacked for so many reasons. Even religious types will try to kill creativity in order to control others. Over the years, I have learned to give everyone a chance to express themselves through music and creativity, and you will hear and see deeper into what they are trying to say and how they are trying to connect with the world.

"In the matter of using hate music, whether it be in therapy or just for people to express their thoughts, it is our right to create it and use it. I will use it if I see that it is a benefit to making a connection or being able to communicate again with a patient. I think that the world has a right to use it or do away with it as they see fit. If a company does not want to see it or produce it, it is their right to do so as well. Even if I do not agree with the 'hate' content of the music, it doesn't mean that it is not allowed to be produced or created in general. Everyone has a right to speak and this is just another medium to do so. I know that this 'hate' can be spread easily to the younger generations listening and be influenced by the lyrics, but it is up to the parent to protect the youth from this influence."

I have not met Morrow, but some photos of her show a smiling young woman with shoulder-length brown hair. Videos of her work with Giffords and years of interviews show that her hairstyles change over time. She told me that some people have mistaken her for being Hispanic. She is a single mom, sharing parenting duties with her first child's father, a "drummer" and a "rock star," who has been gigging since the age of nine in rock, punk, and metal bands. He is currently a drummer with the rock groups Sonder and Dpat.

As a single mom, she feels that she has great support from her family, friends, and community. During Hurricane Harvey, Morrow told me that she and her daughter were safe, but she was having difficulty reaching her mother, who was transitioning from a hospital to a skilled nursing facility—still dealing with the effects of substance abuse and eating disorders. Morrow was not hesitant to share her family's challenges and difficulties, telling me that we all have problems and that she was willing to include this information as her part of humanity.

Her preparation for work in the field of music therapy included both a college degree and post-college certifications. She studied music therapy at Sam Houston University, under the direction of Mary Ann Nolteriek and Karen Miller. She completed her required music therapy internship in Austin, Texas, at the Center for Music Therapy, with Hope Young. She received additional training to become certified as an NMT Fellow at the Unkefer Academy at Colorado State University. At TIRR Memorial Hermann, she received on-the-job instruction as a brain injury specialist. On the music front, Morrow has performed Christian rock, played in several bands, studied opera, and teaches guitar.

Following her internship, Morrow started her music therapy career working in schools in the greater Houston area. Thirteen years ago, she was hired at TIRR Memorial Hermann, working in the area of physical medicine and rehabilitation. She works with a team of physical therapists, occupational therapists, speech and language pathologists, neuropsychologists, and physicians, serving patients recovering from brain injuries, spinal cord injuries, strokes, Parkinson's disease, and other neurologic disorders.

When I talked to Morrow about hate music, her responses did not surprise me. She stated, "I use all music. I use many genres depending on what is requested. Whatever music is familiar to the patient, I will use for the purpose of creating stimulation in the brain and some type of functional outcome."

She explained that if patients are familiar with hate music, and prefer hate music, she will use it in their therapy. She said, "I do have some clients that prefer music that contains hate language or lyrics, whether they like it for that reason or not, I do not know. I do not pay attention closely to the lyrics all of the time, but I do notice lyrics against cops and derogatory words concerning women and sexuality. I know that some of these lyrics are a way to lash out at other races or take out their pain and anger on different groups."

I asked Morrow if her experience with Giffords has changed any of her thinking on political issues. Raised in a conservative environment, she said that she now considers herself more Libertarian, leaning in a liberal direction. She still strongly supports the First and Second Amendments of the US Constitution. She reflected that she was raised with guns in her home and that Texas is a gun-friendly state, but she now believes there is a need for some regulations related to gun control. People do change, in response to their experiences.

Morrow received a great deal of recognition for her work with Giffords. She saw the media attention as an opportunity to provide a voice for the field of music therapy and to create some jobs for other music therapists. She was also quick to recognize her entire multidisciplinary team. She pointed out that music therapist Amy Marroquin is another neurologic music therapist who has worked at TIRR Hermann Memorial for over seventeen years. Morrow's team was awarded the Caring Heart Award from the Institute for Spirituality and Health. On March 6, 2015, David Muir—referring to the work with Congresswoman Giffords—celebrated music therapists as "persons of the week" on *ABC Evening News*.

Finally, Morrow shared a part of her and her team's treatment philosophy.

Based on an article by two medical doctors, Sunil Kothari and Kristi Kirschner, the philosophy challenges the concept of "do unto others as you would have them do unto you." The authors present the case that practicing the

Golden Rule makes healthcare providers assume how their patients want to be treated, based on their preconceptions, not the patients.' They advocate for a different approach, which focuses on listening to the voice of the patient: Treat others as they wish to be treated.

This intersecting pair of stories taught me more about hate music. First, music interpreted as encouraging violence is even found in mainstream music, as evidenced by Drowning Pool's song, "Bodies." While a large percentage of it may be considered extreme and outside normal variation, even popular songs by popular artists may contain some of the common characteristics of hate music. Also, satanic music sites and festivals, such as Mayhem Fest, can reinforce hateful ideas in unstable, vulnerable minds.

Second, hate music can have a profound, negative influence on individuals who may already be experiencing problems with drug or alcohol abuse, or mental illness.

Third, music therapists have been a part of the treatment teams of victims of hate crimes. This includes treating patients with traumatic brain injuries. Hate music may even be used to open new pathways in the brain, facilitate physical rehabilitation, regain speech, and increase motivation during difficult recovery.

I looked for another example of a music therapist who treated victims of hate crimes. National headlines turned me toward an event that happened on the East Coast.

Congresswoman Gabby Giffords and music therapist Maegan Morrow. Used with written permission from Maegan Morrow.

Chapter 5

Charlottesville

Jim Borling

A s I previously shared, clashes between the Patriot Prayer group, Antifa, and the police continued in my state. I was beginning to see similar clashes in other geographic locations. Chants were heard, and participants were inspired by hate music. This next pair of stories demonstrates the interactions between racists and nonracists at community protest events, as well as the story of a music therapist who was involved in the aftermath of one of those events. They describe the use of chanting as a form of hate music.

Charlottesville

News media provided widespread coverage of events on August 11 and 12, 2017, in Charlottesville, Virginia, when a group of protestors and counterprotestors clashed over the removal of a statue of Confederate General Robert E. Lee from a public park. Heather D.

Heyer was killed after being struck by a car driven by a white supremacist, Alex Fields Jr. Fields was charged with twenty-eight counts of hate crimes, not only for the death of Heyer, but also for the others who were struck by his car. He was convicted and given a prison sentence of life plus 419 years.

A national debate followed the events —in the media, in Congress, on radio and television talk shows and news programs, by late-night comedians, and in the general public—about the makeup and intentions of the two groups of protestors. Reports claimed that the group of original protestors consisted of neo-Nazis, white supremacists, KKK members, and white nationalists. They were reported to have a permit to demonstrate, and some accounts said that their main purpose was to protest the removal of the statue, a symbol to them of their history and Southern heritage. The counter-protestors saw the statue as a reminder and symbol of a culture that included slavery, oppression based on race, and the fight to break up the United States—the Civil War. Violence broke out, with both sides expressing their viewpoints in more than words.

President Trump made a statement that there were good people on both sides but was criticized for his equivocating comments. Even members of both political parties in Congress shared that the counterprotestors had a higher moral position and condemned the makeup and beliefs of the original protestors.

Was hate music heard in Charlottesville? There were reports of the original protestors singing "I Wish I Was in Dixie" and "Dixie," and carrying Confederate flags. I discovered that there were many versions of "Dixie" written and performed before, during, and after the Civil War. There were pro-Union versions and pro-Confederate versions. "Dixie" became a vehicle for expressing hatred.

An example of a version from the North, sometimes referred to as the "Union Dixie," included these lyrics:

> *"Away down south in the land of traitors,*
> *Rattlesnakes and alligators,*
> *Right away, come away, right away, come away.*
> *Where cotton's king and men are chattels,*
> *Union boys will win the battles,*
> *Right away, come away, right away, come away.*
> *Then we'll all go down to Dixie,*
> *Away, away.*
> *Each Dixie boy must understand*
> *That he must mind his Uncle Sam"*

In contrast, here's a Southern, Confederate version, with lyrics by Albert Pike:

> *"Southrons! Hear your country call you!*
> *Up! Lest worse than death befall you!*
> *Hear the Northern thunders mutter!*
> *Northern flags in South wind flutter!*
> *Send them back your fierce defiance!*
> *Stamp upon the cursed alliance!"*

In addition to the right-wing groups singing "Dixie" in Charlottesville, both groups of protestors expressed their free speech in Charlottesville through yelling, flags, banners, slurs, slogans, shields—and chanting.

At Charlottesville, and at an earlier "Unite the Right" march at the University of Virginia, there were chants that could certainly be interpreted as a form of hate music. The statue-removal protestors were recorded as chanting, "Blood and Soil," a translation of the chant, *Blut und Boten*, used in the past to advocate for German nationalism and also interpreted as meaning "race and place."

Other chants were broadcast on national news programs, including: "You will not replace us/Jews will not replace us," expressions of anti-Semitism; "White Lives Matter," a white supremacist reaction to the "Black Lives Matter" movement; "The South will rise again," an obvious white supremacy, Southern heritage chant; and "Russia is our friend," support for President Trump's efforts to develop a better relationship with Russia, and a nod to totalitarianism or fascism.

Seeming remarkably out of place, they also chanted, "Harry Potter is not real," apparently a slap at the theme of multiculturalism and tolerance in the famed series of books by J. K. Rowling. Both protestors and counter-protestors argued that their "Lives Matter" chants were not racist but represented their desire to advocate for equal treatment of a specific race, heritage, and/or culture.

Chants have existed for a long time. They can be described as spoken or sung words, sometimes using simple melodies with few notes. Often used in various religious ceremonies, such as Gregorian Chants sung by monks centuries ago, or acapella chants in Latin (or other languages) in present-day churches, chants and songs have also been used at political protest rallies and in other settings.

Chants can even be heard at sporting events. For example, at basketball games, you can hear chants of "air ball" when a player makes a poor shot that doesn't even reach the rim. (Interestingly, studies have shown that when fans chant, "Air ball," it is always on the same notes, F and D, and in perfect rhythmic unison. This has been labeled as an example of "spontaneous large-group precision chanting.")

You may have also heard words from the Ray Charles song "Hit the Road Jack" when a player fouls out, or someone is ejected from a game. The purpose is to shame or humiliate the opposing player or team, even when sung in "good fun," in "a competitive spirit," or to support the home team. When racial overtones are thrown in, these innocent-sounding and intended chants can be viewed as examples of hate music.

In Poznan, Poland, soccer fans were reported to shout out, "Go Jews. Get out. Go to Auschwitz," and "Send you to the gas chamber" at the opposing team. Some of those fans were taken to court for violating anti-hate statutes. Interpreting Polish laws, the local prosecutor determined that the chants were not racist, because none of the opposing team was Jewish, and there were no Jewish people in the stands. I checked YouTube and found many examples of racist chants being used at sporting events.

In 2012—unable to play in the United States due to a lockout in the National Hockey League—many American hockey players had contracts with European teams. A skater with the Philadelphia Flyers, Wayne Simmonds, was playing for the Liberic White Tigers, in the Czech Republic. During a match, a fight broke out between the White Tigers and players of the opposing team. Following the ruckus on the field, Simmonds, who is black, was subjected to chants of *opice*, which is the Czech word for "monkey." Company honchos from both teams issued statements condemning the chants.

In their statements, they wrote, "We damn this behavior and do not identify with it. We do not consider our fans people who participated in racist chanting." Simonds previously had a banana peel thrown at him at a soccer match in London, Ontario.

During a 2016 soccer match between Sporting Gijon and Athletic Bilbao (two Spanish teams), player Inaki Williams was called for a foul. Williams, who is the first black member of the Athletic Bilbao team in its 118-year history, was then subjected to continuous racial chants from fans until the referee refused to let the match continue. Members of the opposing team urged their fans to discontinue the chants, and a public address announcement reminded fans that racist chants would not be allowed. Eventually, the match continued, but this was not the first-time racist chants had marred a soccer match in Spain. A previous incident at a Sporting Gijon match, in 2008, had resulted in the team receiving a fine of 3,000 euros.

Charlottesville, with its singing of "Dixie" and its chants, punctuated the polarities in the United States. It showed extremism along the political spectrum—North against South. Whites against other races. Left-wing versus right-wing. Efforts to honor heritage, and efforts to put negative aspects of history to rest.

After Charlottesville, songwriter Paddy Tarleton (also identified as Patrick Corcoran), released the song "Charlottesville Ballad (War is Coming)" on YouTube. The melody of the song is from an old 1920s Irish protest song, "Come Out Ye Black and Tans." Tarleton frequently uses old folk melodies in his songs. Tony McAleer, a former white supremacist and co-founder of the organization Life After Hate, says that those melodies are powerful, because "they can carry thoughts and memories and emotions through the generations."

The lyrics to Tarleton's song, published in an SPLC article, contain many of the common elements of hate music, including name calling, anti-Semitic language, threats of violence, placement of blame, and conspiracy theories. One of Tarleton's goals is to document, in song, an "alt-right" perspective on clashes between white supremacists/white nationalists and counterprotestors. He is proud that his music inflames liberals but sees that it intrigues disaffected whites. He is quoted in the article as saying, "Fortunately, for us, we are growing, and the opposition's hatred for us is exactly what is helping us grow."

Tarleton would probably be proud of the use of his music as propaganda. In February 2020, the ADL released a report on the growing propaganda efforts of white supremacists. Those activities included the use of rallies, protests, fliers, stickers, banners, posters, leaflets, book clubs, and unannounced, quickly dispersed flash demonstrations. Music, unfortunately, was not listed as a propaganda method. It should have been.

The ADL reported 2,713 cases of propaganda incidents in 2019, which were twice the number of cases of the previous year. College campuses were widely targeted. Organizations carrying out the propaganda campaigns included Patriot Front, American Identity Movement, New Jersey European Heritage Association, Daily Stormer Book Clubs, The Base, Feuerkrieg Division, Hundred Handlers, Revolt Through Tradition, National Alliance, Atomwaffen Division, Church of Creativity, Folks Front, Racialist National Party, Creativity Alliance, Iron Youth, Legion of Saint Ambrose, American Vanguard, League of the South, National Socialist

Movement, Shield Wall Network, and Rise Above Movement.

Ideas espoused by these groups included Holocaust denial, white supremacy, anti-Semitism, and attacks on Jews, Blacks, Muslims, nonwhite immigrants, and the LGBTQ+ community.

The ADL report did not mention the use of music to spread propaganda. Yet, my research was exposing the potent role of music in promoting and reinforcing hateful ideologies, and Charlottesville was just one example.

In their book, *American Swastika* (Rowman & Littlefield Publishers, 2010), Pete Simi and Robert Futrell detail what they call the "hidden spaces of hate." Here is one quote from their book:

> "Music is an integral part of the white power move-ment. Aryans use music to convey ideas about their righteous struggles, focus movement activities, and unite racists in Aryan free spaces, which range from house parties to bar shows and festivals to music websites. In these free spaces, Aryan members dis-play their style and share attitudes and emotions that bind them as racial extremists."

(Remember, Clifford Trahan, as Johnny Rebel, claimed that whites did not form attitudes like blacks did.)

Simi and Futrell also quote a California skinhead girl, who shared with sociologist Kathleen Blee, "How I really started believing, thinking, in that white separatist sense and then got all white supremacist, it was really through the music…. It gives you an identity…you're special, you know, because you're white."

Jim Borling

I LEARNED THAT MUSIC THERAPY PLAYED A ROLE IN THE aftermath of Charlottesville. Jim Borling, a long-time music therapy professor at Radford University in Virginia, was contacted to provide post-trauma counseling and debriefing for individuals who had been counterprotestors. Several of them were experiencing depression and grief, especially over the murder of Heather Heyer. A number of those seeking help had also been injured by the passing car that hit Heyer or had fallen as they ran. Several had bruises on their bodies. Due to confidentiality issues, Borling could not share specific stories about those individuals.

Without sharing personal, protected information, Borling told me that he had worked with about twelve individuals in a single, multisession treatment group. All of his clients were white, both male and female, and between the ages of twenty-two and thirty-five. He described the group as having "a PTSD (Post-Traumatic Stress Disorder) posture with several expressing emotional distress."

According to Borling, the group was very private and could "be easily described as part of the ANTIFA movement." To help them, Borling utilized relaxation training, guided imagery, mindfulness experiences, song lyric discussions, and some rhythm-based drumming techniques—all, evidence-based music therapy methods. Treatment goals included uses of music to form group cohesion, learn skills for coping with stress, process the Charlottesville incident, and debrief the resulting trauma reaction.

I decided to contact Borling, to hear his personal story. We had known each other for years but had little contact since we lived on opposite coasts. We had copresented at a national music therapy conference, on the topic of uses of music in treatment programs for substance abusers, and I had read some of his articles. I researched his background on several websites and then we scheduled time to chat.

Borling was aware of the chanting in Charlottesville and other hate music. When I asked him about the uses of hate music, as a music therapist, he said that he did not believe that it should be censored. He said that if he had a client who brought hate music to a therapy session, he would ask the person to enter into a conversation about why that might be a focus for them, and what could be gained by using that music in therapy. What would the hoped-for outcome be?

He added, "If I sense resistance, denial, or a need to win me over, I would likely state that hate music is not appropriate for our work together at this time."

The youngest of three brothers, Borling grew up in Glen Ellyn, Illinois, a western suburb of Chicago. He described his childhood as "normal," with parents who "were together." He was the youngest of three brothers. His older brother became a Lutheran minister but, unfortunately, his middle brother died from cancer at the age of forty-nine. Growing up, the three brothers were competitive. Borling participated in music but also played basketball, football, and baseball.

Borling uses a quote from the Dalai Lama at the bottom of his emails:

"This is my simple religion. There is no need for temples, no need for complicated philosophy. Our own brain, our own heart is our temple; the philosophy is kindness."

I asked him to explain the quote. He shared that spirituality has played a big role in his life and music therapy practice. While he was raised a Lutheran and studied other religions, he believes that there is no need to be restrained by any specific religion, that people should strive to have full emotional experiences, and that it is important to be compassionate.

Borling shared that his own, personal experiences with addiction and recovery have informed and shaped who he is. He denied having any major traumas in his life, except for addiction struggles that led him to survive some life-and-death situations and forced him to "face the dragon." The moments and milestones along his journey from addiction to recovery are memorialized in tattoos across both arms and covering his back and chest.

When he was a junior in high school, Borling first heard about music therapy when some visiting college professors presented information about possible careers. The music therapy profession resonated deeply with him, and he said that he instantly knew that was what he wanted to do for his life's work. He admitted that he made the decision based purely on hearing the words "music therapy," without knowing what the profession entailed.

Still an athlete, football earned him a scholarship that paid for an undergraduate music education degree at DePauw University in Greencastle, Indiana. From there, he completed a master's degree in music therapy from the University of Miami in Coral Gables, Florida. He completed his required internship at the Georgia Mental Health Institute in Atlanta, where he worked with adolescent and adult psychiatric patients.

Following his internship, Borling returned to Florida,

where he worked in the Miami school system with emotionally disturbed children and adolescents, as well as with individuals with developmental disabilities. A colleague told him about a second music therapy faculty position opening at Radford University in Virginia. At that time, Miami was a tough town, with the "cocaine cowboys" creating a culture of drug wars and violence. Borling was anxious to leave that environment, so he investigated the job at Radford.

Radford University, located in southwestern Virginia, appealed to Borling. Its website states (https://www.radford.edu/content/radfordcore/home/about.html):

"First and foremost, the university emphasizes teaching and learning and the process of learning in its commitment to the development of mature, responsible, well-educated citizens. Radford University develops students' creative and critical thinking skills, teaches students to analyze problems and implement solutions, helps students discover their leadership styles, and fosters their growth as leaders. Toward these ends, the university is student-focused and promotes a sense of caring and of meaningful interaction among all members of the University community."

As an institution, Radford promotes a code of ethics that focuses on the principles of respect, honesty, integrity, communication, stewardship, excellence, responsibility, and accountability. These qualities impressed Borling, matching his own ethics and ideas. I wondered if hate musicians have a code of ethics.

Borling applied for the job and was hired. He and his wife fell in love with Radford, viewing it as the perfect place to settle down and raise a family.

Borling's principal instrument in college had been the trombone. He played in school concert bands, jazz bands, and marching bands and performed professionally. He remembers being on the road with bands, performing covers of songs by the bands Chicago and Blood, Sweat, and Tears. Later, when he moved into the faculty position at Radford, Borling taught music therapy courses but also continued to teach trombone. Music therapy and other personal and professional obligations eventually filled his days, and he finally gave up teaching the trombone. But he also expanded his musical chops by gaining additional training in the methods of Guided Imagery with Music (GIM) and the use of drumming as a healing medium (rhythm-based music therapy).

Even while teaching full time at Radford, Borling remained clinically active as a music therapist. He offered music therapy services at Lewis-Gale Hospital in Salem, Lewis-Gale Chronic Pain Center in Roanoke, The Center for Behavioral and Rehabilitative Medicine in Roanoke, The Life Center of Galax Drug and Alcohol Treatment Center in Galax, and at Avenues to Recovery in Roanoke.

Borling and his wife, Nannette, also run MusicVisions, a company providing outpatient treatment. His wife is now a nursing professor but also has a background in music therapy. They are both fellows of the Association for Music and Imagery, trained in the Bonny Method of GIM.

A method developed by music therapist Helen Bonny, GIM uses classical music to facilitate deep relaxation and journeys into the imagination. The technique and its adaptations have been shown to benefit mental, emotional, physical, and spiritual aspects of well-being. Nannette is also a Reiki Master (Reiki is a Japanese technique that uses relaxation and stress reduction to promote healing.)

Borling has been active in professional music therapy associations—giving presentations, publishing journal articles, writing book chapters, and conducting workshops. His workshops have taken him to Germany, Mexico, Korea and, most recently, to Spain. He has served both AMTA and the Certification Board for Music Therapists.

You can also find Borling riding his motorcycle as a member of the Patriot Guard. If you are not familiar with that group, here is some language from its website:

> "The Patriot Guard is a diverse amalgamation of riders from across the nation. We have one thing in common besides motorcycles. We have an unwavering respect for those who risk their very lives for America's freedom and security including Fallen Military Heroes, First Responders and honorably discharged Veterans. If you share this respect, please join us.
>
> "We don't care what you ride or if you ride, what your political views are, or whether you're a hawk or dove. It is not a requirement that you be a veteran. It doesn't matter where you're from or what your income is; you don't even have to ride. The only prerequisite is Respect.
>
> "Our main mission is to attend the funeral services of fallen American heroes as *invited guests of the family.*"

One of the things that I learned about hate music, while conducting my research, was that some hate musicians were recruited into the hate movement because they were seeking a place to belong. Many of them had been victims of parental neglect or abuse, bullying at school, rejection by the opposite sex, or lack of acceptance by their immediate peers.

For some, mental health issues existed, or personal or familial substance abuse played a role. They just wanted to feel a part of something important and were vulnerable to being groomed and recruited to extremist groups. Some of them never fully understood or accepted the beliefs of the groups that they joined. Granted, others who have survived negative circumstances did not turn to racism or violence, and some hate group joiners believed in the ideology. In Borling's case, he found a music therapy community that was accepting and inclusive. And he found other organizations, such as the Patriot Guard, that welcomed his involvement.

For his books *Angry White Men* and *Healing from Hate: How Young Men Get into and Out of Violent Extremism* (Nation Books, 2017), Michael Kimmel interviewed forty-five active white nationalists and seventy "formers." While many believed and supported racist causes, some did not. Like some of the lyrics to the Phil Everly song, "When will I be Loved" (sung by Linda Ronstadt and others), they felt ignored, and strove to fill the need for affection in their lives. They were adrift and isolated.

An example of this is Chris Harper-Mercer, who, at age twenty-six, shot and killed ten people, including himself, at Umpqua Community College in Oregon on October 1, 2015. He left behind a manifesto in which he shared,

"My interests include listening to music, watching movies, internet piracy…," and, "I have always been the most hated person in the world. Ever since I arrived in this world, I have been under siege from it. Under attack from morons and idiots…. My whole life has been one lonely enterprise. One loss after another. And here I am, 26, with no friends, no job, no girlfriend, a virgin. I long ago realized that society likes to deny people like me these things. People who are elite, people who stand with the gods."

Harper-Mercer lived with his mother, and both of them had been diagnosed with Asperger's syndrome, a high-functioning condition along the autism spectrum. I wondered what his music playlist included, and how much it influenced his eventual progression into mass murder.

In his book *The Cure for Hate* (Arsenal Pulp Press, 2019), Tony McAleer makes the point that anger, left unchecked, eventually leads to murder. A former leader in the white supremacist movement, McAleer entered therapy to gain insights into his own hateful ideas and to learn to forgive himself. In his book, I read about the power of compassion, forgiveness, and making amends as strong tools to help check anger. From recovering haters, I began to see some options for addressing root causes.

The majority of Kimmel's interviewees were young men, and they didn't feel like they were living up to societal expectations placed on men. They were victims, and they were ripe for someone to tell them whom they could blame. They just wanted to find a group to belong to. Many of them were recruited, with promises of protection, inclusion, and respect. They were in search of a way to contribute to something important. And hate music was often a part of the recruitment process and culture.

The tattoos on Jim Borling's body attest to his personal struggles, but he successfully made choices to move away from anger, hate, and substance abuse. He took the musical road less traveled, to help others.

Charlottesville produced another incident related to hate music and recovery. Following the death of Heyer, former hate musician Picciolini, lead singer of the band White American Youth, arranged to introduce a white power, white nationalist follower to Heather's mother. Picciolini is now a founding member of the organization Life After Hate. A YouTube video documents the meeting, where Heyer's mother respectfully greets and talks with her visitor. It appears that he listens, and gains insight into the pain and grief caused by the white power movement.

Jim Borling, Radford University, Radford, Virginia.
Used with written permission

Chapter 6

Skrewdriver

Vally Weigl

I don't want to be hated.
They harmonized in Hebrew about how Jews
have prevailed despite persecution through
generations. They wrapped each other in their
arms. They swayed. Their music, from the
Maimonides' Thirteen Principles of Faith, told
of a time free of war and full of peace.

From *USA Today*, October 29, 2018,
after Robert Bowers killed eleven people
at Tree of Life Synagogue in
Pittsburgh, Pennsylvania

There could be no greater contrast between two stories than those of a British male rock singer/ songwriter with a white nationalist band, who was labeled a "Nazi Rock Star" by one biographer, and a female composer who fled from Austria to avoid the Nazis and later became a music therapist in the United States.

Despite their differences, they also had some similarities. Both of them became politically active. Both of them used music to express their opposing values and beliefs. Some of the years of their lives overlapped. I wondered if they ever heard each other's music. I doubt it.

Skrewdriver

ONE OF THE MOST WELL-KNOWN HATE MUSIC BANDS IS Skrewdriver, led by front man Ian Stuart Donaldson. Although the band went through numerous lineup changes, Ian Stuart, (his stage name dropped his real last name), was the constant. As I read books and articles about hate music, Skrewdriver was mentioned in almost every reference.

Ian Stuart Donaldson was born on August 11, 1957, in Lancashire, England—northwest of London. His family lived in a well-off part of town. A neighbor, close friend, and future bandmate was John Grinton. The two boys took an early interest in music, especially the music of The Rolling Stones and The Who. From an early age, both boys got into scuffles and skirmishes, and during some of those fights, Donaldson exhibited a lack of tolerance for foreigners and immigrants.

As teens, both Donaldson and Grinton (a.k.a. "Grinny") read about the skinhead movement and started to adopt the skinhead image. This bothered their families, which blamed each other for their sons' troublesome, adolescent attitudes and behaviors. But the boys remained friends, getting deeper into the skinhead image, violent culture, and Oi! and punk music. Oi! Music created songs that were more antiestablishment and anticonformist. They were rebellious. From the perspective of democratic free speech, they forced people to think. They expressed the feelings of disenfranchised youth. They challenged the status quo and ignored political correctness.

Grinny was in a band, The Warlocks, and Donaldson took guitar lessons from one of the group members. When The Warlocks broke up in 1975, Donaldson convinced Grinny and a few other friends to form a new band named Tumbling Dice—a nod to The Rolling Stones song of the same title, which had been recorded in 1972. Playing only a smattering of original songs, sets performed by Tumbling Dice were heavy on Stones covers, with some songs by other groups thrown in. Grinny missed several rehearsals, and Donaldson fired him from the band. Grinny returned to the reformed Warlocks, but his firing from Tumbling Dice created a strain between the two boys.

As Tumbling Dice developed a local following, they were offered a chance to record for a company in London. However, some members of the band balked at moving south to London, so Ian dissolved the band. He reconciled with Grinny and invited him to rejoin the band. After months of rehearsing, apparently with Grinny being present this time, the band recorded a demo in the setting of Donaldson's father's workplace, a factory.

Based on the demo and a letter from Donaldson, London-based Chiswick Records sent a representative to watch the band perform what had evolved into a more "punk" music set. They were offered a recording contract. The original line-up of the band included Donaldson, Phil Walmsley, Ron Hartley, Kev McKay, Dirk Deem, and Grinny. Chiswick sent a list of new band names for the group to choose from, and Donaldson chose Skrewdriver, with a "k."

Skrewdriver almost immediately began to develop a fan base, both on their home turf of Blackpool, Lancashire, and in London. Their set list included both sides of their new Chiswick single, "You're So Dumb," an antidrug song, and "Better Off Crazy"—as well as another song, "Antisocial," foreshadowing things to come.

When they applied to provide a farewell concert at a park in Blackpool, before moving to London, the Blackpool Council denied approval. Parks Director Fred Mathews stated in the local paper, "Punk rock groups are on the way out extreme, and while I have never seen one performing, it is well known that their music can be offensive. They attract a section of people that other park users may consider undesirable."

After the request to perform in the park was denied, a committee of the Blackpool Council additionally banned the band from future concerts. It was also reported that the British Broadcasting Corporation had banned them. The negative publicity only served to increase interest in the band, especially with young fans who favored the antiestablishment fervor of the punk music scene—many of them young skinheads.

The boys moved to London, playing on concert bills with the Sex Pistols, The Police, Sham 69, the Nine Nine Nine, The Boomtown Rats, The Damned, and others. Some of the early concerts resulted in violent clashes with anti-punk "Teddy Boys." Donaldson admitted to a reporter that he liked fighting, and Skrewdriver intensified the skinhead image and continued to draw skinheads and members of the National Front (NF, an extreme conservative, right-wing group) to its concerts. They were beginning to see bookings canceled due to their skinhead image, racist audience, the presence of violence, and the perception that they were aligned with the NF.

Following the success of the band's initial releases, Chiswick agreed to record a second, full album with Skrewdriver. They were booked to appear with some well-known bands and received some invitations to perform on radio and TV. However, there was negative backlash, and Donaldson wrote a letter to the press to try and defend the group. Skepticism was still present—both in the music industry and in the press. The band's reputation had turned dark, and many of their new bookings were canceled.

Of the dates that remained, the press either ignored them or wrote many unflattering reviews. They could not shake their reputation for being a skinhead band that attracted violence. There were changes in the band's lineup and periods of frustration. Chiswick severed its ties to the band, the second album was canceled, and members of the band returned to the north.

In a letter to *Melody Maker,* Donaldson claimed, "The biased information that appeared recently in your paper, and which RAR [Rock Against Racism] seems to be responsible for, is false. The news that Skrewdriver is reforming to do NF gigs is complete and utter bulls**t. I have no interest in politics and never have. I've also been told that RAR has solid links with the Anti-Nazi League, an organization who, it seems, are backed heavily by the Communist and Marxist parties, who in their way are just as much a threat to this country as the NF or BM" [British Movement, later called the British National Socialist Movement].

Donaldson stated that he was forming a new band that "doesn't intend to do gigs for the RAR, NF or any other political organization." The future proved differently. By

July 1981, Donaldson announced that Skrewdriver would go on a national tour, sponsored by the NF. However, due to anti-punk, anti-skinhead feelings of some older NF leaders, the tour did not materialize. Donaldson moved back to London and fell in with the NF crowd.

Skrewdriver was again reformed under Donaldson's direction, with a new lineup of musicians, which did not include his old friend Grinny. The band immediately recorded songs for the Boots and Braces label, a label devoted to skinhead music. After an absence from performing, Skrewdriver reappeared on the scene and became a hot commodity. They sold out shows at London's 100 Club and did a short, disastrous tour to Holland.

Following the tour, the group geared up for more recording, this time with White Noise Records, which was connected to the NF. Donaldson wrote new songs, more fascist and racist in content. New songs were titled "Tomorrow Belongs to Me," "White Power," "Smash the IRA," and "Soldier of Freedom." When performing, Donaldson often expressed his political views between songs, including discourses that were anti-immigrant, anti-black, and anti-Semitic. His speeches drew Nazi *Sieg Heils* from the audience. So much for being apolitical. The NF was pleased.

It is not clear what led to Donaldson's transition. How did a punk rocker with supposedly no political leanings evolve into a racist, far-right extremist? Did he have negative experiences with members of minority groups? Did he read and believe propaganda? Were there significant people in his orbit who influenced him? Were opposing viewpoints ignored or kept from him?

Was he seduced by the power and limelight of being a rock star? Did he receive enough feedback from similar-thinking fans to convince him that his opinions were widely accepted?

Was the fun, camaraderie, and excitement too reinforcing? Did he feel more like a man? Did he feel like he was involved with something important that would make the world better for others?

Hypothetically, all of the above.

It was the 1980s but, like today, there were "opposite and equal" reactions to Skrewdriver's new hate music. Members of the music press criticized them, the general press panned them, other bands denounced them, and some venues refused to book them. RAR supporters targeted them and some left-leaning bands would not play on the same stage with them. Anti-fascist groups countered skinhead violence with their own brand of violence. The police were caught in the middle, trying to enforce laws and control criminal assaults. Just like Patriot Prayer and Antifa on the recent streets of Portland.

Despite the negative reactions, the NF and its supporters stuck with Skrewdriver. Their popularity with a particular subgroup of the population was growing. Live performances at select venues were selling out, and record sales through nonmainstream outlets—a few select retail outlets and mail order—were robust.

Donaldson was working—when not songwriting, rehearsing, recording, or performing—as the NF organizer for Central London, recruiting new members. Some NF officials were not fans of Skrewdriver, but they welcomed both new NF members and increased revenues. The music of Skrewdriver and Donaldson's notoriety played a pivotal role in the recruitment process.

Skrewdriver was not the only band in the NF corner.

Other bands, such as the Ovaltinees, Brutal Attack, Indecent Exposure, and Public Enemy, were also promoting far-right, conservative, extremist, NF sentiments. Full of hatred for various demographic groups and advocating for white nationalism.

In 1984, Skrewdriver experienced another, major personnel change. The new lineup consisted of Murray Holme on bass, Adam Douglas on guitar, "Scotty" on drums (Scotty had produced their earlier recordings), and Donaldson. The quartet prepared to record a compilation album for a joint venture between the NF-supported White Noise Records and Rock-o-Rama Records. The latter record company had developed a specialty in right-wing hate music recordings in Europe and would release most of Skrewdriver's future recordings. Artwork for the compilation album showed a Viking shore raid.

(Note: For my research, I was able to easily order a copy of another Skrewdriver compilation album, containing songs from their later albums, *Boots and Braces* and *Voice of Britain*. The album was on Rock-o-Rama Records and included a Rock Against Communism sticker.)

Skrewdriver headlined some outdoor festivals, which were carefully planned to attract like-minded audience members—mostly skinheads—and minimize counterprotestors. Violence in the skinhead music scene continued to draw negative attention in the press and with the general public. Several publications of the NF and other right-wing organizations included stories about Skrewdriver and provided information about the band's upcoming appearances. Unable to advertise through conventional media outlets, concerts were often promoted via word-of-mouth.

Even though several of the more popular NF bands landed Rock-o-Rama recording deals, profits from record sales seemed to benefit mainly the record company and the NF. The financial benefits to musicians were low, and some were being stiffed. It is not known how much compensation Donaldson received for song or performance royalties, or if he even cared about money. Today, Skrewdriver recordings are still producing sales and profits. Donaldson was more interested in promoting "the cause." His onstage diatribes attacked blacks, Jews, gays, and immigrants—any group that was not heterosexual or white.

In 1985, Donaldson and one of his NF roommates were involved in a fight with a black gang, resulting in the two of them being arrested, convicted of violent disorder, and sentenced to twelve months in prison. Donaldson's first stop was at Wormwood Scrubbs prison, which had an inmate population that included many blacks. Given his reputation, it was not a safe situation for him.

Within a few weeks, he was transferred to a lower-level, predominantly white prison. With decreased security at the new prison, he was allowed the use of an acoustic guitar. He filled some of his time writing new songs. In prison, he also wrote and received hundreds of letters and had many visitors who kept him informed about current events.

In early 1986, the NF newsletter published an article by Donaldson, sent from prison, in which he presented his white nationalist beliefs. He referred to his race as having an "infinitely superior history," attacked politicians and laws that benefited minorities and immigrants, pontificated against the United States and Soviet "war games," and stated that American capitalism had become a "vulgar, drug-sodden, multi-racial mess."

Donaldson finally broke from NF in 1987. He was tired of internal politics and squabbling between sub-factions, and especially of how some NF leaders tried to control, use, and take advantage of the successes of Skrewdriver and other bands. He wanted an organization that would remove others from controlling the music and would bring together groups and fans from diverse right-wing corners. Perhaps ironic was the fact that Donaldson's opinion of the NF seemed to match his similar views on the controlling nature of the government, the police, and some racial groups. The new entity was called Blood and Honour, its name drawn from the inscription on weapons of Adolf Hitler's SS. (SS stands for *Schutzstaffel*, German for "Protective Echelon." The SS started as a small group of Hitler's personal body-guards, but eventually grew to more than two hundred fifty thousand members.)

Blood and Honour was also the name of the organization's first publication, a paper which introduced the new organization as representing independent "Rock Against Communism (RAC)," with management by "people who really care about the nationalist music scene." (RAC, in fact, did little to fight against communism. Instead, it evolved into a very racist organization, its initials only lacking the letter E.)

Donaldson's decision to separate from the NF seemed beneficial to him and the band. New concerts were booked and well attended, merchandise flew off concession stands, and records were being stocked and sold, even in some mainstream shops. One record shop named Cutdown—owned by Andrew Benjamin, who was Jewish—offered a variety of anti-Semitic products, including Skrewdriver records. Both the press and the Jewish Board of Deputies criticized him, but he offered a common defense in the hate music industry that he was just meeting a demand for the products. The business was lucrative. In 1991, Benjamin was convicted of "behavior likely to incite racial hatred" and spent time in jail.

Already gaining followers in England, Skrewdriver's popularity spread to Germany, Sweden, and other parts of Europe and Scandinavia. Skrewdriver and Blood and Honour appeared to be uniting a disparate skinhead culture, which had been the goal. When the band appeared on stages, they were greeted by mostly young men yelling, "Sieg Heil." The Nazi salutes were followed by racist chanting between musical numbers, similar to the more recent chanting in the United States, in Charlottesville.

The NF, somewhat stunned by the creation of Blood and Honour, began to lose some of its power and became antagonistic toward the new organization. In addition, liberal groups tried to disrupt the white power music move-ment, but legal challenges were usually ineffective due to freedom of speech protections. White Nationalist skinhead bands as far away as Australia and Japan began to emulate Skrewdriver and cover its songs.

Donaldson was again arrested for violent disorder after a pub fight with a group of gays. He remained in prison for three months, standing trial five times. He used the time to write, read, and correspond with his fans. He was finally released, due to a judge's finding of insufficient evidence. Rock-o-Rama, taking advantage of the publicity and Don-aldson's new songs, signed Skrewdriver and several other bands to new, three-year contracts—requiring two new albums of material per year. The pressure was on to meet those contractual requirements.

For at least one booking, Skrewdriver used an assumed name, Strike Force, and was able to advertise the appearance in leading music publications, which, when discovered, was an embarrassment to some editors and publishers. Donaldson also formed a second band, The Klansmen, which listed its members as Jeb Stuart, Jed Clampett, and JB Forrest—all fake stage names.

The band recorded some songs in a rockabilly style, including lyrics that echoed racist sentiments from the United States. Donaldson was even photographed with Confederate flags as props or in the background. Donaldson did some solo recording and, for a short time, fronted another band named White Diamond. Rock-o-Rama Records, wanting to capitalize on the movement, gave Donaldson the green light to produce anything that could be sold.

As Skrewdriver continued to record and perform, antiracist and antifascist groups continued to dog them, especially Donaldson. Living in London was becoming a challenge and, at times unsafe, so Donaldson left the big city and moved back north. Skrewdriver limited concerts during this period to venues in cities such as Stafford, Derby, Newcastle, and Nottingham, the part of England known as the Midlands. The area had a strong conservative base, some skinheads, and a population that seemed more accepting and friendly to Donaldson and his band.

Sound familiar? What about Johnny Rebel's song "Move Them N****rs North"? Seems that even hate musicians must sometimes change geographic location for their own safety.

When the band was not in the Midlands, they performed in Europe, especially in Germany and Italy, where the band had devoted fans. Donaldson was worshiped and swarmed by fans at some concerts. In some venues, he eagerly mixed with his fans after performing, sharing beers, autographs, and promoting white power.

In 1991, Donaldson announced his engagement to Diane Calladine, sister of Skrewdriver's lead guitarist. Previous female friends had often been one-night stands and were viewed by some as distractions from his work for the white power cause. Diane was seen in a similar light, as taking advantage of Donaldson because he reportedly showered her with gifts.

On a trip to Germany to participate in a white pride event, Donaldson and Diane returned to their hotel one evening, leaving other Skrewdriver members to party with local skinheads. Violence broke out when beer-saturated skinheads attacked a socialist club. Police arrested six people following the melee, four of them being members of Skrewdriver.

With his band in a German prison, Donaldson enlisted a German skinhead band, Stuerkraft, to back him up at the planned concert. When he took to the stage at the event, Donaldson was given an ovation by the two thousand skinheads in attendance.

Nineteen ninety-two brought a new scandal. One of Skrewdriver's security team, Nicky Crane, came out as a gay man. Donaldson and the band were shocked and outraged. Seeing homosexuality as a perversion, Donaldson expressed his anger in the Blood and Honour paper and called for Crane's murder during one of his concert rants. He also told gay skinheads to "keep away from our movement." The scandal motivated disgusted Blood and Honour skinheads to launch attacks on gay bars. Crane died eighteen months later from AIDS.

For the rest of 1992 and into 1993, Donaldson and Skrewdriver continued to perform their racist music. A major concert in London, nicknamed the Battle of Waterloo, pitted the neo-Nazi, white power, Blood and Honour skinheads against both antifascists and the police. Efforts to cancel or disrupt the event failed, but clashes between the opposing groups were featured in headlines in the press. At the concert, Donaldson again vented his anger at blacks, the police, lefties, liberals, opposition bands, and others. Both his verbal tirades and his songs were followed by the usual Hitler salutes from his audience.

Ian Stuart Donaldson died in a car crash on September 23, 1993, at the age of thirty-six. Of the five occupants of the car, three survived. There were conspiracy theories that Donaldson's death was not an accident, but one survivor of the crash said, "It was just a blowout." Thirty-six is a young age to pass away. If Donaldson had lived a longer life, I wonder if any of his extremist views would have changed. If he married Diane and had children, would the innocence of those children and their lack of learned prejudice have affected his thinking? Would he have sought help from a British group similar to the group in the United States, Life After Hate?

In the years since Donaldson's death, his devotees have held annual celebrations in his honor, have written tribute songs, and sales of his many recordings have continued. Bootleg recordings have demanded high prices. The Skrewdriver symbol adorns clothing, patches, pins, and body tattoos. Ian Stuart Donaldson's music still inspires white supremacists and racists everywhere. Others have taken up his cause, spreading hate. People die. Their music remains.

Vally Weigl

SAN RAFAEL, CALIFORNIA, IS LOCATED ON THE NORTH-
west side of the San Francisco Bay, just a short drive from
the Golden Gate Bridge. It is the former location of several villages of Native American Miwok Indians. It is also
where director George Lukas—who produced such films as
American Graffiti, Star Wars, and *Indiana Jones*—located
his company, Lukasfilm, in 1971. It has become a Northern
California mecca for entertainment and high-tech companies. It is also populated with an ethnically and racially
diverse, mostly Democrat, population.

My wife and I visited San Rafael on a road trip in October
2018. We had a dinner appointment but arrived in the city
earlier in the day, so we did some exploring. First, we visited
the Mission San Rafael Arcángel, named after the Archangel
Raphael, the Angel of Healing. The mission was created in
1817 as a hospital for Native Americans who had become
ill due to the cold environments of other missions. Father
Luis Gil was put in charge of the hospital and in leading the
Native Americans to Christianity. History indicates that
the mission was successful in both healing and converting.

After a short walk up the street, we happened upon The
Museum of International Propaganda, which was not previously known to us. The museum presents the collection of
Tom and Lilka Areton, which took them close to thirty-five
years to assemble. Examples of propaganda art and posters are on display from more than twenty-five countries,
including North Korea, Cuba, Nazi Germany, Vietnam,
Iran, the Soviet Union, and the United States.

The museum defines propaganda as "…the calculated
manipulation of information designed to shape public

opinion and behavior to predetermined ends, as desired by the propagandist." In a time when "fake news" has become a commonly used term worldwide, the art on display reinforced how governments, dictators, and special interests use "subjectivity, disinformation, exaggeration, and the outright falsification of facts" to "escalate rage and hatred against a designated enemy, often, a religion, an economic or political system, a race or a special group."

This sounded eerily familiar to what we were observing in contemporary times in the United States. It matched what I was finding in my hate music research. I was surprised to see that the use of music as propaganda comprised an extremely small portion of the museum—represented only by a small stack of foreign recordings tucked onto a bookshelf, below the books. The album covers were written in foreign languages and, with my limited ability to read in other languages, I couldn't translate or interpret them. I concluded that music used for propaganda purposes, or to spread hate, was underrepresented.

After visiting the museum, we continued a walk around the shops and sites of San Rafael. Just around the corner from the museum, I dropped into Red Devil Records, a used record store. I'm always on the lookout for unusual or rare recordings. There, in the bins, behind a divider marked "PUNK," I found two Skrewdriver records—one from their punk period before their neo-Nazi days and another from their racist period. Something about the mission, the museum, the record store, and the reason for our visit seemed more than coincidental. I could see subtle relationships to what I was researching: the healing at the mission, the propaganda of the museum, the neo-Nazi music for sale at the used record shop…and our next stop.

Our real reason for visiting San Rafael was to have dinner with Karl Weigl and Julie Brand, who manage the Karl Weigl Foundation out of their home. Karl is the namesake and grandson of Karl and Vally Weigl, and Julie is a musicologist. We were meeting them to hear more about Vally Weigl, who is the subject of this next story about a music therapist.

I discovered Weigl by accident. While researching the life of Felice Wolmut, I had been trying to find out about Felice Wolmut's early life in Europe. I contacted a researcher in Vienna, Dr. Primavera Gruber. She had been working on a dictionary of Jewish musicians who had been affected by the Nazis.

Dr. Gruber shared some information about Wolmut with me, but also commented, "Of course, you know about Vally Weigl, don't you?" I did not. She recommended that I purchase a copy of her book, *Music Therapy in Exile Using the Example of Vally Weigl* (Edition Praesens, 2003). The book inspired a search for more information about Weigl. For starters, I learned that Wolmut and Vally Weigl may have known each other since I found evidence that Wolmut studied with Karl Weigl, Vally's eventual husband. Their paths may have also crossed when, after immigrating to the United States, they both initially lived and worked on the East Coast. However, I could find no evidence that their later decisions to become music therapists were influenced by each other.

Vally Weigl was born Valery Pick, on September 11, 1894. Raised in what she described as a "...turn-of-the-century good bourgeois intellectual family," Weigl was the first daughter of a newspaper reporter turned lawyer, and his wife, who was twenty-two years his junior.

Eleven months after Weigl's birth, her sister Käthe was born. The two sisters were close and were often required to hold hands, dress alike, and take part in the same activities. They competed for the attention of their parents, especially their beloved father. They had a sibling rivalry that persisted throughout their lives. Weigl felt that she became labeled as the "prettier" one and her sister the "more clever" one. They were both strong-willed, ambitious, and would eventually become leaders and politically active.

As they entered adulthood, their differences resulted in a falling out between the sisters. Later writings by both sisters expressed their regrets for never having the opportunity to reconcile with each other. (Think about that in our current polarized country. Don't wait to reconcile with your family members who may disagree with you.)

The family lost its wealth and the ability to hire household help during World War I and the recession that followed. Weigl's mother tried to maintain their previously enjoyed lifestyle and image. A pianist herself, she noticed that Weigl, at age five, could already "play by ear" music that she heard others play. She arranged for Weigl to take piano lessons. When asked that frequent, childhood question, "What do you want to be when you grow up?" Weigl remembered saying, "*Malerin, Musikerin, und Mutter,*" which translates to "a painter, musician, and mother." By the age of fourteen or fifteen, she had decided: "music was to be my destination."

At seventeen, Weigl began to reject her family's ideas about social expectations and embraced the outdoors—mountain climbing, hiking, and skiing. With strong piano skills, Weigl continued an adolescent rebellious streak when, at age eighteen, she decided to make money by offering music lessons. Her parents objected, feeling that this was below her and did not portray the image they were trying to preserve. She did it anyway, making enough money to buy herself what she called "tourist clothes" to wear when she took her outings to explore nature. Her love of the outdoors was a lifetime passion and reflected in her later music compositions.

Weigl entered the Musicological Institute of Vienna University in 1912, working as an assistant to one of the professors. She played piano in his classes and helped to prepare other students to enter the institute. The two of them went on long hiking and skiing excursions together, which also included—much to the dismay of her parents—other male colleagues from the university. By 1915, during the early years of World War I, one of those men joining them was Dr. Karl Weigl, her composition teacher.

As World War I progressed, Käthe went to Heidelberg, Germany, to pursue a PhD in economics. The war interrupted some of her studies, partially due to her antiwar activities at German munitions factories, but she was eventually granted amnesty and completed her degree in 1918. Käthe had developed new friends during her time away and upon her return to Vienna—many of them were social democrats. Weigl had also developed her own network, in some ways allowing the sisters to grow further apart, but also for each of them to establish their independence and their own separate personalities.

Shortly after Dr. Käthe Pick finished her doctorate in Heidelberg and returned to Vienna, Weigl left home. In 1920, she accepted a job as an assistant to Edo Fimmen, secretary-general of the International Transport Workers Union, in Amsterdam. Weigl's job was to translate materials from four different languages and to serve as Fimmen's secretary. Fimmen was an outspoken antiwar activist, encouraging transport workers to refuse to haul the tools of war.

Weigl wrote in her later memoirs that she sent home funds and food packages to her family and others because the economy had become difficult in Vienna. Her father's legal clients had slowly dwindled. However, she shared that her ulterior motive in going to Amsterdam was to assess if she and Karl could "no longer live without each other." When she returned to Austria, he greeted her at the train station and, after a hike together, they decided to marry. The marriage took place on December 27, 1921, in her family's home. (Note: Karl had a previous marriage to Elsa Pazeller, from 1910 to 1913. He maintained contact with Elsa, and their daughter, for all of his life.)

As Weigl and Käthe entered adulthood, married, and pursued their individual interests, they had strong disagreements along the way. Käthe and her husband were active social democrats, and Weigl, at that time in her life, participated in minimal political activity. The sisters clashed, mostly with Käthe criticizing Weigl for her lack of political involvement. Käthe became an economist, women's rights activist, journalist, and politician, while Weigl focused on music, nature, and her young family.

This story is primarily about Weigl, due to her eventual involvement in the field of music therapy, but I need to offer some limited information about her husband. Karl was born in 1881 in Vienna and began taking music lessons in 1896. He continued music studies at the University of Vienna and the Conservatory for Music and Performing Arts of the Society of Music Lovers. From 1904 to 1906, he served as accompanist and vocal coach for soloists of composer Gustav Mahler.

Karl Weigl rose to a position of high regard among musicians and well-known composers throughout Europe. He received praise for his compositions, performances, and pedagogy. He won prestigious awards and hobnobbed with other prominent musicians. During his lifetime, he composed over one hundred thirty works and collections, including vocal music, piano pieces, chamber music, and lengthy orchestral works. He wrote six symphonies and five concertos. Despite being lesser-known in the United States, he eventually developed a reputation there. His works are still performed internationally, primarily in Europe.

From the time of their marriage in 1921 until 1934, Vally and Karl settled into a comfortable life in Vienna. They performed together and with others, taught, composed, and had a child, Wolfgang Johannes (later called Johnny). They took vacations to the lakes and mountains of Austria, and continued to enjoy hiking, skiing, and relaxing in nature. Their lives were about to change.

As early as 1934, the Central Association of German Citizens of Jewish Faith, in Germany, was protesting to the German government that anti-Semitic songs were being taught to children in schools throughout Germany. One song contained the content: "Put Jews up against the wall… throw the Jewish gang out of our German fatherland, send them to Palestine… once there, cut their throats so that they will never come back." A poem that was also being taught included the line: "Jews are sinners. They slaughter Christian Children. They cut their throats. The damned Jewish filth."

According to a news dispatch published on November 25, 1935, by the Jewish Telegraphic Agency in New York City:

> "Berlin, November 24. (JTA)—"A blacklist of Jewish composers and musicians dating back to 1780 has been issued here under the title 'Jewish Musical ABC.' The pamphlet aims, according to the German press reports of it, "to help combat the Jewish cultural bolshevism of German music."

In 1938, Hitler's army invaded Austria, and life for Jews living there, including Jewish musicians, changed dramatically after Anschluss.

This book shares the stories of musicians who wrote, performed, or sold—and still sell—hateful music. In those cases, the music and/or accompanying words promote hatred toward a demographic group. But there was another way that music was used to spread hate—by blacklisting, exclusion, limitation, or censorship.

Hitler approved only of music that promoted Aryan superiority, German nationalism, or himself. All music composed by Jews or their sympathizers was prohibited. Many non-Jewish composers and other musical artists became employees of the government, producing only "German-sounding" music.

The works of Handel, Bach, Beethoven, Wagner, Strauss, Schumann, Schubert, and other non-Jewish musicians were promoted. All other music was outlawed and considered harmful to the white, German, Aryan culture. Jazz was forbidden and labeled as "non-Aryan Negroid" music. Atonal music, such as the music of Arnold Schoenberg, was also banned.

A photo taken just days after Anschluss shows Vally, Karl, and Johnny in front of a building, looking down the street. I wondered what they were seeing. German soldiers, in full uniform, forcing Jewish citizens to wear yellow stars? Other Jews being forced to perform menial tasks, or being mocked? Friends and relatives scurrying around in a panic? More importantly, what were they thinking and feeling? Fear. Sadness. Loss of their ability to create, perform, and make a living from their music?

Following the Nazi takeover of Austria, Karl and Vally Weigl made arrangements to immigrate to the United States. With the help of Irena Wiley, wife of the US General Counsel to Austria, and Ira Hirschmann, a New York businessman, the Weigls and their son first made the journey to England. Hirschmann, who held executive positions with Lord & Taylor, Saks Fifth Avenue, and Bloomingdale's, was a close supporter of US Congressman and New York City Mayor, Fiorello H. La Guardia. His anti-Nazi efforts included advocating for a boycott of German-made goods. He is also credited with arranging, through political maneuvers, for the escape of close to one hundred thousand Jews from the Transnistria concentration camp in Turkey. In New York, he was involved with early television and radio shows, offering classical music concerts.

From England, the Weigl family came to the United States aboard the SS *Statendam* in October 1938. The Society of Friends, also known as Quakers, sponsored their escape from Nazi persecution. As both Karl and Vally sought employment for themselves, their son lived with three different Quaker families until he finished school. Vally felt at home with the Quakers and saw them as "like-minded." She was to become greatly involved with these new-found friends.

Sad news was to follow. Vally Weigl's mother committed suicide in 1939, possibly due to the circumstances of her two daughters. Weigl and her family were now far away in the United States. Käthe had become involved in the antiwar and anti-fascist activities of the Social Democrats. Following Anschluss, her family succeeded in fleeing from Austria, coming to the United States. For some reason, Käthe stayed behind, intending to catch a later train out of the country.

Käthe's granddaughter, Kathy Liechter, is quoted as commenting about her grandmother's failure to leave Austria with her family:

> "So, as you trace her story, you want to shout at her all the time: "Get on that train. Go on, get on it. Why were you not leaving, for God's sake? Leave, Käthe! But she doesn't."

The Gestapo arrested Käthe on May 30, 1938, during her last visit to see her mother. On that date, she was interrogated at the brutal Gestapo headquarters on Morzin Square. While incarcerated in solitary confinement, she wrote *Kindheitserinnerungen* (childhood memories), which she dedicated to her two children, and in which she expressed regret at never reconciling with Vally, her only sister. By 1939, she was sent to the Ravensbrück concentration camp in Germany. In her book *Ravensbrück*, Sarah Helm shared bits about what Käthe's life was like in that camp:

"Käthe Leichter had delighted the Jewish block with her poems and storytelling from the moment she arrived in 1939 and had since made a name for herself in the camp."

And,

"She used to sing to us as we heaved the stones and made us forget the pain."

Helm tells of Käthe cocreating a play that was performed for others in the camp. She and others involved in producing the play were punished by spending six weeks together in a small cell in a bunker.

In 1942, she was transported to Bernburg Euthanasia Center, where she was murdered in a gas chamber. She had never been able to reconnect with her older sister.

Karl's adjustment to exile in America was not easy. His grandson shared with me that the Weigl's apartment in New York City, in an attempt to make them feel more comfortable in the United States, was filled with their furniture from Vienna. Family members have no idea how the furniture arrived in New York from Austria.

Karl continued to compose and teach, but he missed the life and recognition that he had achieved in Austria. He and Vally performed together, and he wrote some of his best compositions in America, but his reputation seemed diminished. He died in 1949, a victim of cancer. Following his death, Vally continued to promote his music and protect his legacy for the rest of her life. A photo shows her chatting with Leonard Bernstein at a Mahler/Weigl benefit concert at Carnegie Hall in 1979.

At this point in her story, I stopped to reflect on her later life. Here was a woman who was forced to leave her family and home due to extreme anti-Semitism and Nazi persecution, lost her sister to a Nazi concentration camp gas chamber, lost her mother to suicide, watched her husband lose his livelihood and reputation, then saw him die from cancer, and suffered her own injury that prevented her from making music.

She could have become depressed, even despondent, possibly hateful. Instead, after 1949, Weigl became a driven multitasker. Her later life could be described as including four competing roles: composer, inventor, political activist, and music therapist.

Weigl had done some composing in Vienna, but the bulk of her musical compositions were written in the United States. She created over one hundred eighty compositions, most of them in a polyphonic chamber music style. Themes for her music and lyrics often dealt with nature or reactions to events in the news—and peace. She wrote many of her own lyrics, but also set poems by other authors—including Edith Segal, Carl Sandburg, Kenneth Boulding, Marion Edey, Vera Wallis, and others— to music.

A book of her shorter compositions, *Songs for a Child,* first appeared in 1962 but was later republished by the New York State Department of Mental Rehabilitation to help institutionalized children during their treatment programs. That collection of songs was recorded by an organization named Records for Recovery.

In 1973, she received grants from the American Composers Alliance and the Mark Rothko Foundation to record her compositions "Nature Moods" (1956) and "New England Suite" (1951). She also received a fellowship grant from the National Endowment for the Arts in 1976. She wrote, "Requiem for Allison," (1970) to honor a student shot at Kent State University while protesting the Vietnam War. Also, in protest to war, she composed "Peace is a Shelter" (1970) and "The People, Yes!" (1976), the latter which was based on poems by Carl Sandberg and dedicated to President Jimmy Carter.

In 1981, Weigl won three first-place prizes in a contest sponsored by the Composers, Authors, & Artists of America organization. Her three prizes were awarded for "Beyond Time" (a vocal solo song cycle), "Desert Lullaby" (for vocal ensemble), and "New England Suite" (for instrumental ensemble).

Weigl's compositions were recorded and published by leading music publishers including E.C. Schirmer, Theodore Presser, Jelsor Music, Arsis Press, Mercury Music, Merrymount Music, C. F. Peters, M. Witmark, and Westminster Press. Around 1981, Weigl received a Commendation of Excellence from one of her music publishers, Broadcast Music Inc.

The American Composers Alliance website includes a special page devoted to Weigl. Her grandson, Karl, told me that he still receives requests for permission to perform the music of both of his grandparents' music, especially Vally's. Readers can hear samples of their music on the website of the Karl Weigl Foundation. Their compositions are also available on numerous CDs and can be found on YouTube.

It is important to point out that Weigl often considered the nonmusical aspects of her composing and the venues that she chose for approved performances. Consider these passages from a brief biographical sketch of Weigl written by Sophie Fetthauer and translated into English by Juliane Brand:

"In exile Vally Weigl reoriented not only her professional life but also her political engagement. She remained a lifelong member of the Quaker community, whom she owed her escape, and was involved in the founding of the Society of Friends' Arts for World Unity Organization. For many years she served as president of this organization, reaching out to politicians, organizing concerts, theater performances, lectures, and exhibits in churches, synagogues, colleges, and cultural centers of all confessions. She believed in the power of music to bring people of all backgrounds together. This was also the foundation of her music making. Clearly she thought works of art to have more lasting effect in this regard than political pamphlets.

"Many of Vally Weigl's works express her strong love of nature. Others are strongly influenced by her engagement with pacifism, which she pursued in the United States. She wrote her 'Requiem for Allison' after President Nixon's invasion of Cambodia sparked the student uprising on 4 May 1970 at Kent State University in Ohio that left four students dead and nine injured. In a television program commemorating the victims, Vally Weigl heard a poem by Peter Davies about Allison Krause, one of the students who had been killed. Weigl set Davies's poem for mezzo-soprano and string quartet, and "Requiem for Allison" was subsequently performed at commemorative programs in New York's Trinity Church and St. John the Divine. Another politically motivated work of significance is the chamber cantata "The People, Yes!" based on twenty poems from the cycle of that name by Carl Sandburg. Weigl dedicated the work, which was awarded a National Endowment for the Arts prize, to Jimmy Carter."

Here are Weigl's own words, describing some of the thoughts that went into her composition "The People, Yes!":

"In the early 50s, more than twenty years ago, I first got acquainted and fell in love with Carl Sandburg's beautiful poems and selected four of them, 'Cool Tombs,' 'Grass,' 'Under the Harvest Moon,' and 'Shenandoah' to be combined to a brief cycle, which I set to music and called 'Four Choral Songs on Death and Man.' I sent a copy to Mr. Sandburg, who wrote me a very appreciative letter, allowing me to set these and other poems of his to music and to enter them in the American Composers' Facsimile Edition. This cycle became the nucleus for my cantata 'The People, Yes!'

"Some 10 years later I started some research on Carl Sandburg in various libraries and found more and more exciting and strikingly timely poems, which I began selecting for a larger, meaningful context outlining the "American Revolution" and some of its recurring problems, ideals, and hopes."

"I finished the cantata on election day, November 2, 1976. And it struck me that the last words were so very much in keeping with the situation of mankind, and also America today, that I thought it would be very timely, especially since President-elect Carter had mentioned many of these problems that are very close to my heart and that are also mentioned in the cantata. He had mentioned them in his campaign speeches, and I was very much hoping that he, as President, would go on and develop these principles and carry them out and bring the world really closer to peace."

A reviewer wrote:

> "The first part of the cantata traces the evolution of the American people as they settled the new land. The second part is more ideological. It includes a strong anti-war theme expressed in Sandburg's poems 'Shenandoah'—based on the American Civil War—and 'Killers'—written after World War I. The theme is set with the poem 'Choose.' As Mrs. Weigl sees it, many must choose to settle things peacefully, reasonably, or by war."

I found another example of the use of Weigl's music for nonmusical reasons. In my own state, a 1981 ad for a National Public Radio program titled "The Struggle for Women's Suffrage: A History in Song," included choral music composed by Weigl. Her sister Käthe would have been proud.

As mentioned above, it was hard to determine Ian Stuart Donaldson's motivation for becoming more political in his music. The same is true for Vally Weigl. Possibly it was the death of her sister in a Nazi concentration camp. Maybe it was the course of her own life—being forced to leave her home, country, and family due to extreme racism, political strife, and approaching war. It may have been the suicide of her mother, who had been a strong role model for her.

Another possibility is the influence of the Quakers who rescued her from persecution. Losing her husband also left her feeling alone and thinking about how to spend the rest of her life. These are all guesses. For whatever reason, she chose to make her music compositions more direct and full of messages.

Unlike her young adult years in Austria, Weigl became more politically involved as she grew older in the United States. She was active in several organizations, including the Friends' Arts for World Unity, the Fellowship of Reconciliation, the Women's International League for Peace and Freedom, the Women's Strike for Peace, and the United Nations Educational, Scientific, and Cultural Organization (UNESCO). One article about her bore the title "Vally Weigl: Musical Peacemaker." Another labeled her, "Vally Weigl: Music's Renaissance Woman." Those titles provide a striking contrast to Paul London's book about Ian Stuart Donaldson, *Nazi Rock Star*.

Ed Snyder, chairman of the Friends Committee on National Legislation, told Weigl that she should register as a lobbyist, due to the number of letters that she wrote to elected officials. Her grandson shared that when he visited her in New York, he often found a stack of carbon copies of letters on her piano. Her letter-writing was not limited to politicians. During my research, I found a letter she had written to the editor of the Binghamton, New York, *Press and Sun Bulletin*. The letter, published June 2, 1961, praised the Freedom Riders in the South, recognized their courage and nonviolent approach, and wrote in opposition to the "Ku Klux Klan, Nazi Rockwells, and other racists."

Through her work with the Women's International League for Peace and Freedom, Weigl had formed a friendship with Ava Helen Pauling and her husband, Linus Pauling. The special archives collection of Oregon State University, where Dr. Pauling taught, includes correspondence between Weigl and both Paulings. The cache of documents found there includes annual holiday cards and Weigl's year-end, annual summaries of her various activities.

One document showed minutes from a meeting of the Friends Committee on National Legislation, which advocated for the impeachment of Richard Nixon, who was also a Quaker. In another letter, she shared that there was a "Linus Pauling for President" movement on the East Coast. In response, Ava wrote that her husband could do much more good outside of the government. In 1962, Linus Pauling received the Nobel Peace Prize.

As an inventor, Weigl contributed one item: her "typewriter keyboard." It was her idea to spread the keys of a traditional piano out into buttons on several parallel levels, like the letters on an old typewriter. She felt that this allowed people with neurologic limitations to play the keys without mistakenly hitting adjacent keys. Schematic drawings of the adapted keyboard exist, but a prototype was never manufactured. Weigl secured a patent for the instrument.

Incredibly, while Weigl carried out her many other activities described above, she was a true pioneer in the field of music therapy.

In 1949, the same year as her husband's death, Weigl fractured her right shoulder in a fall. Unable to lift her arm to play piano, she used music to accompany her physical therapy routines. She observed that listening to music and performing exercises to various rhythms helped in her recovery. Following nine months of physical therapy and the use of a splint that she named "Ivan the Terrible," her interest in music therapy was born.

She put it this way:

> "This painful but instructive experience encouraged me to take up more intensive studies in special education and rehabilitation and to devote, since then, much of my time to work as a music therapist."

She wanted to learn more about how to apply her own experience to the physical and emotional problems of others. She returned to school, earning a master's degree in recreation and rehabilitation from Columbia University in 1953. Combined with her previous music education and some supplemental continuing education courses, the degree qualified her to become a Registered Music Therapist, at the age of sixty-four, with the NAMT RMT Number 208, granted in 1958. She would work as a music therapist, advocate for the field both domestically and abroad, and publish articles about music therapy for the remainder of her life.

Clinically, she worked with several healthcare organizations near her home in New York. While some music therapists provide their services to a single population, Weigl offered services in the New York City area in a variety of settings with several different client groups. She served as Chief Music Therapist at the New York Medical College, working with mentally retarded children; engaged with psychiatric patients at Mount Sinai Hospital; taught at the Roosevelt Cerebral Palsy School in Long Island; provided services at the Home for Jewish Aged; and had other involvements at Doctors Hospital and Flower Hospital.

As her work and reputation grew, she became a strong representative of the music therapy profession. Documentation exists of her speaking engagements in Ohio, California, Washington, Virginia, Connecticut, Colorado, Hawaii, and Indiana. Linus Pauling, through a grant from the Ford Foundation, authorized payment for at least one of her speaking engagements at Pacific State Hospital in California.

Weigl also passed the California Civil Service exam for music therapy and attended continuing education events at San Francisco State College—one of them taught by E. Thayer Gaston, the "father of modern music therapy." He was probably proud of her music based on "the tender emotions."

At the international level, she spoke and gave presentations in Austria, Finland, and Denmark—mostly representing the field of music therapy, but also advocating for peace. In 1953, she visited clinical sites in seven European countries, including Norway, Denmark, Switzerland, and England.

By 1962, she presented on "The Rhythmic Approach to Music Therapy" at an Orff Conference in Toronto and participated in a panel discussion with the famed composer, Carl Orff, and others. Orff then invited her to speak at his Orff Institute in Europe. She published an article about a goodwill trip to Russia in 1966. She has been credited, by some, as being a prominent bridge between the field of music therapy in the United States and early, similar developments in Europe.

In addition to her involvements with political and peace organizations, Weigl was active in several music associations, including memberships in the American Composer's

Alliance, the National Association for American Composers and Conductors, the Composer's Group of New York, the Urban Federation of Music Therapists, the NAMT, the Society of the New York Medical College, the National Federation of Music Clubs, and the American League of Composers from Austria.

Weigl wrote several articles about music therapy, which were found in such diverse publications as *Bulletin of the National Association for Music Therapy, American Journal of Mental Deficiency, The Crippled Child, Cerebral Palsy Review,* and *Long Island Jewish World.* The Karl Weigl Foundation website includes a list of both her published and unpublished articles related to music therapy.

As Weigl became older, she wrote, "I oppose all kinds of discrimination and segregation, including discrimination by age. I have many young friends with whom I am as comfortable as they are with me. I say, 'What generation gap?' Where there's a gap, it's an understanding gap—and that doesn't depend on age."

In my mind, I imagined her in spirited debate with Ian Stuart Donaldson. Their lives overlapped for twenty-five years (1957 to 1982).

Vally Weigl died on Christmas Day, 1982. Following her death, her ashes were scattered in Yosemite National Park in California, which had reminded her of the mountains surrounding Vienna.

As I studied Weigl's life and traced her career, she struck me as a true music therapy pioneer in the United States. Her articles were cited three times in Dr. Gaston's early music therapy textbook, *Music in Therapy.* It amazed me that her story was almost unknown to my music therapy colleagues in the US. How could someone so inspiring be forgotten?

As I had previously searched through the historic sheet music archives, I was surprised that I did not find many examples of early anti-Semitic music in the United States. It seems to be a more recent phenomenon, during and after World War II—imported from Europe. Sure, there were Jewish songs, many of them with lyrics written in Yiddish. But I did not find many early examples of works that expressed hatred toward Jews.

That's not to say that anti-Semitic music does not occupy a major space in today's hate music scene. White power musicians view Jews as the root of current problems. They blame Jews for giving civil rights to blacks, opening borders to evil immigrants, promoting Affirmative Action, and supporting efforts that weaken the white race. Jews are viewed as nonwhites who secretly conspire to control the mainstream media, financial institutions, entertainment industry, public education, and government—all to the detriment of the "more deserving, superior" white population. In the song "Aryan Child" by the band Brutal Attack, the lyrics express the common white supremacy belief that Jews control the world of finance. Listeners are encouraged to wise up to this belief. To attack Jews is considered a self-defense strategy, to prevent white genocide.

One recent Wikipedia site lists the following neo-Nazi, anti-Semitic bands: Absurd, Blue Eyed Devils, Definite Hate, Die Lunikoff Verschworung, Goatmoon, Grand Belial's Key, Honor, Kolovrat, Landser, Macht and Ehre, Nokturnal Mortun, No Remorse, Prussian Blue, Race War, RAHOWA, Skrewdriver, Skullhead, and Stahlgewitter. The site states that the list is incomplete and asks for additions to be made.

There are other more recent instances of anti-Semitic music. In 2013, an article by the *Huffington Post* reported that Ulf Ekberg, a member of the Swedish pop group Ace of Base, had previously been a member of a Nazi band, Commit Suicide. One of that band's lyrics included lines advocating for beheading blacks, hating immigrants, and murdering non-Nordic persons. Ekberg, referring to that earlier time, apologized, expressed regret, and stated, "I want to be very clear that Ace of Base never shared any of these opinions and strongly oppose all extremist opinions on both the right and left wing."

Another 2013 report shared that police in Germany were developing a software smartphone app that would allow them to identify outlawed neo-Nazi music being performed live or over the airwaves. Germany currently has laws that prohibit the use of far-right music. Germany's laws against hate music, especially music associated with Nazi ideology, are stricter than US laws.

In 2014, a music video uploaded to YouTube was titled "Runaway oh Zionist." The lyrics advocated for the murder of Jews by vehicular homicide. Similar anti-Semitic music videos have been viewed by thousands of people.

In Germany in 2017, six thousand people attended a neo-Nazi music festival in the state of Thuringia. The festival resulted in reports of forty-six crimes, including the display of Nazi symbols, bodily harm, threatening behavior, and assorted weapons charges. Six individuals were arrested, and an additional four hundred forty problematic individuals were identified by the police. Over one thousand policemen were present to try to prevent clashes between neo-Nazis and anti-Nazi counterprotesters.

As recently as 2018, in Austria, secretive youth fraternities, Germania zu Wiener Neustadt and Bruna Sudetia, were reported as having an anti-Semitic song in their organization's official songbooks. As a result, Udo Lanbauer, a member of the far-right Freedom Party—and a member of one of the fraternities—resigned from all political affiliations. Austrian Chancellor Sebastian Kurz advocated for punishing the songwriter, due to lyrics that advocated for killing an additional million Jews, beyond the six million victims of the Holocaust.

Anti-Semitism remains active in Austria, but a new phenomenon has been observed. Now some factions of the population are advocating for protecting the Jews from Muslims. Sociologist Robers Brubaker stated, "The far right has come to redefine Jews as fellow Europeans and exemplary victims of the threat from Islam." Still hatred but changing directions.

A report from England in early 2018 described the trial of Alison Chabloz for writing, performing, and broadcasting three anti-Semitic songs on the internet. During the trial, the prosecutor, Karen Robinson, described the songs as "...anti-Semitic, targeted at Jewish people as a whole. They use content and tone to ensure offence (*sic*). The songs are designed to provoke maximum upset and discomfort." Chabloz claimed that her rights to free speech were being violated.

These examples of anti-Semitic songs demonstrate that hate music still exists in Europe. Not only is some of that music exported to the United States, but new hate songs are being written, performed, distributed, and sold within our country. As this book demonstrates, hate music is found in many American music genres. Probably the most prolific contributing category is white power, white nationalist, neo-Nazi skinhead music.

On January 30, 2020, the ADL issued a press release

announcing an online "Tracker of Anti-Semitic Incidents." The tracker is connected to the ADL's H.E.A.T. (Hate, Extremism, Anti-Semitic, Terrorism) Map. The heading of the map states, "In 2018 and 2019, there were 7,067 incidents of extremism or anti-Semitism in the United States." Those incidents can now be viewed and sorted by state or city, incident type, ideology, or years. A search for resources on the ADL website also produced one thousand forty results related to the keywords 'hate music.'

Felice Wolmut and Vally Weigl had been immigrants, choosing to leave their beloved Austria to escape from extreme hatred. Deforia Lane's ancestors had come to America as slaves, forced to leave their African homelands. I was growing curious about anti-immigrant music and about to learn more about hate music directed at individuals coming to America.

Vally Weigl and her sister Käthe, Vienna, Austria, early 1900s.
Used with permission, Karl Weigl Foundation,
San Rafael, California.

Vally Weigl, late 1920s, Vienna, Austria. Used with permission, Karl Weigl Foundation, San Rafael, California

Vally, Karl, and Wolfgang Johannes (later called Johnny) Weigl, March 15, 1938—just days after Hitler's invasion of Austria. Used with permission, Karl Weigl Foundation, San Rafael, California

Vally and Karl Weigl performing together in exile, in the US, ca. early 1940s. Used with permission, Karl Weigl Foundation, San Rafael, California

Vally Weigl and Leonard Bernstein chatting at a Mahler/Weigl concert at Carnegie Hall, 1979. Used with permission, Karl Weigl Foundation, San Rafael, California

Vally receiving the BMI Commemoration of Excellence, ca. 1981.
Used with permission, Karl Weigl Foundation,
San Rafael, California.

Chapter 7

ANTI-IMMIGRANT MUSIC

OLGA SAMSONOVA-JELLISON

Give me your tired, your poor
Your huddled masses yearning to breathe free
The wretched refuse of your teeming shore
Send these the homeless tempest-tost to me.

From the song "Give Me Your Tired, Your Poor" by
Irving Berlin and Emma Lazarus.
(lyrics were written in 1883 and are in the public domain)

O pinions about immigration and immigrants are being expressed, left and right, in our current environment. I wanted to learn more about how music might be fueling the attitudes and beliefs about immigrants. Was music being used to spread hate against certain immigrants? Were any music therapists working with immigrants or refugees in the United States? This next pair of stories provided new information related to these questions.

Anti-Immigrant Music

ONE OF THE THINGS I LEARNED ABOUT HATE MUSICIANS is that most of them claim they want to honor their heritage. In some cases, they want to recognize their ancestry, protect their culture, and defend their history. For some, this means excluding, attacking, or discounting the heritage and cultures of anyone outside their demographic group.

At its extreme, this can also mean ignorance of the wonderful heritage of others. For some haters, it means separatism, segregation, or isolation. It's like, "I don't care how you dress, what you eat, how you worship, where you came from, what language you speak, what your culture is, what your contributions have been, or what music you listen to—as long as you don't force those ideas on me, or do those things around me. Go back to your country of origin or stay away from me."

Some hate musicians—as well as members of the general public—don't care for illegal immigrants. Others don't care for any immigrants, either legal or illegal. Immigrants are considered "others" who don't belong here. Members of other races are called "muds." Some believe "They are bad, they steal resources from us—the "deserving"—and we are their victims."

For male haters, they felt emasculated by society and were looking for a way to feel like a man. Not all of them bought into the ideologies of their chosen groups. They just bought into being in a group that accepted them. Not all of them agreed with hatred. Some just wanted to feel close to others and included in something that mattered. They discovered groups that made them feel better about themselves.

They were recruited by others who told them, "Here's something that will prove that you are a man—that you have a purpose." They also enjoyed the partying, the alcohol, fighting with others, sex with women, and sometimes drugs. They also soaked in the hate music. They created it, partied to it, celebrated to it, committed violent acts because of it, and were inspired by it.

Female haters also exist, but not in the numbers of their male counterparts. I will share more about women in other stories.

As a subgroup of the hater universe, I found that hate musicians were more devoted to the ideology, as expressed through their lyrics and songs. Fans of hate music also seemed to have strong convictions to racist and hateful beliefs.

To discuss hate music in the context of immigrants, I felt I had to know more about my own genealogy and heritage. I didn't want to pass judgment on how other people view their background and heritage unless I took a good look at my own family history. As a hobby, I began to delve into my family's past.

I wanted to understand hate musicians and possibly meet some of them for interviews. Even if I disagreed with them, I wanted to gain an understanding and some insight. I thought that I might have more credibility with potential interviewees if we shared some of the same heritage. I found three things that surprised me.

The first discovery came from working on my family tree. I'm the descendant of an immigrant. I have not determined if he was originally a legal immigrant, or undocumented, but he eventually became a US citizen.

My four times grandfather, Jacob, was born in 1818, in either Gyhum or Wehldorf, Germany—about an hour southwest of Hamburg. He came to the United States alone, in 1836, arriving in Baltimore, Maryland, aboard an unknown ship. The original ship manifests were destroyed. I could not find out why he left Germany, but he may have followed his girlfriend and future wife. Another possibility is that he was avoiding military service that, if drafted to serve, could have been for life. (Similar to the "blood in, blood out" rule of the mafia, or of neo-Nazi skinheads.)

During the 1830s, more than 1.5 million Germans immigrated to the United States. He might have heard that America was a land of opportunity. He and his wife eventually settled in Huntingburg, Indiana. He was a farmer and, by some accounts, an excellent woodworker and cooper (barrel maker). He appeared on the official census reports and paid taxes. I could find no evidence that he applied for any handouts or other benefits from the government. I have yet to determine if he fought in the Civil War and, if so, which side.

If Jacob had come to the United States alone, what had become of his relatives who stayed in Germany? I traveled to Gyhum and Wehldorf and visited a cemetery where many of my ancestors are buried. I went to their church and a farm that had been owned by various members of the family for over three hundred years.

In the immediate area, I noticed both World War I and World War II markers and memorials, with several of my ancestors and others with the same last name listed as having served in the German military. It took some time for the significance of that fact to sink in. My ancestors fought on the side of Germany in both world wars and were probably Nazi soldiers during the Second World War.

During the world wars, Germans in the United States felt some discrimination and were often suspect. My grandfather, born in 1884 in Indiana, taught German at a private college in Ohio for over forty years. He also served as a Methodist minister. He kept his head down but was aware of anti-German sentiments.

He might have been aware of the music during World War I, including "All Together: We're Out to Beat the Hun" (1918) and "What Kind of an American Are You?" and "What are You Doing over Here?" (1917). During World War II, he might have heard "You Can't Win This War Through Love" (1943), which had stereotypic representations of both German and Japanese soldiers on its sheet music cover.

How is that possible, I wondered? Could my ancestors have been involved in the Second World War and complicit in the murder of millions of innocent Jews, disabled individuals, gays, gypsies, immigrants, Poles, Russians, and perceived non-Aryans? Were they too weak or afraid to confront what was happening around them? Were they victims of their environment and propaganda?

I wrote to a distant relative in Germany, and his response answered some of these questions:

> "Of course my father and his brothers had to be soldiers in the war. They were recruited to different times during the war. They all were soldiers on the lowest level. Most time they were in East-Europe, especially the Soviet Union. One of his brothers was killed in action near St. Petersburgh (*sic*). Two other brothers became prisoners in the Soviet Union still in the last weeks of war. My father lost his left arm in a battle of encirclement near the river Dnjesti (*sic*), but he came home before war came to an end.
>
> "I am sure that many people can't imagine how to live in a country leaded (*sic*) by a dictator (like Hitler

or Stalin). There you have no rights, but always fear. Of course it is necessary to see and to judge all happenings in the temporal context of history."

My second surprise came when I had my DNA tested through ancestry.com.

When I received my DNA test results, the report showed that I was 53 percent Scandinavian, 42 percent English, Welch, and Northwestern European; and 5 percent Germanic. Not only Aryan but also Nordic. The report included the lines, "Looks like you might have some Viking blood in you," and "…the Vikings were feared by the coastal towns of medieval Europe as seaborne raiders and violent pillagers."

I could conclude that the Central European part of my background was from my father's lineage. The Scandinavian portion was from my mother's side. Probably my mother's ancestors were the Vikings, and perhaps those ancestors invaded the region where my father's ancestors resided.

This reminded me of some recent talk of caravans "invading" our country from Mexico and other South American countries. It is funny how immigrants can be labeled as invaders, even when they are not Vikings. Or even when they were white settlers inhabiting the homeland of Native American Indians.

Further research told me that the Vikings were slave owners, violent murderers, rapists, and conquerors. A 2017 article in *National Geographic* included this passage:

"Viking raiders prowled the coasts of Britain and Europe, striking with sudden, shocking brutality. In northern France they sailed up and down the Seine and other rivers, attacking at leisure and filling their ships with plunder. Spreading terror far and wide, they extorted nearly 14 percent of the entire economy of Western Europe's Carolingian Empire in exchange for empty promises of peace. Across the channel in England, sporadic raids expanded into total warfare, as a Viking army invaded and conquered three Anglo-Saxon kingdoms, leaving bodies to rot in the fields."

I encourage all readers to explore their heritage. You may find details that surprise and shock you. You will learn more about your ancestors—their lives, challenges, and traumas. You will gain more understanding about family values and might discover that your pride in that history may need to be reconsidered.

My third surprise came when I was researching my grandfather's brother, a dentist who had lived in Evansville, Indiana. His name was Arthur, and he lived from 1881 to 1954. Preliminary digging into old documents revealed that he had conducted a church choir and was an accomplished musician. I was having difficulty discovering more of his story, so I wrote to a librarian in Evansville and asked if there was anything in the library that could inform me.

She sent me a two-page write-up about him, mostly talking about his dental career and his involvement in the Indiana Dental Association. But...within the document, it stated that before his career as a dentist, he had worked as an attendant at a local insane asylum and had conducted a choir there. Maybe my music therapy identity is at the cellular level, in my family blood.

With a heritage that included Vikings, Nazis, an immigrant, and a dentist who used music with the mentally ill,

I became more intrigued with the changing perceptions of immigrants. Were past characteristics passed down genetically? Did people change when they immigrated to a new geographic location? Where would I be if a family member had not immigrated to the United States? Or, would I even exist, if a Viking warrior had not invaded the region of my ancestors in Germany?

As I write this, immigration reform is a hot topic. There are chants of, "Build the wall." (Remember, chanting, like old Gregorian chants sung by monks, could be considered another form of unaccompanied music—in some instances, hate music.) Just the same as Vikings, modern-day immigrants have been called drug pushers, rapists, criminals, bad hombres, and other negative names. Depending on a person's position along the political spectrum, that person may view immigrants as hurting our economy, unjustly using available governmental resources, unable to assimilate, stealing jobs from others, non-English speaking, criminals, or inferior.

This is the belief of most white supremacists. Some propaganda, including hate music, demonizes all immigrants, especially those who have entered our country illegally. Some citizens blindly accept that propaganda, with little question. Others push back, and welcome newcomers in search of a better life. Still, others study the issues and make informed decisions with less confirmation bias.

We are all either immigrants or descendants of immigrants. Our ancestors, some from many generations ago, came to the land of "others." Unless you are a descendant of one of 567 Native American Indian tribes recognized by the United States Bureau of Indian Affairs or speak one of the languages of those tribes, you are related to immigrants.

Even Native Americans probably were immigrants from distant lands, centuries before white settlers came here.

You either came here voluntarily, in search of a different life, freedoms, and privileges. Or, in the case of servants or slaves, you came here involuntarily. We were all thrown into an existing, yet ever-changing, melting pot. Variety is the spice of life. A mixed-breed mutt is sometimes the best of dogs.

But this is a book about hate music and music therapy. How has music been used to foster anti-immigrant leanings? What negative stereotypes of immigrants are sung into our minds? Does music initiate and spread negative messages about immigrants, as a form of propaganda? Did the negative perceptions of immigrants exist first and were then expressed through music? Or did hate music play a role in spreading hatred toward immigrants?

The American Immigration Council claims, "Immigration policy is frequently shaped more by fear and stereotype than by empirical evidence." Has music played a role in shaping that fear and those stereotypes?

An early example of anti-immigrant music targeted the Irish. They were variously described in England as backward, lazy, violent, alcoholic, ape-like, wild, reckless, filthy, incestuous, and inferior. In 1862, a song appeared, titled "No Irish Need Apply," which advocated for employment discrimination against Irish immigrants. It was first published in England and was written by John F. Poole. However, the song and its variations also appeared in the United States and several other countries. Discrimination against Irish immigrants continues to this day, in some quarters.

Anti-immigrant thinking is not new in the United States. During the Great Depression of the 1930s, with hundreds of

Americans out of work, foreigners were not welcome. Even then, Mexicans and Mexican Americans were discriminated against and deported. Immigration quotas limited the number of immigrants from southern and eastern parts of Europe, Mexico, and Asian countries.

In 1938, ethnomusicologist Sidney Robertson Cowell began collecting the music of immigrant groups in California, as a project of the New Deal Programs—programs intended to improve the economy. Cowell found and recorded songs from Armenian, English, Cornish, Hungarian, Russian, and Mexican immigrants. In her field notes, Cowell wrote:

> "Local pride in the preservation of the cultural things that belong to the old days should be stimulated wherever possible, particularly in the minority groups. Remember that the Anglo-Saxon music which we are inclined to think of as the only "American" kind is a relatively recent importation on this continent, exactly as the Hungarian, Finnish and Armenian folk musics are. The Portuguese and Spanish have been in California three times as long as the "Americans."

Inspired by Cowell's work from the 1930s, the Sounds of California project was initiated in 2015 by the Alliance of California Traditional Arts, with support from Radio Bilingüe and the Smithsonian. The project expanded Cowell's collection by including the music of immigrants who were black, Asian, Latin American, or members of indigenous groups.

A student at San Francisco State University, Isik Berfin, contributed songs from her Kurdish heritage, and stated,

"We're not just telling the stories of the past, but we're also trying to spread what's going on right now." As the music of immigrants is being preserved, I wondered about existing pressure for immigrants to give up their native music and assimilate into the United States by adopting "American" music.

As I began my search for examples of more recent, anti-immigrant hate music, the first YouTube example that popped up was "Get Back" by the Beatles. Turns out there was a bootleg recording of early session outtakes of the song, which included the line, "Too many Pakistanis living in a council flat." A London publication, *The Sun*, labeled the recording as racist.

Paul McCartney defended the song, and explained, "There were stories in the newspapers then about Pakistanis crowding out flats—living 16 to a room, or whatever (the lyric) to me was talking out against overcrowding for Pakistanis." Full disclosure: McCartney is a long-time supporter of music therapy and has received recognition from the Nordoff and Robbins Music Therapy organization.

My investigation turned up many songs about immigrants. My analysis indicated that there were three main categories:

- neutral songs about the challenges that immigrants faced, including some songs that honored and accepted immigrants but were not taking either a pro-immigrant or anti-immigrant stance;

- songs that presented negative stereotypes of immigrants, including some song parodies and attempts at humor; and

- songs expressing negative attitudes or hatred toward immigrants.

The two latter categories included some prominent characteristics of hate music.

The presence of songs on a particular topic, along a continuum, seems common. When considering hate music, songs could be categorized as ranging from least hateful to most hateful...the most hateful falling "in the tails" of a normal bell curve—outside of expected variation and requiring investigation.

Even the least hateful may be considered as microaggression, which the *Merriam-Webster* dictionary defines as "a comment or action that subtly and often unconsciously or unintentionally expresses a prejudiced attitude toward a member of a marginalized group (such as a racial minority)."

It is important to consider the intent of the songwriter and the use and influence of the song by, and on, others.

Examples of positive or neutral songs about immigrants include "The Immigrant" by Neil Sedaka, "America," by Neil Diamond, "Ellis Island" by Mark Cohn, "Eyes of the Immigrant" by Eric Andersen, and "City of Immigrants" by Steve Earle.

These songs don't present negative stereotypes, nor do they assign derogatory labels to immigrants. They just state the reality that immigrants come to our country and reflect what is going on. Listeners and fans are challenged to think, which is the strength of the First Amendment. There are references to what newcomers have left behind and what they hope to find in America. Ugly judgments against immigrants are not apparent. The songs try to present the experience of immigrants, not necessarily their motivation—either positive or negative—for coming to the United States.

A second group of songs moved into the realm of hate music. Like Coon songs from the past, these songs presented negative stereotypes, and assigned less than honorable reasons to why some immigrants make their way to our country. Similar to "comic" Coon songs, some songs in this category were presented as song parodies or attempts at humor, albeit not always funny.

Examples included "Illegal Immigrant Song" by Alvin Rhodes, which is sung from the viewpoint of a migrant farm worker, complaining about working conditions and lack of credit for hard work.; "Immigration" by Jesse Goldberg, in which he talks about the negative motivations of immigrants. He claimed, "I just wanted to poke fun at the issue in a light-hearted way instead of taking sides." Yet, he sings about immigrants hurting the healthcare system and abusing welfare programs.

Singer Ray Stevens, known for novelty songs such as "Guitarzan" and "Ahab the Arab", contributed "Come to the USA" to the anti-immigrant songbook. The lyrics start by saying how immigrants are treated in other countries, such as China, Iran, Mexico, and North Korea. He then encourages immigrants to avoid those countries and come to the United States, where they can get almost unlimited benefits and support for criminal activities. Negative stereotypes. Yep. Accusations of criminality. You bet.

Author Stephen Lemons ridiculed Stevens' song, calling it a "retarded redneck song," and presented data to support counter arguments to the song's claims. He quoted findings from the Federation for American Immigration Reform

(FAIR) and *Wall Street Journal* editorial board member, Jason Riley (author of the book *Let Them In: The Case for Open Borders*) that refuted the song's perspective that immigrants take advantage of government-funded benefits, such as welfare. Negative stereotypes. Check. Criminality. Check.

I listened to more songs about immigrants: "Illegal Alien" by Genesis, "The Immigrant" by Merle Haggard, "Immigrants (We Get the Job Done)" by K'naan, "Fight to the End" by Youngland, and "When the Boat Comes In" by Skrewdriver. The first two songs talked more about the plight of immigrants, based on the opinions and perceptions of white songwriters. The latter two songs, from the perspective of white nationalists, did not even mention immigrants, but the lyrics implied something in opposition. The Youngland song encourages white supremacists to continue to believe in, and fight for, their cause. In the Skrewdriver song, Ian Stuart Donaldson attacks African Americans and, in harsh, racist language, tells them to leave Great Britain on boats. He described "When the Boat Comes In" as an anti-immigrant song in response to black immigrants making white Brits feeling ignored and "second class."

I FOUND A LIST PUBLISHED BY THE *ORANGE COUNTY Weekly* titled "The 10 Best Songs About Illegal Immigration." Except for the song "Deportee (Plane Wreck at Los Gatos)" by Woody Guthrie, the others on the list were in Spanish and performed by Mexican artists. The songs, from several decades, presented a variety of viewpoints on immigrants, mostly by non-American songwriters.

The Guardian published a story about the song "La Bestia," which translates to "The Beast" in English. According to the report, the song has been on the playlists of twenty-one radio stations south of the American border and was devised by an advertising agency for the US Customs and Border Protection. Lyrics, set to spirited music, tell the story of how horrible a train trip headed north can be and is intended to try to dissuade Central Americans from making the effort. The story reported that the song was "part of a multi-million dollar anti-immigrant campaign to halt the influx of migrants from Honduras, Guatemala and El Salvador."

One of the most hateful songs I discovered was "Anti Immigrant Song", from the album *Brand Damage* by the group Capitalist Kids (released July 6, 2017, on Brassneck Records). Immigrants are referred to by negative labels and adjectives throughout the song. It also contains other elements of hate music: Name calling. Uh-huh. Negative stereotypes. Yes. Direct expression of hate. Absolutely.

My exploration had revealed that music was being used as a tool by both pro- and anti-immigration advocates. Just another path to self-expression, stimulating thought, and discussion? Or for perpetuating negative stereotypes, spreading hate, and ignoring other valid reasons for immigration? Who was listening to anti-immigrant hate music?

Was it Patrick Crusius, who killed twenty-two people and wounded twenty-four others in El Paso, Texas, on August 3, 2019? A manifesto attributed to Crusius expressed a white supremacist ideology. While in high school, he had posted the following on LinkedIn:

"I'm not really motivated to do anything more than what's necessary to get by. Working in general sucks, but I guess a career in Software Development suits me well. I spend about 8 hours every day on the computer..."

Was he visiting hate music sites? Authorities hypothesized that he was radicalized online.

Olga Samsonova-Jellison

As a balancing story to anti-immigrant music, I wanted to include the account of an immigrant to the United States who explored ways to use music to help his or her own kind. I had nobody in mind and searched my memory and professional contacts in the hope of finding a person with a good story to tell. I was sure there were probably music therapists who had moved to America from other countries but couldn't think of any current person who became a music therapist after arriving and settling in the US.

In early March 2017, I attended a music therapy conference in Denver, Colorado. It was a special joint regional conference, bringing together music therapists from both the Midwest and Western Regions of the AMTA, with members from a total of eighteen states. It was my first opportunity to kick around ideas for my book with colleagues and hear their reactions to my book's concept. I was starting to collect comments and stories, and I felt nurtured by their enthusiasm. It was also an exciting conference for me because, after the event, I had an opportunity to visit an old childhood friend and to reconnect with my very first music therapy intern from 1974.

These types of conferences almost always include pre- and post-conference sessions. These before-and-after events include business meetings for the association's officers, committee work, special task forces' work, and extra-cost courses offered for continuing education credits. Board-certified music therapists must complete one hundred continuing education credits every five-year cycle to maintain their credentials. In states where music therapists are licensed, there may be additional requirements.

I was planning to leave the conference after the official closing session and had not registered for any post-conference courses. I wanted to visit my childhood friend and also my former intern. However, in the program, I noticed a session scheduled for the morning following the main conference. It was titled "Immigration, Acculturation and Music Therapy" and approved for three continuing education credits for $89, a bargain. I was not familiar with the presenter, Olga Samsonova-Jellison, but I was anxious to meet her and learn from her. And hear her story.

There were only six participants in Samsonova-Jellison's session, and she started by having them introduce themselves and explain why they were there. Samsonova-Jellison began her story by saying that she was an immigrant from Russia and that she had begun researching immigration due to her own experience. During the workshop, she only told bits and pieces of her story.

She had emigrated from Russia in her early thirties. When she arrived in Southern California, she worked as a waitress at two different restaurants, although she did not speak English and could not read the menus. She eventually learned English by watching television and old movies.

Samsonova-Jellison described her immigration trauma, which included symptoms such as six months of nausea, a year of migraine headaches, inability to sleep, and a feeling of isolation. She felt like her body was failing her, and that she was in a constant feeling of overload. She ascribed an anxiety disorder and five major surgeries to her immigration experience. It was not an easy transition. The marriage that brought her to America did not last. Eventually, Samsonova-Jellison met a man and happily remarried.

After describing her transition challenges, she explained that, based on her research, her reactions and adjustments were similar to many other immigrants.

The bulk of Samsonova-Jellison's workshop included sharing her research on immigration trauma, exercises to help the participants gain empathy for what immigrants experience, and a discussion of how music could be used to help immigrants through their transitions to a new culture—while preserving their cultural psyche from their country of origin. Citing the works of researchers whom she had reviewed, Samsonova-Jellison provided a detailed glossary so that everyone was clear on the definitions of acculturation, alloplastic activity, cultural competency, culturally informed music therapy, emigration, immigration, social stigma, and other relevant terms.

In one hands-on activity, participants were divided into two groups and asked to observe a member of their group attempt to translate a Russian phrase into English. She allowed the individuals doing the translating to use their smartphones, but the exercise was timed, so there was a sense of urgency. As one of the translators, I barely succeeded interpreting a few words during the allotted time. I now remember the phrase as, "Is there bread?" The phrase, in fact, was "Buy some bread." My group gave me feedback on my facial expressions and behavior during the time period. Using an unfamiliar language, alphabet, and phrase was difficult and illustrated one of the challenges of immigrants.

A three-hour workshop didn't provide enough time to learn Samsonova-Jellison's story, so I contacted her several months later to see if she would be willing to share more with me through emails and Skype. I wanted to get her opinion about hate music and see if she had experienced anti-immigrant music. She agreed to communicate with me, and her story started to unfold in more detail.

Olga was born and raised in the town of Verkhnyay Salda, in Sverdlovsk Oblast, located in central Russia, about eight hundred eighty miles east of Moscow. It is known for being the base of VSMPO-AVISMA, a corporation that is the world's largest manufacturer of titanium. It is also considered to be the "rock 'n' roll capitol" of Russia.

Samsonova-Jellison left Russia when the effects of *perestroika* were in full swing. A movement first proposed by Leonid Brezhnev in 1979 and supported by Mikhail Gorbachev with his *glasnost*, or "openness" policies, perestroika included reforms within the Communist party in the 1980s and early 1990s. The movement created a restructuring of political and economic systems, aimed specifically at improvements in automation and labor efficiency.

Referring to when she left Russia as "the wild nineties," Samsonova-Jellison said that many people left Russia at that time "looking for something better." In her case, she wanted to continue her post-graduate education but could not afford it there, so she came to America thinking that it might be possible in the "dreamland." Samsonova-Jellison later shared that it was a myth that education is cheap in the United States. When asked why she chose Southern California, she replied that she had no idea. "It just happened," she said.

Before coming to the United States, Samsonova-Jellison had years of musical training, starting around age six. Through private lessons and attendance at the municipal School of Arts, she studied piano, ensemble playing, music theory, choir, and music history and literature. She attended the School of Arts in addition to her regular school. Following graduation from the School of Arts, she continued with piano and choir in college and added private guitar studies.

Arriving in the United States, she found herself in a new culture, with a basic, minimal support system. During her workshop in Denver, I asked her if there was a Russian community in the Los Angeles (LA) area that offered comfort and help as she acclimated. I shared that I was aware of a large Russian community in my home state, Oregon.

Samsonova-Jellison said that she was unaware of that type of support where she first settled. Other attendees of the workshop pointed out that, like the United States, different geographic regions in Russia have very unique cultures and customs. Just because Oregon had a Russian community did not mean that a Russian group in LA would match her need for cultural familiarity.

Hate music was new to Samsonova-Jellison, so she did some of her own homework before sending me an email. She visited the home page of the SPLC and other websites. She wrote:

> "Music is such a powerful tool that can do both healing and harm. We discussed it in undergrad and grad music therapy studies. However, my personal encounter with this side of music is limited to my childhood memories of singing in a choir the songs that would praise Lenin and 'our collective path

to communism.' Surely, the examples of radicalized groups turning to violence during their music festivals sounded alarming. I have to say that any kind of radicalization is against my personal beliefs. And, I am aware that music may serve as a powerful tool for brainwashing and radicalization of young generation."

Samsonova-Jellison shared two interesting examples of what she considered to be hate music from her Russian perspective. The first was "The Internationale," a left-wing socialist anthem. The song was written in France in 1871 by Eugène Pottier, but the French lyrics have been rewritten and translated into many other languages. It has been used in support of liberal causes worldwide.

Samsonova-Jellison showed me a YouTube clip of a movie, depicting Russian soldiers singing the song to their Nazi soldier captors during World War II. The Russians were threatened with death unless they stopped singing. They continued, raising their voices high. She was taught that the scene depicted the Russians' hatred of the German invaders—hatred so strong that they would risk loss of life. The song strengthened them and mobilized them.

The second song came from another YouTube video. The scene was a concert, with the singer, Elena Vaenga, enthusiastically singing "The Sacred War." Here is an English translation of some of the lyrics:

"Let our noble wrath
Seethe like Waves
The national war is going

The Sacred War
Let us put a bullet into the brow
Of rotten fascist vermin
Let us make a strong coffin
For such breed"

These two songs from the World War II era were very different from the hate music examples I was finding in the US, but they illustrated how the love for a song in one country could convey hatred for the politics, soldiers, or governments of another country. In some ways, "The Sacred War" reminded me of George Burdi and his band RAHOWA (short for "Racial Holy War").

I asked Olga if she had experienced anti-immigrant sentiments, or had been told, "Return to where you came from." She said that she had felt marginalized and had sometimes been viewed as being from France, Germany, or even Mexico.

To my eyes, she was a white woman, which turned out to be false. She was both a book being judged by its cover and a voice being judged by its unfamiliar accent.

She said that some people thought she was Jewish when, in fact, she had been baptized in the Russian Orthodox Church, a Christian faith. She explained that she has a complicated relationship with official religion but "believes in a higher power." Once people discovered that she was Russian, she heard, "I don't know what you did in Russia, but here we do it this way…"

Samsonova-Jellison eventually told me that she is not white. She is half Chuvash, one-quarter Russian, and one-quarter Chechen. So easy to make false judgments of people, based on how they look and how they sound.

Samsonova-Jellison had left all of her family behind in her home country and cannot afford to visit very often. Her parents are still there, benefiting from stock in the titanium company where they both worked. She wanted to be a legal immigrant so, after marrying her first husband, she returned to work in Russia for nine months, until her paperwork was approved in the US. She had bachelor's and master's degrees from her earlier studies in Russia, so she worked as an educational psychologist.

When she legally returned to Orange County, by necessity, Samsonova-Jellison began looking for a new field to pursue. Walking past some coworkers at the Lifetime Music Academy in Aliso Viejo, California, she overheard them use the words "music therapy." The combination of the two words was new to her, but they seemed to fit her background and skills as both a psychologist and a musician.

"Voilà," she would have said, had she been French. "Eureka," in English. Or, possibly, "эврика," in Russian. (See how hard it is to think and speak, using a foreign alphabet and language?)

Because she already had two college degrees, Samsonova-Jellison was accepted in 2003 to complete an equivalency to a bachelor's degree in music therapy at Chapman University, in Orange, California. During one music therapy class, students were asked to select a song to share something about themselves. She was not familiar with enough American music to make a choice, but she remembers being encouraged to choose the song "California, Here I Come." She had no idea what it meant.

Samsonova-Jellison completed her required music therapy internship at Mobile Music Therapy Services of Orange County, in Garden Grove, California, under the direction of Roberta Adler. They co-authored a book together. Between 2000 and 2011, she worked in a variety of jobs under the titles tutor of music and English language, teacher of Russian language, music educator, and finally, music therapist.

Between 2011 and 2015 she completed a master's degree in music therapy thru St. Mary-of-the-Woods College, which is based in Indiana. Wanting additional clinical skills in music therapy, she pursued training in neurologic music therapy, strength-based improvisation, and Guided Imagery and Music.

In 2003, Samsonova-Jellison founded Rainbow Bridge Music Studio, in Costa Mesa, California. In 2006, her future husband, also a musician, joined her in developing the business. She is proud that they are "job creators" and did not take jobs away from other US citizens.

They not only created jobs for themselves but also created a job for another American. Their studio provides a variety of music services including traditional lessons, recitals, camps, and a rock band program, as well as music therapy for children with learning disabilities and Down syndrome and elderly patients with Alzheimer's disease and other forms of dementia.

Today, Samsonova-Jellison continues to do work with immigrants and refugees. She has established a partnership between her Rainbow Bridge Music Studio and the Home for Refugees USA program (https://www.homeforrefugeesusa.org/ourpartnerships/ and http://rainbowbridgestudio.com/music-therapy-with-immigrants-refugees/) She shared some interesting insights about that work:

"My brother-in-law served in the Soviet-Afghan

War. I've lost several friends in that war. The Soviet-Afghan War for the Russian nation is like the Vietnam War for the American nation: very complex feelings including the feelings of powerlessness and hatred. Now, I am happy that I had the opportunity to participate in the matter from a totally different perspective. There is an amazing musical exchange happening during my visits with the Afghan families."

Samsonova-Jellison is working on her PsyD degree at California Southern University, and she shared a passage from a paper she wrote for a Cultural Diversity class within that program:

"I would like to use the habit for critical thinking in my current practice with Afghan families who are considered to be newly arrived immigrants. They have been living in the United States for less than five years. Working with Afghan families is particularly meaningful for me. I was twelve years old when the long Soviet-Afghan war started. Several of my acquaintances came back home in *zinc coffins*, as we used to say then. When my supervisor informed the cultural ambassador that their music therapist was Russian, she could see a strong emotional reaction. I have to admit that every time the Russian war is mentioned in the discussions of the Afghan families at the team meetings, I feel a bodily reaction. At the same time, I enjoy working with the Afghan families that I got to know. I sincerely hope to contribute to their successful adaptation in the United States. I believe that goodwill and knowledge may help in generating a favorable psychological climate and in establishing cross-cultural bridges of mutual respect and understanding. It is especially important in the multicultural areas where your neighbors may happen to be from the other side of the Globe."

In closing, Samsonova-Jellison shared the lyrics to one of her original songs, which is quite a contrast to Ian Stuart Donaldson's song, "When the Boat Comes in," above:

"Taking a Mulligan"
(By Olga Samsonova-Jellison, 2017, used with permission)

We cannot choose a place we're born,
But we can choose the place to live.
Your wish is granted and you're here,
In magic place where freedom rings.
The ocean rolls its emerald waves,
The sun is hot in turquoise sky,
The palms are toll in bursts of winds,
But paradise comes with a price.

Chorus:
Second chance in life,
Happy chance in life.
Smile, you've been granted
A better chance in life,

Now...
Stigmatized forever with exotic accent

Concealing sharpness of your thoughts,
You'll have the days when Disney is a torture,
Because like Ariel you've lost your voice.
You're trapped in myth of economic freedom
And labeled firmly "uninvited guest."
Learn to be smart with words like trust and credit
And do not ever get them mixed.

Chorus:
Second chance in life,
Happy chance in life.
We pay a price for the
Second chance in life.

Bridge:
Alas, you've come too far, you cannot turn your boat:
Those whom you left behind believe you and support.
Years quickly go by, you look and reach for something
That justifies yours leaving place you've once
belonged:
A bigger house, written book, child's education,
Worldwide travel, whiter smile or stylish look…
Engaged in daily, never ending battle for your life,
You've learnt to cope anxiety of the survival mode…
Meanwhile, your lonely parents getting older
Far, on the other side of Globe.

Chorus:
Second chance in life,
Happy chance in life.
Smile, you've been granted
A Second chance in life.

Immigrants represent just one group that is attacked through hate music. I had already learned about anti-Semitic music and anti-African American music. I would learn that other groups are also targeted.

Olga Samsonova-Jellison, Rainbow Bridge Music Studio, Costa Mesa, California. Used with written permission.

Chapter 8

RESISTANCE RECORDS

RUSSELL HILLIARD

I n combining these next two stories, I landed on the theme of death. On the one hand, a record company concerned with the perception of the death of the white race and culture—white genocide. On the other, a music therapist working in one of the largest hospice companies in the United States—helping individuals die with dignity.

Resistance Records

ONE OF THE MOST SUCCESSFUL AND LONG-LIVED HATE music companies has been Resistance Records. On the website titled Encyclopedia Metallum, Resistance Records is described as selling music with "extreme right-wing ideologies." Other publications have used the following labels to describe the music it promotes: neo-Nazi, white separatist, white supremacist, hatecore, Goth metal, white power, skinhead, white nationalist, and death metal. In 2012, the ADL claimed that, based on filling approximately fifty orders per day, the record company could produce close to one million dollars in annual revenue. The music could be used to recruit young listeners to hate philosophies, and the money from sales could be used to support various hate groups.

To tell the story of Resistance Records, it is important to review the cast of characters and organizations affiliated with the company.

George Burdi was born in 1970, in Canada. Also known as "Reverend George Eric Hawthorne," he created Resistance Records in 1993, in Windsor, Ontario. The label also became incorporated as a company in Detroit, Michigan, in 1994. Burdi was a member of the band RAHOWA.

He is quoted as saying, "Music alone cannot save our race, granted, but our music is precious to us and highly effective as a recruitment tool." The Resistance Records catalog described its music as "searing, relentless, scorching, grinding, hate-filled, and unbelievably aggressive."

Burdi was also a leader of the Canadian chapter of the World Church of the Creator, which was affiliated with another white nationalist organization, Heritage Front. He wrote several articles for the Church of the Creator publication, *Racial Loyalty,* including a 1992 cover story titled "Enter the Racial Holy War." Resistance Records was owned by Resistance LLC and had a strong relationship with the National Alliance, which operated another publication, *Resistance.*

After an Ottawa RAHOWA concert in May 1993, anti-racist protestors were present to challenge the band's performance and message. Burdi, along with a leader of Heritage Front, Wolfgang Droege, led a march of their sympathizers to Parliament Hill, "chanting sieg heil, making racist remarks, and giving Roman Salutes." Violence broke out, and Burdi was identified by an antiracist protestor as being an individual who kicked her in the face, giving her a broken nose and reportedly dislodging some teeth. During the ensuing court case, he was ruled out as the kicker but was still charged with leading others in the march. In 1995, he was charged with assault and causing bodily harm and given a prison sentence of twelve months, of which he served four.

Another person involved with Resistance Records was Tony McAleer, who convinced Burdi to let him develop one of the first white power music websites in 1994. Noticing the success of that initial Resistance Records site, McAleer was soon approached by other groups, including a Holocaust-denial group. Despite their successes, both McAleer and Burdi eventually questioned their involvements in the movement.

After leaving prison, Burdi denounced white nationalism. He formed a new multiracial band, Novacosm, and decided to change his life and tell his story through his music. One of their songs is titled "Everyday Love." However, Novacosm also re-recorded an old RAHOWA song, "Ode to a Dying People," which laments the death of the white race and its culture. There was skepticism about his true conversion, and some believed that he performed for his own self-interest and profit. His early fans felt that he sold out, and some labeled him a "race traitor."

While George Burdi was having legal problems, ownership and management of Resistance Records had been assumed by some of his Canadian business associates, Jason Snow and Joe Talic. They coordinated with an American, Mark Wilson, and then, Eric Davidson. The company faltered and was temporarily put out of business, due to a tax dispute and violation of Canada's hate laws. Since the

Canadian offices of the record company had closed, operations were moved to the United States, with headquarters in Milford, Michigan. Federal officials were directed by the Internal Revenue Service to seize Resistance Records business records and inventory there, which they did.

In early 1997, Burdi again faced legal problems. During April of that year, Resistance Records was raided by the Oakland County, Michigan Sherriff's Department, the Michigan Department of the Treasury, and the Ontario Provincial Police. The company's inventory and other business items were seized. While the raid was taking place, Burdi was arrested in Windsor for violating the Canadian Criminal Code against promoting hate.

Following a trial and conviction, Burdi was spared a jail sentence but required to cut his ties with both RAHOWA and Resistance Records. He quit his band. His Canadian partners, Jason Snow and Joe Talic, had taken control of Resistance Records but sold it to Willis Carto in 1998. The American branch of the record company was directed first by Mark Wilson and, by 1997, Eric Davidson.

Willis Carto was the next major player to own and grow Resistance Records. Born in 1926 in Fort Wayne, Indiana, he was to become a major player in far-right politics in the United States. During the Second World War, he served in the Philippines and was wounded twice, earning a Purple Heart. Returning from the war, he lived for a time in Ohio and took some college classes at the University of Cincinnati Law School. He worked for the Proctor and Gamble Company in Cincinnati and then the Household Finance Company in San Francisco.

Carto created Liberty Lobby in 1955, which he dubbed a "pressure group for patriotism." As Carto became more involved in politics, he developed a reputation for advocating anti-Semitic conspiracy theories and was a Holocaust denier. He began a publication, *Right*, to share his beliefs.

Carto was influenced by Francis Parker Yockey, who wrote the book *Imperium: The Philosophy of History and Politics*. (Wermod and Wermod Publishing Group, 1948). Yockey favored Adolf Hitler's German nationalism, protested the influence of Jews, and supported other fascist ideals. Yockey had traveled widely, spreading his racist philosophies. He had served as a prosecutor in the Nuremberg trials following World War II, but resigned, due to disagreement with the prosecution.

Carto met with Yockey in a San Francisco jail in 1960, where Yockey was serving a sentence for passport fraud. According to a story about Carto's death, published in 2015, he "was convinced that Yockley was a genius." A week after the two had met, Yockley was found dead in his jail cell, having swallowed cyanide. At that point, Carto began efforts to preserve and spread Yockley's beliefs.

During the 1960s and 1970s, Carto became politically involved in several right-wing, racist organizations and publications. He joined the John Birch Society, only to be dismissed by its founder as a "pointless diversion." He assumed control of a magazine, *The American Mercury*, in 1966, and used it to spread his ideas. He supported the campaign of George Wallace for President in 1968. In 1979, he founded the *Institute for Historical Review*, another publication pushing racism, nationalism, anti-Semitic philosophy, a variety of conspiracy theories, and other right-wing extremist beliefs.

Also, in 1979, based on his denial of the Holocaust, Carto offered $50,000 to anyone who could prove that Jewish individuals had been gassed at Auschwitz. Mel Mermelstein, an

Auschwitz survivor living in California, provided evidence including photographs, eyewitness accounts, documents, and even a can that had contained Zyklon B—the gas allegedly used in murders of Jewish prisoners. He reported watching his mother and sister being taken to the gas chambers.

When Mr. Mermelstein was not paid for providing proof, he sued. The trial lasted eleven years. The final settlement resulted in the $50,000 being awarded to Mermelstein, plus an additional $40,000. The courts also asked the defendants, including Carto, to apologize and acknowledge acceptance of the court's findings that the Holocaust had happened and was undeniable.

During the 1980s, Carto refined his philosophy, labeling it "Jeffersonian" and "populist." In 1982, he wrote the book *Profiles in Populism*, which presented stories of Thomas Jefferson, Andrew Jackson, Henry Ford, and Father Charles Coughlin, a fan of the policies of Adolf Hitler and Benito Mussolini. In 1984, Carto's offices were burned, but his office, containing four busts of Hitler, survived.

The conservative, William F. Buckley sued Carto for libel in 1985. Following the trial, which Buckley won, Buckley referred to Carto as representing "the fever swamps of the crazed right." Buckley was one of many conservative leaders who denounced Carto. In 1988, Carto formed the Populist Party, running David Duke for President.

Over his life, Carto used many publications to spread hatred. These included *Spotlight, Journal of Historical Review, The Barnes Review, The Noontime Press, The American Mercury,* and *The American Free Press.* Despite Carto's expressed views in many publications and his political activities, like many others, he was in some ways very secretive. He often wrote under pseudonyms, seldom spoke in public, was reluctant to participate in interviews, conducted business using payphones, and was not listed on the mastheads of his publications.

A few years later, Carto would blame the 9/11 attacks in the United States on Israel. In 2007, he openly attacked supporters of the Iraq War, including Vice President Dick Cheney and cable news commentator Bill O'Reilly. He expressed that American citizens were being encouraged to support the invasion of Iran as a way to establish Israel's dominance in the region.

By the late 1990s, Resistance Records was going through many quick changes. It was incorporated in Washington, DC, with a new operations manager, Todd Blodgett. He and William Luther Pierce became co-owners. By 1999, Carto and Blodgett sold their shares in Resistance Records to Pierce, who had previously been head of the National Alliance, a far-right organization. Pierce then fired Blodgett, moved the record label to West Virginia, and purchased another white power record label, Nordland Records, based in Sweden. The purchase doubled the roster of hate music groups represented by Resistance Records.

Eric Davidson, who had been one of the previous owners of the American branch of Resistance Records, resigned. He eventually started his own record company, Panzerfaust Records, in Minnesota. Todd Blodgett—who, before coming to Resistance Records, had previously worked for the Reagan White House press office, the Bush-Quayle election committee, and other Republican state campaigns—eventually became an FBI informant, infiltrating white supremacist organizations. After leaving Resistance Records, he claimed that he worked there because he was "opportunically" driven and greedy.

Trying to trace the location of Resistance Records was a challenge, because its location kept changing—from Toronto, to Detroit, to California, to Washington, DC, to Minnesota, and to West Virginia.

Resistance Records branched out to include some smaller record labels, Cymophone Records and Unholy Records. In addition to selling CDs, the three labels sell flags, clothing items, and computer games. Of note are the two computer games, *Ethnic Cleansing* and *White Law*. Both games feature racist themes and are won by committing murder. Both have hate music soundtracks.

The current manager of Resistance Records appears to be Erich Gliebe, also with ties to the National Alliance. With the nickname "The Aryan Barbarian," he has continued to profit from the label's roster of white power music groups. According to the website Discogs, Resistance Records is currently selling eighty different albums, cassettes, test pressings, and CDs.

Represented in that inventory are the following bands: Max Resist, Aryan, Aggravated Assault, Berserkr, New Minority, No Remorse, RAHOWA, Aryan Terrorism, Blue Eyed Devils, Bound for Glory, Angry Aryans, Extreme Hatred, Prussian Blue, Brutal Attack, Fueled by Hate, Kremator, Code of Violence, and others. The band names speak for themselves. A "Who's Who" of white power bands.

Album names were also suggestive of the content: *Against the World, Born to Hate, Crush the Weak, Racially Motivated Violence, Old School Hate, Filled with Rage, Cult of the Holy War,* etc. Many of the recordings were from the 1990s, but there were items from as recent as 2017. What an inventory.

I turned to YouTube to listen to music by some of the bands. What I heard was mostly loud, pounding, punk-style anthems, with lyrics almost impossible to understand. Testosterone-fueled, angry music. It was difficult to distinguish between the bands. Many of them sounded remarkably alike. Album covers on YouTube contained Nazi symbols and images of heavily tattooed skinhead musicians. One photo depicted a German soldier shooting a man standing in what appeared to be a grave.

In 2001, Burdi spoke to the *Intelligence Report* of the SPLC. He shared:

> "Racism is wrong because...I should probably say hatred is wrong, anger is wrong. Hatred and anger are wrong because they consume what is good in you. They smother your ability to appreciate love and peace. Another reason that racism is wrong is that you attach yourself to the accomplishments of white Europeans, instead of developing yourself and actually contributing to the society you live in."

He was confronted with the lyrics that he sang in the song "Third Reich", which referred to African Americans with the N word and advocated for their murder along with Jews, gypsies, and communists. He responded that he had not written the lyrics or the music for that song, but he had sung it. He admitted feeling ashamed about singing those words and said that it would be impossible to offer an adequate apology.

I spoke to a researcher at SPLC and asked why Resistance Records was still on its list of hate music outfits, because it seems to be inactive. The response was, "Yes, they don't seem to be very active. We think they might just be selling off their inventory." Quite a large inventory, for a company that is inactive.

In November and December 2017, an "exclusive inter-view with George Burdi" was published in two-parts in *Veriyhteys,* described as the "information channel of the Finnish counterculture." Burdi had been less visible since severing his ties with Resistance Records twenty years earlier. In the lengthy interview, Burdi clarified his beliefs. Referring to two of the founders of the organization Life After Hate, he said, "I can accept that Christian and Arno have become left-wing in their views, as long as they can accept that I never stopped being right-wing." He went on to explain his philosophy:

> "I do not accept those self-styled leaders—I was once one too—who claim to speak for white people yet do so in a way totally misrepresenting our ethos, values, traditions, and good qualities. My leader overflows with love for his people, for his culture. He loves children, and animals, and isn't capable of brutality. He believes in the laws of nature, acts in harmony with dharma, and is a humble servant of God and his fellow man.
>
> What I find hard to accept, however, is the idea that all organizing by white people for their group interests is 'racism' and 'hate,' which conflates mas-sive historical forces into a narrow psychological 'defect of humanity.'
>
> It characterizes all white group identity and organizing as 'hate,' which is a massive mistake. If the only way that white people are permitted by society to organize for their group interests is characterized as hatred, then a psychological syph-oning occurs where only people sufficiently frus-

trated enough to wear these labels and the resulting social stigmatism step forward. It's sort of an anti-selection. Then these elements create a doomsday mentality where there is no recourse other than mutual destruction."

Those last two sentences seemed to fit the music and musicians still being promoted by Resistance Records.

As of 2017, Burdi was working with a new band, Ueber-volk (Überfolk), readying the release of their debut album *Music for Nations*. On the Überfolk website (https://uber-folk.com/askdfaskldlkas-blog/), Burdi wrote:

"Fighting for narcissistic rulers, the war stage became our constantly repeating act of egoistic materialism, where we butchered one another over nearly irrel-evant distinctions, because we lacked the knowledge and wisdom to project a different future. Let us not repeat this destructive arrogance."

Russell Hilliard

RESISTANCE RECORDS HAS A RELATIONSHIP TO DEATH in several ways. First, many of its artists have been concerned with what they feel is the death of the white, Euro-pean, Aryan race and culture. They advocate for white supremacy, white separatism, and a racial holy war.

Second, some of those musicians advocate for violent responses and sometimes murder, for those who disagree with them. They want to awaken whites to the threat of extinction and, paradoxically, even clash with, maim, or kill whites or members of other races who challenge their racism.

To Resistance Records' artists, whites who don't join them in their twisted set of beliefs are "race traitors." Finally, some of the Resistance musicians still deny the deaths of millions of Jews and others during the Holocaust.

Some experts have described a "death attitude system," which includes how we think, feel, and behave in relation to living, dying, and grieving. Songs exist about dying, heaven, hell, killing, and angels. Funerals and memorial services include music of all types. Some hate music includes lyrics about violence and death, even genocide. And music therapists use music to assist the dying with relaxation, pain reduction, life reviews, reduction of side effects of medications, to counteract insomnia and, among other things, improve quality of life.

A music therapist whose career has also involved a relationship to death and dying is Russell Hilliard.

Hilliard was born in West Palm Beach, Florida. At the age of two, he had his first experience with death when his father passed away. Growing up without a father was not easy, but Hilliard describes his mother as a loving, religious, nurturing woman. During his childhood, she encouraged him to strive for the "life of Christ." Hilliard's family was spiritual, musical, and involved in church—first as Baptists, and then, Methodists. When he encountered early challenges in his life, he was taught to "let God sort it out." He told me that he has often felt divinely inspired and that he learned that music was a tool that allows for forgiveness and peace. At the age of sixteen, he came out as a gay man.

Hilliard took up music and played double bass. He first heard about music therapy when his forty-seven-year-old mother experienced a brain aneurism and required treatment and rehabilitation. He witnessed an occupational therapy session where music was used. He remembers his mother singing "You are My Sunshine" and the hymn "How Great Thou Art." For Hilliard, he strongly felt that music contributed to his mother's therapy in a positive way.

Staying in his home state, Hilliard completed his bachelor's degree in music therapy in 1994, graduating cum laude from Florida State University in Tallahassee. As a student, he volunteered at an HIV/AIDs hotline, fielding calls and providing information. He wanted to work with children and did additional volunteer work with terminally ill children undergoing hospice care. He considered becoming a hospice worker, but originally considered it a weird profession.

His college professor, Dr. Jayne Standley, told him that working with dying patients would be good volunteer experience, but cautioned him that he would never find secure employment with that population. "They'll never hire you," she said. Despite her warning, by 1995 he was giving his first presentation to a national music therapy conference titled, "Hospice and Music Therapy: Creating Jobs and Fulfilling Needs."

While a music therapy student, Hilliard continued to build his music skills by playing double bass with the Imperial Symphony Orchestra, the Florida Southern College Requiem Series, the Albany (Georgia) Symphony Orchestra, the Tallahassee Symphony Orchestra, and several Florida State University ensembles.

His mother passed away in 1997. Hilliard said that was a turning point—it was the last time he wanted to focus on being a performer.

Like other music therapists, Hilliard decided to add more clinical skills to his repertoire by next pursuing a master's degree in social work from Florida International University. He continued to gain clinical experience both after his bachelor's degree and while attending social work graduate school. He served as music therapy manager for Renfrew Center of Florida, Hospice of Palm Beach County, and Hospice of the Great Lakes—all in Florida. These were programs offering music therapy services for the first time, and Hilliard helped them use that fact to their advantage, in marketing materials and promotional efforts.

Immediately following receipt of his master's degree, Hilliard quickly returned to Florida State University, completing his PhD in both music therapy and social work in 2002. As he took classes and fulfilled other requirements for his doctorate, he continued to work at Big Bend Hospice in Tallahassee. There he designed the music therapy program, hired additional therapists, created and supervised an internship program, and helped market the music therapy services—all while carrying his own music therapy and social work patient caseloads.

Although Hilliard has devoted his career to providing services to terminally ill and dying patients, he has pursued many additional music therapy involvements. He has been an active teacher, helping students study and develop as music therapists.

Starting as a graduate teaching assistant at Florida State University, he then became a professor and director of the music therapy program at the State University of New York at New Paltz. While teaching at SUNY/New Paltz, he also worked clinically at Hospice, Inc., in Poughkeepsie, and Metropolitan Jewish Hospice and Health System. He has also served as a guest faculty member at Eastern Michigan University, Berklee College of Music, University of Missouri/Kansas City, and the Institute for Traditional Music in Toronto, Canada.

As a board-certified music therapist, Hilliard fulfilled an active professional role. He provided interviews for a variety of media, including the *New York Daily News, the British Broadcasting Company (BBC),* the *Los Angeles Times, FOX NEWS,* the *Minneapolis Star,* and others. He delivered close to thirty refereed research presentations, nationally and internationally. He published a book and book chapters, as well as thirty refereed journal articles and seven non-refereed articles. He served on the editorial boards of three professional journals: *Music Therapy Perspectives, Journal of Palliative Care, and Social Science & Medicine.* Hilliard remains in demand as a speaker and presenter at numerous professional conferences.

Hilliard founded the Center for Music Therapy in End of Life Care (CMTELC) in 2005. The organization offers continuing education courses to music therapists who want to earn an additional credential—HPMT, or Certificate in Hospice and Palliative Care Music Therapy.

Hilliard joined Seasons Hospice and Palliative Care Services in 2008. His current job title is "Senior Vice President for Patient Experience and Staff Development," but previous positions included executive director, vice president of operations, vice president of quality assurance and performance improvement, and vice president of supportive care and patient experience.

Seasons also supports his ongoing role directing the CMTELC. In 2018, the center offered classes in Las Vegas, St. Louis, San Diego, Boston, Denver, and Milwaukee. That same year, to foster international outreach, the center offered a ten-day training in Bangkok, Thailand.

Seasons is one of the largest hospice companies in the United States. It offers services in nineteen states and is exploring international expansion. Its mission is stated as "Honoring Life—Offering Hope." A positive vision for the company expresses the following: "recognition that clients usually know what's best for themselves, supporting employees and encouraging them to put patients first, fostering creativity, striving for excellence and exceeding standards, and increasing awareness of hospice as a part of the healthcare continuum."

I interviewed Hilliard at the national music therapy conference in St. Louis in 2017. We had scheduled the interview for an early morning time slot, but Hilliard asked to reschedule it later so that he could participate in a yoga session. I had done some homework and was familiar with his career, so we reviewed that part of his life quickly. We focused on other aspects of his life, and then Hilliard wanted to tell me a story about one of his clients.

Hilliard shared that he believes there is an important five-step process that family members go through when a loved one is dying. I thought of Elizabeth Kübler-Ross's familiar stages of grieving—denial, anger, bargaining, depression, acceptance—but that was not what he was referencing. He said family members need to do the following:

1. Tell each other that they are loved.

2. Let family members forgive the dying person for some past behaviors.

3. Let the dying person forgive others for things they have done.

4. Say "thank-you" to each other.

5. Say "good-bye."

He told me the story of a man whose father, a former "tough guy," was dying. His relationship with his father had survived some rough periods, but he wanted to patch things up and have closure. Hilliard worked with him to write a song to his father, to the melody of a Methodist hymn, "Blessed Assurance." (The family was Methodist, and the son selected that melody.) They wrote the lyrics in five minutes.

When the son sang the hymn for his father, the dying man gave him a "thumbs up," and then sobbing, embraced and rocked his son. They were able to talk about their lives together and peacefully say good-bye. The song seemed to help them break the ice to relate to each other at that very difficult time. The father passed away three days later. Hilliard made it clear that his role was to help the son write the song, but not to intrude on this final, family experience.

Hilliard and I talked briefly about hate music. He said that he was not very familiar with music that spreads hate. The only example he could think of was "Goodbye, Earl," written by Dennis Linde and sung by the Dixie Chicks. It is the story of two women who conspire to murder the abusive husband of one of the women—not the best way to end what had once been a loving relationship.

Hilliard said that if he ever has a client who prefers a form of hate music or brings up that kind of a song in a therapy session, he would learn the song and use it to let the client express his or her feelings. He would then use his relationship with that client, and his therapy skills, to process the feelings and what the song represented to them. He would use cognitive reframing to try to help them through the negative associations so that they could die with dignity.

Hilliard has had a long and distinguished music therapy career. He helps his clients and their families deal with pain, end-of-life issues, and closure. Like other music therapists, he has chosen to use music as a helpful tool. His services do not discriminate based on race, ethnicity, religion, gender identity, or disability.

Seasons Hospice and the Center for Music Therapy in End of Life Care use music in a unique and needed way. It is possible that some hate musicians, at the end of their lives, may require hospice care—and receive services from a music therapist.

Russell Hilliard, Seasons Hospice and Palliative Care.
Used with written permission.

Chapter 9

ANTI-DISABLED

ALICE AND JOE PARENTE/ CELESTE KEITH

Included in John Lennon's album *Imagine* (Apple Records, 1971) was the song "Crippled Inside". The lyrics make the point that people can change their appearance and judge others, but they can't disguise any lies that they believe and espouse.

Hate music always targets demographic groups for their characteristics or qualities over which they have no control: the color of their skin, where they came from, their gender, their sexual identity, their age, a disability, etc. Those things cannot be changed, simply because somebody hates them. Individuals with disabilities and handicaps must deal with their circumstances, and societal norms help them by offering some assistance, such as specialized treatment settings, ramps, convenient parking spaces, seating areas at movies and concerts, accessible housing, and disability insurance benefits. Unfortunately, not everyone agrees with or supports these accommodations. For some, the disabled are considered "unworthy of living."

In this pair of stories, I will share what I found out about anti-disabled music, next to the story of music therapists who use music to benefit individuals with disabilities.

As a precaution, I need to mention that there are strong feelings about what terms should be used when describing people with limitations. Words include "disabled, handicapped, crippled, mentally deficient, developmentally disabled," and others. People use phrases such as "Weirdo," "Moron," "Freak," "That's retarded," "Are you off your meds today?", "Why are you so blind?", "Somebody call the doctor," "You must need hearing aids," "Are you crazy?", "That's so lame," and others.

Some of these words are used casually in songs, movie scripts, TV shows, and everyday conversations. Words are important, and care should be given to consider their effects and the intent of the speaker—or singer. Some people cautioned me that it is currently preferred to use the descriptor, "individuals with cognitive, sensory, or physical differences." It is not my intent to be 100 percent politically correct, because some of the non-preferred words are not my own but come from literature that I reviewed or song lyrics. My intent is not to offend, but I will use various descriptors to avoid being overly redundant.

Anti-Disabled Music

IN 1920, PSYCHIATRIST, ALFRED HOCHE, AND JURIST, Karl Binding, published an article titled "Permitting the Destruction of Unworthy Life." This publication was later used by the Nazis as grounds for their treatment of persons with disabilities.

The Nazis killed approximately three hundred thousand disabled individuals. It was the first group that they systematically murdered, through a program called T4. The T4 program was named for the address of the offices in Berlin that directed the program—Tiergartenstrasse 4. Also known as the T4 Euthanasia Program, it officially ran from 1939 to 1941, but unofficially continued until 1945.

When T4 was first implemented, it was described as a "wartime measure," giving physicians the authority to identify patients with "incurable" conditions and grant them a "mercy killing." The program targeted psychiatric patients, the hearing- impaired, psychopaths, mentally retarded, the elderly, the blind, children with Down syndrome, those with microcephaly or hydrocephaly, anyone with bodily malformations, individuals with Huntington's chorea, people with terminal neurological conditions, and others.

Treatment centers—including hospitals, homes for the elderly, asylums, and nursing homes—were required to complete reports on all of their patients. A panel of at least three physicians then determined which patients were "unfit for life." Today, some hate musicians would have supported the T4 program—or, conversely, would have been on the list for mercy killings.

During the T4 years, patients were starved to death or their needed medical treatments were withheld. Experiments were conducted on them. Some were gassed to death, some were shot, and others died by lethal injections. Some of those who survived the program were sterilized, to prevent any future births of children with disabilities.

The Nazi regime kept some of these practices secret, but that was impossible. One of its strategies was to sell the program as economically necessary to preserve limited resources for others. They argued that the program was compassionate, helped to reduce unnecessary suffering, helped with ethnic cleansing, and saved money for other priorities. These beliefs were put forward in a coordinated propaganda campaign that included leaflets, movies, and speeches. Even some parents agreed that it was best for their handicapped children. Viewed as survival of the fittest, Nazis sometimes referred to the victims as "burdensome lives" and "useless eaters."

There was resistance to the program. Churches, family members, and some physicians took actions to protest the crusade and protect the innocent targets of T4. Knowing about the program, some physicians discharged patients back to the care of their families, so that they did not have to file the required reports. One Catholic bishop, Count Clemens August von Galen, said that Christians needed to oppose any taking of human life, even if it required sacrificing their own.

Some of these details were new to me, and I was only vaguely aware that some of the same practices had been present in the United States. I had either forgotten or had made assumptions that those programs only happened in the past and that the disabled were no longer treated as individuals unworthy of human life.

The disabled have fought against discrimination for centuries. During the 1800s, in the United States, disabled individuals were displayed in circuses, exhibitions, and freak shows. Many were locked away from society, in institutions, sometimes for their entire lives.

As early as the 1860s, several states had statutes called "ugly laws," which made it against the law for people considered "unsightly or unseemly" to be visible in public. This included individuals with disabilities. It took until 1974 for these laws to be repealed.

These laws reminded me that musicians have also been insensitive to individuals with disabilities. For example, John Lennon reportedly made fun of handicapped individuals at early Beatle performances and asked that they be seated out of sight. More recently, at a concert in Melbourne, Australia, Kanye West would not perform until all of his audience members stood. He even had the IDs of seated people checked to verify that they were legitimately disabled—not only insensitive but possibly illegal. Audience members had purchased tickets for a seat and should not have been forced to stand.

Following World War I and World War II, disabled veterans began to demand medical care and rehabilitation in return for their service to their country. Even President Franklin Delano Roosevelt—himself, in a wheelchair—supported more treatment for those with handicaps. Still, parts of the general public viewed these "different" people as odd, freakish, abnormal, and in need of being fixed or cured. There was still little or no access to public transportation, adaptive telephones or communication devices, restrooms, or retail outlets. Many could not find rewarding employment.

During the sixties, disability rights advocates joined forces with other civil rights groups, bringing further public education to the inequalities facing the disabled. By 1973, Congress passed the Rehabilitation Act, which offered protections to individuals with disabilities. The law provided for equal opportunity employment, access to public transportation, and vocational training. It was followed in 1975 with the Education for All Handicapped Children Act, which allowed some disabled children to be mainstreamed into schools, provided their disabilities were not so severe as to limit their ability to participate and benefit.

In 1990, the Education for All Handicapped Children Act was renamed the Individuals with Disabilities Education Act. The newly named law expanded how mainstreaming could occur, allowed for parents to participate, and required that Individual Education Plans be developed for each child. Also, in 1990, the Americans with Disabilities Act was passed, mandating the full rights of disabled individuals to participate in all levels of society.

But biases, prejudice, and discrimination remained. These laws and others that offered support for the disabled did not come easily. They were brought about by the ongoing efforts of advocates, using a multitude of strategies and tactics.

During the twentieth century, thirty-two states implemented eugenic laws, allowing institutionalized individuals to be involuntarily sterilized. This included those living in state facilities for the mentally retarded and mentally ill, as well as state prisons.

Even the Supreme Court supported the program in its 1927 ruling from the *Buck v Bell* case, in which Judge Oliver Wendell Holmes wrote: "Three generations of imbeciles is enough." The court ruled that sterilization was constitutional. It was viewed as supporting the reproduction of certain groups while eliminating the reproduction rights of "unfit" individuals. The "unfit" included promiscuous young women, the sons and daughters of some immigrants, children from poor families, and men and women who fell outside of sexual norms. Some families fought against the sterilization of their family members, while others consented.

In California, one study showed that patients with Spanish surnames were 3.5 times more likely to be victims of sterilization than other institutionalized persons. As recently as 2006 to 2010, 146 females in California's women prisons were given tubal ligations. The majority of these women were African American or Hispanic, many of them first-time offenders.

Even in my state, Oregon, over two thousand five hundred citizens were sterilized in state institutions between 1917 and 1983. Former Governor John Kitzhaber issued an official apology in 2003. Some former patients accepted his apology, while others demanded compensation for their forced mental and physical pain and suffering.

FBI crime statistics show that there was an increase in hate crimes against persons with perceived disabilities between 2016 and 2017. Crimes included theft of special assistive devices, vandalism, physical abuse, verbal abuse, assault, murder—or any crime that demonstrated bias against another person due to their disability. Some of these crimes were committed by family members or caregivers. Others were committed by strangers.

As I contemplated these discoveries, I searched for music that played a role in anti-disabled sentiments. I began looking into songs that spread negative stereotypes about the disabled, advocated for limiting their rights, discriminated against them, or openly expressed hatred toward them.

Visiting websites that allowed searches of song lyrics, I plugged in keywords and reviewed what came up. Some songs included the keywords "wheelchair, retard, handicapped, disabled, crippled, blind," and "put you in a wheelchair." Not all of those songs expressed hatred, but they certainly were insensitive, uninformed, and presented negative stereotypes.

There were sick songs about wanting to have enough sex with a woman to put her in a wheelchair, songs in protest of handicapped parking spaces, a song about wanting to abuse the bodies of elderly patients in a nursing home, a lot of name-calling, and casual use of derogatory terms to describe individuals who have cognitive, sensory, or physical limitations.

Ableism is defined as discrimination against disabled people, and it takes many forms in the world of music. Concert venues may not be totally accessible. Restrooms may be located where wheelchairs cannot reach them, or they may lack handicapped stalls. Maybe there's an appropriate restroom on the second floor but no elevator. Some performers don't even check to see if their disabled fans can be safe and/or comfortable during a concert. Other musicians might take social justice seriously and insist on accessibility, accommodation, and safety—but then not follow up to assure compliance. Sam McBride, member of the punk rock band, Fang, told me about an organization in Portland, Oregon, *Half Access*, which advocates for making live music venues accessible to disabled individuals (more about Sam below).

A YouTube video presented a compiled list of songs that demonstrated ableism. Songs included:

- "Kids on Holiday" by Animal Collective

- "Can't Hold it Back" by Dred Scott

- "Faith No More" by Zombie Eaters

- "Party for Two" by Guttermouth

- "Retard Girl" by Hole, which includes language about hating a disabled girl

- "Let's Get It Started" by the Black Eyed Peas, originally titled "Let's Get Retarded"

- A song by Naughty By Nature that contained a list of negative terms to describe disabled individuals

- "Amp Hymn" by Pungent Stench, singing about loving the stubs of women who are missing limbs

- "Lifeboat" by Steve Taylor, which includes a teacher asking students who they would throw out of a lifeboat, and describing handicapped individuals as being unproductive in society.

The songs made me cringe. Negative stereotypes, extreme insensitivity, and, in several cases, hatred on display. This was just one small collection of songs, from thousands of songs that mentioned disabilities in some way. Combining disabilities with other factors, such as race, religion, sexual identity, etc. escalates the levels of mocking, bias, discrimination, and hatred.

Like songs about immigrants, those about individuals with disabilities ran along a continuum, with some being less hateful than others. Others were even designed to make us think, to question stereotypes, or in jest. For example, Randy Newman's "Short People," which included lyrics that questioned whether short people were worthy of living, seemed obviously satirical.

Another example might be Joe Raposo's "It's Not Easy Bein' Green," sung by Kermit the Frog on the *Muppets* TV show. By dehumanizing the issues, Raposo shines a light on the difficulties of individuals who are "different."

Do some songs go too far? When rappers DMoney N Smoove sang their song, "Wheelchair Shawty," were they trying to make us think about the challenges facing disabled individuals, or were they really making fun of those individuals? In the video for the song, able-bodied men and women create a dance appearing to mock how somebody in a wheelchair might dance.

I read about and listened to other songs that related to disabilities:

- "My Generation" by The Who, which featured Roger Daltry singing with a stutter

- "Ruby" by Kenny Rogers and the First Edition, which expressed how it is difficult to love a handicapped person.

- "Mongoloid" by Devo

- "In Northern California (Where the Palm Tree Meets the Pine)" by Danny O'Keefe, about a one-night stand with a woman who had braces and crutches

- "November Spawned a Monster" by Morrissey, which described a disabled child as ugly.

- "Acute Schizophrenic Paranoia Blues" by the Kinks (with a mental illness theme)

- "4st 7lb" by Manic Street Preachers (about anorexia)

- "Symphony of Tourette" by Manic Street Preachers (about Tourette Syndrome)

- "Crippled and Blind" by The Vandals

In a previous story, I wrote about the use of hateful chants at sporting events. This was also true with anti-disabled chants. One example occurred when soccer fans sang "mong" chants at the opposing team's player, Harry Kane, at a match in Great Britain. Kane's daughter lives with Down syndrome. Kevin Kilbane, a BBC reporter, whose daughter also suffers from Down syndrome, commented, "You cannot sweep it under the carpet and label it as ignorance. It is visible and clear, and like racist or homophobic chanting, it is intended to cause offence (*sic*)."

These were just a few, from an avalanche of song possibilities. There were hundreds, if not thousands, of songs about individuals with disabilities and handicaps. Some were supportive, inclusive, accepting, and empathetic. Some were real and told authentic stories through the eyes of disabled individuals. Others were the opposite—perpetuating negative perceptions and images—and hateful.

Perhaps the most extreme song I encountered was "Destroy the Handicapped" (Boner Records, 1989) by a Northern California punk band named Fang. Lyrics repeated the song's title multiple times, with the addition of negative comments about disabled individuals. On the surface, hate music.

I spoke to the songwriter, Sam "Sammytown" McBride,

on the phone. He explained that the composition was not written as a hate song. He clarified that the punk music of that time, and presently, was to create a social revolution to challenge aspects of the status quo. He said he wrote the song "tongue in cheek," to "call out hate culture." In fact, he said that disabled individuals often requested the song and sang along with him at Fang concerts. In his words, "They got it."

Following a long prison term for a horrendous crime, Sam now works for Transformation Care Detox in Gardena, California, further proof that people change. He told me about a second song, "Crippled Children Suck," by Meat Men (*Touch and Go* Records, 1983), which presented one of the most politically incorrect uses of humor to challenge attitudes toward the disabled, and featured an album cover depicting a disabled child being beaten. The album also included the song "I Sin for a Living", and tunes about gays and women. Again, McBride explained that punk rock was often meant to be satirical, pointing out that it is important to consider the context and intent of songs. Still, there are people in the environment who will take songs like these on face value, and that could be dangerous. Individuals who don't "get" satire can be influenced to hurt others.

Of course, there was an opposite perspective—the songs that uplifted and encouraged persons with special challenges. Bob Kauflin wrote a song titled "Song for Those with Disabilities." In a similar vein, Lady Gaga wrote, "Born This Way". Both songs encouraged self-acceptance and love.

Songs are not the only way that the music industry discriminates against persons with disabilities and limitations. Many music clubs, organizations, choirs, bands, orchestras, dance troupes, and other music ensembles do not fully include disabled participants. Some segregation of disabled musicians still remains.

Even in schools, some music teachers resist having "special" students in their music ensembles. They haven't learned how to accommodate those students or adapt their teaching methods. They only want to work with "normal" students. They are afraid that disabled musicians will be unable to rise to certain levels of music skill or may detract from performances. On TV shows, musical performers are often shown moving around. It is rare to see artists who are unable to move.

There are plenty of examples of disabled individuals who have demonstrated high musical skills. Beethoven was deaf. More recent examples include Stevie Wonder, Jose Feliciano, Ray Charles, Itzhak Perlman, Andrea Bocelli, Django Reinhardt, Rick Allen, Jerry Garcia, Mel Tillis, and Teddy Pendergras.

Another musician who has received broad media attention is Derek Paravicini, who is blind, autistic, and severely disabled. He can't read standard written music or even music written in braille. But sitting at a piano, he can instantaneously play almost any song, in any key, in any style. He is a shining example of a person with advanced musical skills, despite his other limitations. His abilities outshine any disabilities.

There are bright spots on the horizon. I found examples of efforts to include disabled musicians. The Bournemouth Symphony Orchestra, in England, created a new ensemble led by disabled musicians. In the world of rock, the band, Portugal the Man, includes a guitarist in a wheelchair. One US-based organization, Krip-Hop Nation, has initiated its Hip Hop for Disability Justice Campaign. The Coalition for

Disabled Musicians, another organization in the United States, set the following goals for itself:

- Introducing disabled musicians to each other
- Providing access to rehearsal spaces and recording studios
- Creating systems and adaptive techniques to help with pain, endurance, and other limiting factors
- Setting up studio and stage bands for both amateur and professional, disabled musicians
- Hosting live performances, recordings, workshops, and seminars
- Increasing public awareness of the disability community as a source of talent and ability

Despite these efforts, music has been used to spread hate against individuals with cognitive, sensory, or physical differences. Songs demean, ridicule, demonize, mock, protest, and fuel hatred against the disabled. But there is one other field that counters these negative, insensitive forms of music: music therapy.

Alice and Joe Parente/Celeste Keith

ALICE BALL, FROM SANTA ROSA, CALIFORNIA, STARTED playing piano when she was five-and-a-half years old. Her mother insisted that she continue lessons until she graduated from high school. During her adolescent years, she began volunteering at Sonoma State Hospital and a camp for children and adolescents with developmental disabilities. She found that she loved working with kids with special needs. She also knew that she had perfect pitch and musical talent.

A part of her could not wait to get away from the mandatory piano lessons that her mother demanded, so when she left for college at the University of the Pacific (UOP) in Stockton, California, she stopped the lessons and initially chose to major in English—that is, until she heard about music therapy.

She switched her major to music therapy, graduating with a bachelor's degree from UOP in 1973. After working for a few years at Fairview State Hospital in Costa Mesa, California—a facility for people of all ages with severe and profound development disabilities—she returned to UOP to earn her master's degree in education in 1980. She desired to learn more techniques and skills to help the population she loved.

On the opposite coast, Joe Parente, from Scranton, Pennsylvania, started accordion lessons at age six. As he grew up, he joined local accordion bands and started to get into music. He remembers liking the play *Fiddler on the Roof* because it had an accordion player in it. He credits that play with giving him his first taste of the musical theatre. He had developed music skills and interests, but when he entered college, he earned his first degree in psychology—then he heard about music therapy.

Deciding to pursue a master's degree, Joe chose music therapy as his major and was accepted into the program at Loyola University in New Orleans. He had read about the program, saw that the director of the MT program, Dr. Charles Braswell, was the current president of the NAMT, and decided that it was "the most outrageous place to go." He was seeking a change of geography and an adventure.

For one of his classes, Joe wrote a paper about the musical preferences of children, which was published in the journal *Perceptual and Motor Skills*. Since his first degree was in psychology, he was required to complete additional music classes, as well as the full music therapy curriculum. He took composition courses and gained experience working at a recording studio in New Orleans. At the studio, he helped with arrangements and developed a network of friends—some with ties to the musical theatre. With their support and encouragement, Joe composed a musical version of Shakespeare's *As You like It*.

As a student, Joe attended a music therapy conference in Kansas City, where he saw a play, *Snow White and the Seven Dwarfs*. The lead character roles were taken by two music therapists, while the roles of the Seven Dwarfs were filled with children who had Down syndrome. For Joe, something was amiss. He decided to write a musical where children with disabilities had the lead roles, performed at a professional level, understood all aspects of the theatrical production, and did not play "second fiddle" to nondisabled cast members.

He approached Charles Braswell with the idea and proposed that he wanted to make the project the basis of his master's thesis. After discussion within the program hierarchy, it was decided that this would be acceptable, provided that it included a research aspect. He composed a new musical, *Fatso*. Now he was going to need an appropriate setting to produce the play.

Joe wrote the musical as an allegory for the "costume" that we all wear. The musical illustrates, through songs, different kinds of hate and how to replace that hate with self-acceptance and healthy relationships. Rehearsals allowed cast members to improvise dialog between songs until a final script evolved. The process held the key, because the actors learned to express to others that they had something to offer the world.

Alice Ball had completed two college degrees in Stockton and had gained a couple of years of clinical experience as a professional music therapist working with individuals with developmental disabilities in Southern California. The next step in her career was at the Alan Short Center, also in Stockton. Alice describes the Alan Short Center this way:

> "Alan Short Center had been chosen as one of ten model sites by the National Committee Arts for The Handicapped—started by Jean Kennedy Smith—which later evolved into National Very Special Arts and now Very Special Arts. Alan Short Center was set up to be a role model program for quality, professional arts, visual and performing, for adults with disabilities. All programs were 'people first' and meant to bring attention to the talents and capabilities rather than the limitations and 'handicaps' of the students. They were artists and people with artistic talents who just happened to have a disability."

The Alan Short Center, in one of its own theatre programs, went further:

> "The unique approach of the Alan Short Center is designed to enable the handicapped individual to lead a productive and useful life in the community. This is accomplished by enabling the student

to discover and expand his own creative abilities through media such as music, drama, art and photography, and thereby increasing his own self-concept and confidence. A self-confident individual begins taking the initiative to accomplish on his own, which is the ultimate goal of the Center for each student.

"The students are not being held back by prior judgments of what they can or cannot accomplish. Each subject—graphic arts, drama, photography, film making, dry-cleaning and others—carries the possibility of eventual part or full time employment for the students.

"In the American dream of making post-secondary education a universal opportunity, some groups have been overlooked. Delta College is working with the Alan Short Center to help overcome that shortcoming."

Alice found the work at the Alan Short Center very rewarding and quickly saw the facility—located in the old superintendent's house on the grounds of Stockton State Hospital—as a perfect setting to use music therapy as a means for enhancing students' essential living skills and self-esteem. She also recognized that it was an optimal setting to offer an internship for music therapy students who had completed their college coursework. Setting up an approved internship takes work, but she was invested in it. It would pay off, both professionally and personally.

Alice received a call from Charles Braswell. He explained that he had a student who had written a musical for his master's thesis and was looking for an internship site where he could produce the show. Would Alice accept Joe Parente as an intern? He told her, "You can meet Joe at the next national music therapy conference in Milwaukee, interview him, and decide if you are willing to accept him."

The interview, which was held in a hotel's brandy bar, did not go well. Alice's first impression of Joe was that he was egotistical and exhibited a touch of condescension. Joe was of Italian descent and raised Catholic. Alice was not Italian or from the East Coast and had been raised Presbyterian. They didn't jive at first. They were from different coasts, different schools, different cultures. Different, different, different—except for their love of music and their desire to use it in positive ways to help people with disabilities. Alice, with serious apprehension, accepted Joe as an intern in 1977.

One Friday afternoon, the Alan Short Center staff decided to play hooky, cancel their usual classes and go to a movie. It was the last day of the week—TGIF—and, besides, none of the students would notice that classes were not being held. Alice couldn't force herself to go along. She decided to stay behind and hold her music therapy classes as scheduled.

At some point, she heard a piano being played in another part of the building. She investigated and found Joe and a group of students crowded around the piano. Joe was working with the students, teaching them theatre songs, and encouraging them. She saw him treating the students with great respect, honoring their ideas and contributions. It changed her whole opinion of Joe. He had not gone to the movies. He had chosen to work with his students. She was hooked. She had found someone who loved and believed in these special students as much as she did. They began working more closely together, especially on the production of *Fatso*.

Rehearsals were difficult. Joe and Alice wanted to bring their students to the level of good musical theatre. They refused to "dumb down" the expectations. Instead, they wanted to "raise up" the students to good theatre. They wanted the students to be great artists. Alice and Joe wanted them to understand all aspects of each production—lighting, sound, costuming, staging, dramatic effects, and how to win over an audience. Slowly, but surely, the students caught on and learned. They could even explain everything to others and impressed the "normal" crew members with their knowledge.

Fatso was performed at Delta Community College, Santa Ana College, and Chapman College, in California; Fairview State Hospital and Training Center and Chemeketa Community College, in Oregon; a state school and an American Theatre Association conference, in Louisiana; a national music therapy conference in Anaheim; and other venues.

When the cast members were greeted with, "Oh, you're the disabled group," they responded, "No, we're the actors in this musical." They showed their technical support people where to place sets and props; how to light each scene; where to put the piano; where to place microphones for the best sound; what was "upstage," "downstage," or "in the wings;" when to start the overture, etc. They held question-and-answer sessions after performing and could explain all aspects of their production and the significant message: "This musical theatre production focuses on abilities, not disabilities."

They received recognition for their wonderful performances, not just because they were "different." The actors' families swelled with pride and supported ongoing efforts. Each performance of the musical was a game-changer.

Joe collected data about the *Fatso* actors and produced a documentary about the process of putting on the show. His research demonstrated that participants showed statistically significant improvements in standard measurements related to both academic and behavioral skills. They also increased their self-esteem and confidence. These findings were the result of the whole process that led to performances, plus participation in the onstage shows themselves.

Based on *Fatso* and his internship, Joe completed his master's degree in music therapy at Loyola University. But things didn't end there. Joe and Alice have continued to collaborate. They were married in 1980.

Alice and Joe have maintained a focus on additional live theatrical performances, video productions, musical compositions, films, and other arts-based programs—both for "normal" and "other abled" populations. After *Fatso,* there have been additional musicals: *Yoyo's* (1981)), *Companions* (1982), and *Building a Rainbow* (1986). All of their productions have reflected their philosophy that stresses the value of the process of staging a production over the value of the final show itself—and all starring actors with and without disabilities.

In 1982, Alice and Joe cofounded Process Theatre, Inc./ Very Special Arts. Alice serves as the co-administrative director and co-artistic director of the program. From 1986 to 2015, she served as the executive director of I Can Do That!/Very Special Arts program, serving over three thousand children and youth, both with and without disabilities, in Sacramento County, California.

As the creator of the I Can Do That! program, she served as the artist-in-schools coordinator for a consortium of schools in the Sacramento area, bringing in professional artists from the community to work with students both with and without disabilities. Programs integrated special education and general education classes. Her involvement included training teams of professional artists, teachers, and student artists to create professional-level art shows and performances. She also established documentation systems for monitoring student growth. From 2005 to 2010, she served as executive director and director of development for Very Special Arts of California.

Alice's resume reflects numerous awards, publications, professional association memberships, and teaching assignments. She continues her work with Process Theatre, even bringing in hip-hop artists and groups to work in schools with integrated groups of students of all abilities, teaching them hip-hop dance and developing performances for the community. She refuses to let her professional artists teach students to copy what they have seen other artists do. No mimicking Michael Jackson's dance moves. No stealing the words from their favorite rap or hip-hop songs. Performers must create their own lyrics, beats, choreography, and products. They have proven that they have the abilities to do that.

Joe is also a cofounder, co-administrator, and co-artistic director at Process Theatre, which is their private, non-profit, charity (a 501(c)3). As a registered charity, it has a board of directors, its own philosophy, bylaws, articles of incorporation, and a tax identification number. Joe's part of the organization focuses more on media arts—producing videos, recordings, and running a radio station.

Between 1983 and 2000, Joe received more than a dozen awards for his work, including two Emmy nominations— the first in 1986 for his composition "I Got News for You" and the second in 1988 for "I am Somebody." Other awards have been received for films and videos—*The Attendant* (five awards between 1983 and 1986), *I Got News for You* (three awards between 1986 and 1987), *I am Somebody* (1988), *At the Ballet* (1998), *Not Just Child's Play* (1999), and *Life Rhythms* (2000).

Beginning in 1990 and continuing until 2003, Joe worked for the San Juan Unified School District—leading Studio E-3, a program for the distance education of normal students, special education students, lifelong learners, teachers, parents, and senior citizens. Since 2001, Joe has worked as an adjunct professor in the Communications Studies Department at California State University, Sacramento. Between 2003 and 2006, Joe served as producer/director/distance education/digital media consultant for the California Department of Education. From 2006 to the present, Joe has continued those same roles for WestEd, a branch of Process Theatre.

Although the Parentes both have degrees in music therapy, only Alice became a credentialed music therapist. At a point in her career, she chose not to renew any music therapy credentials or memberships. Those things are no longer required for her or Joe to run their own company, Process Theatre. I mention this to recognize the fact that music therapists do not "own" music and are not the only ones using music in positive ways. There are music teachers, musicians, producers, directors, composers, songwriters, organizations, and others that all use music in positive, sometimes therapeutic ways. The general public should support those who do this valuable work, especially those who are appropriately educated, trained, and credentialed.

To offer the perspective of another music therapist who is still credentialed and an active member of the AMTA,

Alice referred me to a Sacramento music therapy colleague, Celeste Keith. She runs The Music Works Music Therapy Service in Sacramento, where she has been providing music therapy services to special populations for over forty years.

Celeste expressed frustration with the "mainstreaming" model of including disabled clients in school settings, which she views as "dehumanizing." She said the mainstreaming model is inherently biased and unfair because it requires persons with disabilities to "prove themselves" first, to gain access.

Celeste noted that even the systems that serve disabled persons of all ages are only as good as the staff members who work in them. In too many instances, those individuals are not adequately trained or supported to understand that significant fragility does not equate to inadequacy. She observed that our collective society arranges persons with disabilities in an "us and them" framework.

She stated, "There is no exposure or education for the public at large about inclusion and what it really means, or what 'these' people look like or sound like, and they are faced with encountering pity over compassion or companionship."

Celeste explained that the current laws and models often force families to either prove that their family member deserves access, or wait until they have failed before help is offered. In her words, it was "damned if they do, and damned if they don't." Parents, in particular, who advocate for their children, often at great personal and fiscal expense, are sometimes viewed as being overly aggressive and "troublemakers," despite advocating for what the law requires.

According to Celeste, part of the problem remains that persons with disabilities are still sometimes viewed as needing to be "fixed" or "cured," instead of being accepted as they are. Needing support and being challenged is completely different. Her agency uses a philosophy that clients are "exactly who they need to be." She and the music therapy colleagues within her agency practice doing things "with" their clients, instead of "to" their clients. Celeste noted this approach levels the playing field, assumes a person is competent, embraces each client's distinctive personal influences and life experience, holds the space for self-actualization, and is inherently respectful.

As an example, Celeste provided the story of one of her medically fragile adult clients who needed to prove that he was eligible for "funding of services"—in this case, music therapy. He experienced a health complication that resulted in respiratory distress and a significant increase in seizure activity. These life-threatening changes required hospitalization and resulted in weeks of care in an intensive care unit. However, this client is also a songwriter and, with Celeste's help, used composition to work through the resulting trauma and begin healing.

Celeste assembled a group of musicians to professionally record some of his songs. In one, he even used sounds from his suction machine as a design for a bass and percussion line. Through rehearsals, recording, and live performances, he was able to show audiences, case managers, his medical team, and the general public that he could be "a person with significant physical and medical limitations 'embedded' with typical able-bodied folks, and not just relegated to 'programs for the handicapped.'"

His bandmates are his peers and "posse of protection." His musical skills, recordings, and capabilities in directing his band were used to demonstrate to authorities that he had abilities and could benefit from services. Funding was

approved. (Readers can listen to his songs on Soundcloud.
com. Search on Forrest Evans or Celeste Keith, artists; In
a Tizzy, band; or the songs "Do B Us," "Trust Account,"
or "Oath.")

As punk bands sing their songs "Destroy the Handicapped" and "Crippled Children Suck," music therapists and
others take the opposite approach, proving that individuals
with cognitive, sensory, or physical differences have lives
worth living.

My research had visited anti-Semitic music, antiblack
music, anti-immigrant music, and now, anti-disabled music.
There were other demographic groups to be considered, and
events in other geographical locations.

Alice Parente, rehearsing clients at Alan Short Center, Stockton, California, ca. 1978. Used with written permission.

Alice Parente, Process Theatre/Very Special Arts, Sacramento, California. Used with written permission.

Joe Parente, leading a rehearsal of Fatso, Alan Short Center, ca. 1978. Used with written permission.

Joe Parente, Process Theatre/Very Special Arts, Sacramento, California. Used with written permission.

Celeste Keith, leading a music therapy session, The Music Works
Music Therapy Service, Sacramento, California.
Used with written permission

Chapter 10

MURDER MUSIC

SPENCER HARDY

I n this pair of stories, I will describe "murder music," a
genre of music that advocates for the killing of members of the LGBTQ+ community. That will be followed
by the story of a mid-career music therapist.

Murder Music

JAMAICA IS KNOWN FOR ITS BEAUTIFUL ISLAND ENVIRON-
ment, Rastafarians, and reggae music. Bob Marley's hit song
"One Love" might bring an image to mind of a culture that
reflects acceptance, tolerance, and love. People sitting under
coconut trees, sipping their multicolored rum drinks, or
smoking marijuana and relaxing on white-sand beaches,
in the shadow of mountains kept green by rain forests and
overlooking beautiful coral reefs. The image is picturesque,
soothing, and peaceful. Full of positive vibes. But there are
other songs that disrupt that image—the songs of Jamaican
"murder music."

Murder music grew out of Jamaica's strongly homophobic culture and the island's dance hall music scene. In 1988, artist Buju Banton recorded and released the song "Boom Bye Bye." It became a huge hit on the island, as well as other parts of the world.

I listened to the song. For me, the words were incomprehensible because they were sung in a Jamaican slang language, a patois. The lyrics talk about killing gays, but with more graphic language. According to an article published in 2011, a video for the song had been viewed over three million times, between its posting in 2007 and 2011—and that video was just one of more than eighty YouTube versions of Banton performing the song. Many of the viewers of the videos were in the United States. It is one of the most well-known songs in the murder music genre, not only in Jamaica but internationally. Murder music took its place as a form of hate music.

Religion played a role. In Jamaica, both the local brand of Christianity and the native Rastafarian beliefs are staunchly antigay. But even if people have an opinion that homosexuality is frowned upon by their religion, it's hard to ignore the commandment, "Thou shall not kill."

People of all religions have sometimes corrupted, warped, cherry-picked, misrepresented, misunderstood, or taken out of context parts of their chosen religion's doctrines. I have heard some people claim that their religion is the one-and-only "best" religion, and that other religions are not legitimate or valid. This is called "confirmation bias," when people only read, or are familiar with, literature or propaganda that supports their pre-existing beliefs.

Hate music that advocates for "white supremacy" or "male supremacy" also practices confirmation bias. A race, gender, sexual identity, or religion are considered superior. The problem is that the strong adoption of a one-sided belief system often denies or ignores contrary evidence.

The United States is a country that was founded on religious freedom. How do we stop judging and attacking each other based on our chosen faith-based beliefs? Several of the dance hall musicians who wrote and sang murder music adhere to Christian or Rastafarian beliefs, which are antigay and advocate for violence, including murder, against members of the LGBTQ+ community. Many Jamaican churches originally took stances against murder music, but others stood in support of the musicians.

Some people in Jamaica are defiant against critics of murder music. First, they say that Jamaica has a very tolerant culture and that the murder of gays is often due to lovers' spats. But they also recognize that murder music is often demanded in dance halls and that attacks and murders have resulted.

Another defense of the music is that, similar to the civil rights movement in the 1960s in the United States, murder music is a phase that must be experienced to create debate and eventual societal change. It sounds like a freedom of speech argument, where music is used to present opposing ideas, informing citizens, and allowing minority groups to express themselves. Possibly, even the good ol' zeitgeist defense.

From another perspective, some of the murder music artists have countered that they do not need to apologize. They claim that protestors should be the ones apologizing because they go against God's "law" regarding gays.

Buju Banton was not the only artist singing murder music. Beenie Man, Sizzla Kalonji, Capleton, TOK, Bounty Killa, Vybz Kartel, Yogie, and Elephant Man are examples of musicians who contributed to the genre. Songs by these artists use terms such as "batty boy," "chi chi man," and "ickie man"—all derogatory names for gay individuals—and encourage their murders. Again, name-calling as a common hate music element.

In a country where parts of the population are poor, dance hall artists enjoy popularity and influence. They are viewed as stars, and citizens from lower economic groups follow their lead. However, as the artists associated with murder music have attempted to broaden their careers beyond Jamaica, they have sometimes had to downplay those songs in their sets, have recorded versions of songs with altered lyrics, or have hidden their messages in newly created slang that is difficult to translate or understand. Slang—another hate music characteristic.

In the United States, we have seen politicians try to use the music of popular musicians to win voters by suggesting that they are aligned with the ideas expressed by those stars. Musicians have protested and even taken legal action to stop the unauthorized use of their songs. In Jamaica, due to the popularity of murder music, it has also been used for political purposes.

In 2002, the People's National Party adopted the slogan "Log on to Progress," which was based on lyrics from the song "Log On" by Elephant Man. Again, the song was written in local slang, but the English translation was, "Log on, and stomp on a fag. Log on, because you know you're not a fag. Log on, and stomp on a fag. We dance and dance and burn up a fag." Advocating for violence against a demographic group—a third characteristic of hate music.

In the ensuing years since "Boom Bye Bye," there has been a push back against murder music. In Jamaica, it has come from an organization named J-FLAG. Workers for J-FLAG have provided resources to gay residents, including safe housing, medical care, assistance with legal issues, and advocacy for civil and human rights. For their safety, employees and volunteers of J-FLAG have sometimes had to work in secret, protecting their own identities. The cofounder of the organization, Brian Williamson, was stabbed to death in 2004, in his residence. Other staffers have been threatened to the point of needing to leave the country. Following Williamson's murder, a crowd of people gathered, singing lyrics from "Boom Bye Bye," and vowing to kill other gays, one at a time.

Other organizations, such as the group Outrage, have protested murder music. Through letter-writing campaigns and protests at concerts, some progress was achieved against murder music by limiting the ability of its artists to make much money. The reasoning was that if hurt financially, maybe they would choose other topics for their songs.

Expressing more defiant views, some defenders of murder music downplay its influence, saying that the local population doesn't care what musicians say—and that the economy is much more important to them. Many forms of hate music claim that its hatred against various groups is because of those groups' perceived effects on the economy. Many of the murder music artists listed above have seen their concert tours in other countries canceled, nominations for music awards withdrawn, and apologies issued by their record companies.

In their home country of Jamaica, that is not the case. Murder music continues to be performed in dance halls without apology. Some of the musicians make their living almost exclusively in Jamaica, so losing revenues from record sales or concerts in other countries doesn't have a large negative impact on their revenue streams. Although some of them have lost income from foreign markets, there are still many places outside of Jamaica where their music remains popular and supported—including venues in the United States.

Another effort addressing murder music has been the Stop the Murder Music campaign, which is worldwide and includes coordinated efforts by such groups as Outrage, Black Gay Men's Advisory Group, and J-FLAG. Among its recommendations, the campaign encouraged people to boycott Jamaica. Since Jamaica depends on a healthy and lucrative tourist market, members of Stop the Murder Music have also been threatened.

Still, the organization has had some success. In 2007, Beenie Man, Sizzla, and Capleton were reported as signing the Reggae Compassion Act, a petition developed by Stop the Murder Music. The petition renounced homophobia, and the artists pledged to remove anti-gay lyrics from their music.

It is difficult to estimate the actual number of murders of LGBTQ+ individuals in Jamaica but, in general, Jamaica is ranked high for both murders and assaults. The Human Rights Watch organization published a lengthy report in 2013, titled "Not Safe at Home: Violence and Discrimination Against LGBT People in Jamaica." That report described fifty-six cases of violence against members of the LGBTQ+ community.

One writer described the culture of Jamaica as one that can't negotiate conflict without resorting to violence. Is this the current norm for our world? If we disagree with each other, is it impossible to mediate and resolve those disagreements without trying to murder the other side? Should murder music be against the law?

If you believe in free speech, as I do, the answer is no. A better approach would be to provide valid counterarguments and songs to produce change. Punish the actual murderers and assaulters, but not those who sing about it, unless they violate legitimate legal restrictions on free speech. In the case of murder music, prevention seems better than punishment.

Despite the ongoing popularity of murder music in some quarters, some Jamaican artists have written and performed pro-gay music. Mista Majah P, Tanya Stephens, Sanjay Ramanand, and Etana are examples. Etana has been quoted as saying, "The only thing I can say that I've done is to openly say that every man has a right to his own destiny, and to openly say that I have no objection with somebody's choice of how they want to live their lives." Referring to Rastafari religious beliefs, she also says, "Rastafari is love, togetherness, oneness, unconditional love, fighting for the rights of people, for the poor, the sick, the elderly, the needy, that's what Rasta is about—loving and caring and sharing."

In December 2018, Buju Banton returned to Jamaica after serving seven years in an American prison for cocaine drug trafficking. The writer and singer of "Boom, Bye Bye" had disavowed his antigay hatred by signing the Reggae Compassion Act petition in 2007. But his recent return to Jamaica brought his former hate music back to the surface.

Jamaican poet Staceyanne Chin—who is a lesbian—was interviewed about Banton's return. She had been gang-raped in Jamaica, either as a way to punish her or in an effort to "turn her straight"—as if rape is the preferred way to change a person's sexual preference or identity. Chin is a fan of Jamaican music and recognizes that another side of

Banton's music "speaks with such truth, with such beauty about the lives of poor people and the struggle to be recognized as human, for blackness and being from Africa to be the center of one's pleasure and one's power."

Although Chin has been living in the United States, she has visited Jamaica. She notes that there are now gay pride marches and visible gay activists, and that gay students meet together on their campuses. She does not see it as her place to forgive Banton for his previous antigay music. She sees change. But even if Banton's view of gays has changed, his song from 1988 lives on. He had planned to tour in 2018.

Spencer Hardy

WHEN THIRTEEN-YEAR-OLD MATTHEW BOGER CAME OUT to his mother as gay, her reaction shattered him. She threw him out of their house in San Francisco. When he later attempted to return, she stated, "F**k you, you little faggot," and hit him so hard he was propelled across the room. He relocated to Los Angeles, where he tried to survive, but was homeless and continuously targeted and victimized. Matthew remembers a day in 1979 when he almost lost his life. He described the incident this way:

> "One day a bunch of punk rockers started chasing me. When I saw them coming I literally froze. Then they started punching and kicking me so hard that I fell to the ground. In those last moments I looked up and saw these Mohawks high-fiving and congratulating each other because they believed they'd accomplished their goal by killing a gay kid. In the years that followed, their words and what I saw on

their faces, were far more painful than the boots and the blades."

One of those "punk rockers," Tim Zaal, also remembers the incident:

> "At my first hard core punk rock show there was anger, fear, and violence in the air. It made me feel elated; the adrenalin rush was like a drug. From then on the people I gravitated towards were Nazi punks. We'd get into fights, go on the rampage and create havoc. On the evening we attacked Matthew there was a heightened level of aggression. We were out to "Kill the faggots."

The incident took place nine years before "Boom Bye Bye." I'll share more about Tim and Matthew below.

In 2009, The Matthew Shepard and James Byrd Jr. Hate Crimes Prevention Act (18 U.S.C. §249) was passed in the United States. This act made it against the law to "willfully cause bodily injury, or attempt to do so using a dangerous weapon, because of the victim's actual or perceived race, color, religion, or national origin." It also went further by including crimes "committed because of actual or perceived religion, national origin, gender, sexual orientation, gender identity, or disability of any person, only where the crime affected interstate or foreign commerce or occurred within federal special maritime and territorial jurisdiction."

This bill was named after Matthew Shepard, a student who was murdered due to his sexual orientation, and James Byrd Jr, a black man who was murdered by being dragged behind a truck by white supremacists.

Susanna Hardy was born female, in the town of Hingham, near the south shore of Massachusetts. Now he is known as Shea Spencer Hardy. Friends and colleagues usually call him Spencer. Shea is his mother's maiden name. Family members often call him Shea. He is a female-to-male transgender individual. I have only known him as Spencer.

His father was an inner-city schoolteacher in Boston. He had grown up in a poor family, in Maine and had Irish roots. His mother's heritage was part Irish and part Czechoslovakian. She was, at times, a stay-at-home mom. At other points, she provided daycare services and later worked as a paraprofessional serving students in local schools.

Aunts, uncles, cousins, and other family members lived in the same neighborhood or nearby. Hardy remembers a strong sense of family, with relatives participating in frequent get-togethers. His grandmother served as matriarch of the extended family, which included several generations. As babies were born and the younger set grew in size, the family reached the point where reunions took the place of previous, smaller, more intimate holiday events. Hardy enjoyed growing up with a large family and felt like his cousins were more like siblings. The neighborhood was full of other children, and Hardy remembers having "the freedom to walk out the front door and run around all day." Block parties and field days were common.

The Hardy family was Catholic and attended church every Sunday. Religion was a big part of the culture, and everyone participated in church events, services, and celebrations of life's milestones. The neighborhood was somewhat self-contained, with approximately one hundred houses. Everyone knew each other, and everyday life, to Hardy, felt grounded in traditional Catholicism.

As a counter-balance to some conservative religious ideology, Hardy remembers that the community was also known as a liberal, Democratic, blue-dog part of the state. The tension between conservatism and liberalism was evident to Hardy. Religious ideas and secular ideas bounced against each other in his head. At church, he was taught that being gay was morally wrong, but at home he experienced what he called "more progressive" thinking. He did not feel that he was pressured to accept any single belief system, but the conflicting messages confused him.

As a child, he felt painfully shy and remembers stammering in school when asked to read. Teachers thought that he was having trouble reading when, in fact, he could read well. He struggled with fitting in and with dressing in the clothes of a young girl. As an adolescent, he began to feel rebellious and tried to make sense of the turmoil he was experiencing. He observed that people who identified themselves as members of the LGBTQ+ community were supported, but some of them remained "closeted." He had a cousin who came out as gay, and Hardy was pleased that open, positive support was displayed for him.

Back then, Hardy struggled with his own identity and the ambiguous messages he received. Now, he states that his current viewpoints are more in line with his parents' beliefs. In other words, he feels that his father and mother had a greater influence on him than the church.

When he finally came out to his family, his parents embraced and wholeheartedly supported him. He first came out as a lesbian, after graduating from high school. Despite the fear, he wanted to share his feelings with his family and friends before heading off to college. His father passed away two years ago, and Hardy still chokes up when recalling the love and acceptance that his father showed him, referring to his dad as "an amazing human being." He remains extremely close to his mother and is grateful for the progressive thinking that both parents instilled in him.

Within a short time, and with the help of therapy, Hardy quickly realized that what he was feeling was more in line with being "trans" and that he was not a lesbian. At the age of twenty, he came out for a second time, as a transgender individual. It wasn't easy. His struggles led him to adopt an activist persona, to help others who were conflicted, fearful, and trying to be authentic to their true selves. He knew that others were in the same boat, being rejected by parts of society, and being told that they were "morally wrong."

Hardy took piano lessons from a young age and also played the saxophone—as did his father and brother. He played in a band at his church's youth service, Teen Life program. While still in high school, he started looking into Berklee School of Music in Boston. His mother told him about music therapy, after seeing a brochure. She brought the brochure home to share with his older brother, but it ended up in Hardy's hands. He arranged to "shadow" a local music therapist, to see what the field was all about. After high school, and because of his music skills, he was accepted into the music therapy program at Berklee. He was a classically trained saxophonist, but Berklee pushed him to learn about jazz saxophone.

He felt that the music therapy faculty immediately supported his decision to identify as a trans. He remembers feeling welcomed, especially by Suzanne Hanser, chair of the program, and other faculty members, Karen Wacks and Kimberly Khare. They respected his using a male pro-noun to describe himself and also his change of name to Shea Spencer Hardy. He was allowed to take a semester off from a music therapy practicum experience, as he initiated his transition to male—which included surgery, hormone treatments, and personal therapy.

Hardy continued to be actively involved with his church, making frequent trips from Boston to his hometown. He served as a youth leader on church summer service trips. A youth minister at the church, who was also an employee at Berklee, assisted Hardy with housing changes on campus, which eventually even allowed him to become a resident assistant on an all-male floor.

The minister was supportive in many ways, but he also told Hardy that he could no longer serve as a youth leader on service outings. So, while Hardy still identified with the "Irish Catholic" culture, he began to reject some of its religious tenets. At the time, his mother remained an active member of their church, advocating for change through Catholic LBGTQ+ support groups.

As Hardy entered the field of music therapy, he discovered an LBGTQ+ community within the profession. He also started to connect with other LGBTQ+ musicians outside of music therapy. With both groups, he started to feel at home and stated, "I felt I could come out of my shell." Similar to musicians recruited into hate groups, he felt accepted, valued, and found comfort within the music therapy and general music scenes.

But even as he gained more confidence within those new communities, he also had fears about how he would be viewed as a music therapist by the general public. Specifically, he wondered if segments of the public would be opposed to him working with their children or other family members. He had professional boundaries that told him, appropriately, not to share personal information about himself with his clients.

To complete his final music therapy degree requirement, he was accepted as an intern at Music to Grow On Music Therapy Services, in Sacramento, California. His supervisor was Bessie Barth. He provided in-home and school-based, early intervention music therapy services to young children with special needs. In Sacramento, he discovered another welcoming trans community.

Following his internship, he obtained immediate employment by the agency as a full-time music therapist. He spent the first year of his professional life there. Next, he moved to Palo Alto, California, to start a private practice named Spencer Hardy Music Therapy Services. He successfully owned and operated that practice for the next four years.

In the high-tech, Silicon Valley environment of Palo Alto, Hardy experienced another supportive trans community. He became the co-owner of a new company, Rainbow Music Therapy Services, combining his services with other music therapists working on the peninsula south of San Francisco.

In 2015, Hardy relocated to Salt Lake City, Utah, where he currently works at Primary Children's Hospital, a part of the Intermountain Healthcare system. He serves patients on every unit of the hospital, including the Pediatric Intensive Care Unit, Cardiac ICU, Neonatal ICU, Neuro-Trauma Unit, Children's Surgical and Medical Units, Infant Medical/Surgical Unit, and Children's Oncology Unit. He has also served on the Intermountain Diversity Council and has helped develop training for staff to improve care to LGBTQ and transgender patients and their families. He currently serves as co-chair, developing a new Employee Caregiver Resource Program for Intermountain LGBTQ staff. That new program is under the auspices of the Office of Diversity, Equity, and Inclusion.

Hardy is proud that he has also started a part-time position as co-facilitator for the Unique Expressions program at the Utah Pride Center—a music and art therapy program serving transgender and gender creative youth. The program helps participants navigate gender identity, sexual orientation, school systems, family dynamics, and peer relationships. It aims to address the youths' resilience and self-esteem through creative self-expression, fostering a sense of community, and the development of adaptive coping skills.

During 2018 and 2019, Hardy happily reached three additional goals. First, he completed his master's degree in music therapy at Berklee College of Music. Second, he was promoted to expressive therapies coordinator at Primary Children's Hospital. And, bringing him great joy, he and his wife, Beth, who is also a music therapist, welcomed their second child into the world.

With so much happening in Hardy's life, it took me over a year to convince him to let me interview him. By the time he responded, I had decided to wrap up the book, without this chapter that considers music that discriminates against LGBTQ+ individuals, including music that advocates for their murder. Hearing that, Hardy convinced me of the importance of telling his story. He made himself available, shared openly, and gave me a green light to include this chapter.

Hardy has witnessed confusion and turmoil in his life but has survived as a person of high morals and ethics, using music to help others. A part of his journey has been a search for an accepting community. He has found that in his involvement with friends and colleagues. He has participated in Team Rainbow, a collective of LGBTQ+ music therapists, but also established strong relationships in the general population at large. I feel that it is due to his warmth, professionalism, acceptance of others, and willingness to live as his authentic self. He has encountered hatred, discrimination, and lack of inclusion during his life. Despite that, he has persevered to be a loving, contributing member of society—a husband, father, therapist, and friend. He deserves admiration, support, and acceptance.

By 2005, Matthew Boger—the gay teen who had almost been killed by neo-Nazi, adolescent punks twenty-six years earlier—was working at the Museum of Tolerance in Los Angeles.

So was Tim Zaal, one of his attackers —the one who had provided the last boot kick to Matthew's forehead, assuming that he had killed a gay kid.

At first, they did not recognize each other. As they gave presentations together and delivered their individual stories, they discovered their shared history. What followed was a drawn-out, difficult recovery process for both of them. They experienced anger, denial, grief, avoidance, and eventually, forgiveness. They have established a program called Hate 2 Hope, and in 2015 their story was told in the movie *Facing Fear*. They now say, "Sharing our story has been our therapy." Their therapy has demonstrated that people change, and that forgiveness is possible.

Spencer Hardy, Primary Children's Hospital, Salt Lake City, Utah. Used with written permission.

Chapter 11

GET SOME 88

RON BORCZON

One literary agent told me, "The topic of hate is very popular right now." In their song, "It's Cool to Hate," the Offspring offer the same sentiment, that some people are finding it in vogue to hate, but also seem to admit that they are fools for thinking that being positive is not in fashion.

This pairing of stories is used to again show how hate music and music therapy can coexist in close geographic proximity to each other, with different belief systems, lifestyles, and uses of music. These stories returned my exploration of hate music to the West Coast, where I live.

Get Some 88

GET SOME 88 WAS SELLING ITS HATE MUSIC AND MERchandise close to an amusement park, Magic Mountain, somewhere in, or near, Castaic, California. Products, including T-shirts and other clothes, were promoted on a Get Some 88 website, which advertised: "Get Some 88 provides clothing for the hate filled mind. We offer clothing and merchandise specialized in white power, white pride, white power skinheads, white power clothing designs."

Right up front, they claimed that their target audience was "hate-filled."

I wondered about the name of the company: Get Some 88. In white power circles, numbers represent many things. The number "8" refers to the eighth letter in the alphabet, "H," and, when repeated twice, as "88," stands for "Heil Hitler." On its website for advertising clothing, the company listed "key words" as "getsome88, skinhead, white power, white pride, Skrewdriver, Stormtroop16, and 88 gear." The number "16" also has special meaning to white power followers. The ADL maintains a list of hate symbols and includes the number "16" with this description:

> "The number combination 23/16 is a numeric symbol used by white supremacists, particularly common on the West Coast. Substituting letters for numbers, the 23/16 equates to W/P or "white power." Occasionally the number 23 appears by itself, as a condensed version. Sometimes the combination is rendered as 16/23, in which case it is usually intended to mean P/W for "peckerwood."

"Peckerwood" is also included as a separate entity on the ADL list and described in this way:

> "'Peckerwood,' derived from an old racial epithet aimed at whites, has evolved to become a term used to refer to white prisoners, particular white prison-

ers belonging to the racist prison gang subculture. Often the term is shortened to 'wood' and all such prisoners in a particular prison might be referred to as the 'woodpile.'"

(Readers interested in hate symbols are encouraged to visit the ADL Hate Symbols Database, which can be easily found, on the ADL website.)

Stormfront.org was one of the earliest white supremacist websites on the internet. Founded in 1995 by Don Black, a former KKK leader, Stormfront.org was reported as being shut down in 2017. Reportedly, a company named Network Solutions blocked the use of the Stormfront.org domain after receiving complaints about the site following the events in Charlottesville, Virginia, in August 2017. However, the site still exists and contains areas where approximately three hundred thousand users could chat and pose questions to each other. When somebody posed a question about Get Some 88, there were several posts by satisfied customers who had purchased its products. One responder wrote, "Great guys and great products." However, others wrote that they had security concerns when their personal information was posted on the internet. A suggested work-around was to deal with the owners through snail mail, or at a show, to avoid the risk of having personal information shared electronically.

As I learned more about hate music, I found that the dominant methods of selling it were either online, at white power or other secretive concert venues or festivals, or at planned rallies and conferences. Several digital music outlets have started to drop hate music products. Most record stores (does anyone still sell records or CDs in a record store?) or CD retail outlets either no longer carry hate music or, if they do, the products are not on display, but may be sold "under the counter."

Bands and record companies that promote and sell hate music and other merchandise are now selling their products almost exclusively online and require submission of payment methods. Competing companies have either limited which artists they stock and sell or have taken action to try to negatively affect the sales of their competitors.

Get Some 88 was a racist organization and proud of it—promoting its beliefs through clothing and other merchandise, including hate music.

At the Discogs website, only two music CDs were listed as being for sale at Get Some 88: *Labeled Racially Deranged* by Stormtroop 16 (2010, Get Some 88 Records) and *Blood of the Martyrs* by Enforcer (2012, Get Some 88 Records).

An earlier Stormtroop 16 recording, *The New Voice of Oi* (Condemned Records, 2006), contained the songs "Cowardice Treachery," "S.H.A.R.P. Scum" (Remember: a S.H.A.R.P. is a Skinhead Against Racial Prejudice), "Nationalism," "We Don't Give A S**t," "White Separation," and others.

Some of the titles reminded me of a bumper-sticker I frequently saw on my drive to work, that read, simply: "Baditude." A bad attitude. Not caring about political correctness. Not caring about being polite, respectful, inclusive, tolerant, helpful, accepting of others, or having other positive characteristics. In the words of Stormtroop 16, "not giving a s**t." Being proud of having a bad attitude. Promoting the white race by attacking others. Being victims and looking for others to blame.

In psychiatry, individuals diagnosed as having Antisocial Personality Disorder can often make statements, or have observable behaviors, of not caring about others. To express this sentiment in its song lyrics may demonstrate a sense of Stormtroop 16's self-insight. However, an ad for the band simply categorized its music as, "Rock, Oi, Hardcore."

I listened to two Stormtroop 16 songs on YouTube. First, I played "Nationalism." The lyrics reflected praise for Adolf Hitler, who is referred to as a man with brilliance. The lyrics also express denial of the murder of Jews and others by the Nazis, referring to reports that six million people were murdered as lies. I discovered that many white nationalists are fans of Adolf Hitler and either deny that the Holocaust ever happened, accept that it happened but deny the high death count, or feel that it was justified.

Next, I listened to "Rank Upon Rank," which is a white power anthem. The lyrics also reflect denial of the Holocaust, referring to factual, recorded number of deaths as untrue. These two songs illustrated common themes found in neo-Nazi music: extreme racial nationalism and war and violence to reestablish or preserve the white Aryan race. Some members, but not all, felt that it was self-defense to attack minorities and nonwhites. The minorities weakened the white culture, crossbred with white women, abused welfare and other tax-supported resources, stole jobs from whites, and conspiried to kill the white race. They had to be stopped. Ironically, some also attacked whites who disagreed with them. The music was loud and intimidating, with pounding drums and power chords, and performers yelled or screamed lyrics. Angry music.

In a 2007 interview in The *European Union Times*, Charlie Boots (a pseudonym) answered questions about Stormtroop 16. He said that the band was formed "around June of 2005." Band members included Charlie (lead singer),

Mark (guitarist), Leo (drummer), and Brian (bassist). No last names were given. The band's music was described as a fusion between classic rock, Oi!, death metal, and black metal. Charlie listed the following bands as being big influences on Stormtroop 16: Skrewdriver, Brutal Attack, Skullhead, and No Remorse—all of them, white power bands. He also said that the musicians in the band were members of the American Front.

Charlie Boots's real name is Charles Gilbert Demar III. In March 2011, he was identified as a person of interest in the murder of David Lynch in Sacramento, California. Lynch was another racist skinhead and leader of the American Front, which was an early and prominent skinhead organization in the United States. At the time of his death, it was reported that he was trying to unite several national skinhead organizations under the American Front umbrella. A response to a question posed to the *Sacramento Bee* newspaper in January 2016 said that Demar was never charged with the murder, and no arrests were ever made.

However, Demar had been found guilty, in 2011, of distributing methamphetamine to raise money for a Sacramento skinhead gang. He had previously been convicted of burglary, manufacturing methamphetamine, and assault. The combination of his 2011 charge with those previous convictions resulted in his being sentenced to seventy-five years-to-life in prison, plus an additional nine years because of California's Three Strikes law. He is serving his time at Calipatria State Prison in California, where, in February 2018, he was a suspect in the murder of another inmate.

Stormtroop 16 no longer exists without Charlie Boots, but its earlier recordings are still sold. Releases include *The New Voice of Oi* (2006, Condemned Records), *Braces Up*

Straight Laces Up (2007, Whitenoise Records), *Steel Capped Justice* (2008, Micetrap Records), and the above-mentioned *Labeled Racially Deranged* (2010, Get Some 88 Records).

This reinforced another of my research findings. Even when hate musicians die, are imprisoned, or even change their ideology and leave their chosen hate movement, their music lives on. Some hate music recordings have become legendary, receiving renewed interest at different points of history, having a resurgence in sales, and providing sources of revenue to hate organizations and causes. In some cases, hate music is a source of income to capitalist entrepreneurs, who may not even agree with the content.

Next, I tried to learn more about Enforcer. I discovered that its lead singer was named Chad Bostwick, a member of Volksfront, another skinhead group. An article about Chad, published in 2014, described a life full of difficulties with the law. His criminal history included incidents of burglary, theft, illegal weapons possession, domestic abuse, and numerous assaults. He was growing marijuana in one of his homes. He reportedly had six children, by three different mothers, and had been delinquent in child support payments.

Documents and affidavits from the mothers of his children alleged several incidents of violent threats. The women claimed that their children were not safe with Chad. One woman wrote, "I do not believe that [my daughter] would be/is safe with Chad and believe that he will only place her in a situation of danger and also to where she is to be manipulated, treated as property and taught that criminal activity, violence and a lack of responsibility are the norm and preferred way of life."

Despite the negative documents and legal issues, Chad managed to connect with his son through music. It was reported that the two played music together. The son, who was tutored at home, joined a varsity show choir. I assume that the show choir did not perform the hate music that had played a role in his father's life.

Another member of Enforcer was Chad's brother, Drew, who was described in one publication as a "Christian identity pastor" and a member of Volksfront. The group's leaders have allowed members some leeway in their religious beliefs, as long as they support white supremacy.

A common thread was that some hate musicians and members of hate groups presented themselves as members of a religion and tried to validate their hate messages through those beliefs. I found that, in some cases, religion was used to either justify their violence and actions or to try to give a presentable, righteous image to the public. They were just trying to be good Christians. Or, they were returning to pagan religions, such as Odinism, which had some racist tenets. In some cases, they took references from the Bible or other religious documents out of context or created entirely new religions.

Despite their stated tolerance of other religions, some Volksfront members were convicted of defacing, throwing rocks at, or firing guns at synagogues. A 2005 Volksfront concert was billed as "Rock Against Islam," demonstrating an early stand against Muslims. I had to remind myself that this was freedom of speech and freedom of religion at play, both of which I support. However, freedom of speech and freedom of religion do not allow committing crimes against others.

A third member of Enforcer was Casey Jo Banyas, its drummer. Banyas was also an active member of Volksfront.

Again, I turned to YouTube to listen to some of Enforcer's recordings. Their only CD listed on the Get Some 88 website was *Blood of the Martyrs,* which included the following songs: "Gather Up Your Guns," "Outlaws Of Old," "One Fine Day," "Hey Mister," "Real," "Blood Of the Martyrs," "Time of Change," "Back With A Bang," and "28's" (According to the ADL, the number "28" stands for "Blood and Honour," an international skinhead group.)

I listened to the entire CD, every song. The style of the songs was heavy metal. I was surprised that I actually liked some of the tunes, even if I did not agree with the lyrics. The music was more varied than other skinhead bands I had listened to. But I could not understand many of the lyrics, and when I consulted websites that maintain archives of song lyrics, the lyrics to these songs were not available.

As I mentioned above, the musicians in Stormtroop 16 and Enforcer were associated with several organizations: Stormfront, American Front, and Volksfront. Those, in turn, were affiliated with other groups: the Hammerskins, Women for Aryan Unity, Aryan Nations, and other skinhead chapters and groups.

An ADL article about Volksfront described some of these relationships and the ever-expanding, international web of white power hate. The organization has been associated with attacks against immigrants, African Americans, Jews, homosexuals, and even homeless individuals.

The publication stated, "Volksfront plays a big role in the white power music scene." Details were presented documenting Volksfront's involvement in the formation and support of numerous white power bands including Intimidation One, Criminal Culture (a renaming of Intimidation One), Jew Slaughter, Aggressive Force, American Standard, Bound for Glory, Cradle Song, Cut Throat, Max Resist, Rebel Hell, Valhalla's Patriots, Wolf's Hook, Youngland, and Down Right Hateful. Volksfront was also pivotal in creating or recommending several record companies: Upfront Records, Panzerhaust Records, Imperium Records, and Free Your Mind Productions.

I began to feel overwhelmed with the number of bands recording and performing this type of music.

Reportedly, Volksfront has produced white power concerts two to three times per year, although crowd sizes have been relatively small. Other concerts have been fund-raisers for racist skinheads who have been killed or imprisoned. For example, one concert was in support of neo-Nazi Ken Mieske, who was convicted of murdering Mulugeta Seara, an Ethiopian immigrant, in 1988, in Portland, Oregon.

One of Volksfront's goals has been to establish a whites-only community in the Pacific Northwest, and it has gone as far as purchasing property in Oregon and Washington for development.

I found that the bands affiliated with Get Some 88, in Castaic, Southern California, had connections to violent skinhead groups in Northern California, which, in turn, had connections to violent skinhead groups in the Northwest, and beyond. Music is prominently used to recruit new members, raise funds for their causes, bring members together, spread their beliefs, and promote and endorse violence against others.

Ron Borczon

LESS THAN THIRTY MILES FROM CASTAIC, CALIFORNIA— where Get Some 88 has run its mail order, online business selling products for customers with a "hate filled mind"—lies Northridge, California, home of California

State University at Northridge (CSUN). Located at the east end of the San Fernando Valley, CSUN has over thirty-eight thousand students and four thousand faculty members. Comprised of nine individual colleges, CSUN offers sixty-eight baccalaureate degrees, fifty-eight master's degrees, two doctorate degrees, and fourteen programs leading to teaching credentials.

Like most colleges, CSUN has a website that includes a wealth of information, including a statement of the following values: commitment to teaching, scholarship, and active learning; commitment to excellence; respect for all people; alliances with the community; and the encouragement of innovation, experimentation, and creativity.

It is at CSUN that Ron Borczon founded its music therapy program in 1984 and has been its sole director ever since. I have known Borczon since those early years and served with him on the executive board of the Western Region of the NAMT (now the AMTA). I wanted to learn more about Borczon's background and career, but also his thoughts on hate music and his proximity to Get Some 88. Borczon agreed to let me interview him via Skype but also chatted with me at conferences during the writing of this book.

Born in Louisville, Kentucky, Borczon's grandparents were Polish immigrants. The family originally lived in Erie, Pennsylvania, but moved to Louisville, where his father was the foreman at a General Electric plant. The family included both of Borczon's parents, a ten-year older brother, and a fifteen-year older sister. Borczon's father was tragically killed in a factory accident, and his mother relocated the family back to Erie.

His mother later remarried, but Borczon recalls that he grew up "mostly without a father." His older siblings were out of the house by the time Borczon was ten years old. Borczon shared that there were private "family issues" that he has had to deal with in his life, but growing up in the absence of his father was one of the most difficult.

When he failed to make the basketball team at school, he was disappointed and felt that he could play better than some of the boys who were selected for the team. His mother told him that some of those boys had fathers who carried some weight with the school because of their financial support. It opened his eyes to the advantages that some people have due to family connections or affluence, and he found the experience to be discouraging and depressing.

Similar to Borczon, a musician who has been labeled as a hate musician by the SPLC, Douglas Pearce, also lost his father at a young age, felt aimless, and searched for direction. He chose a musical career that has been accused of using anti-immigrant, neo-Nazi ideation, symbols, and themes.

Borczon chose a career using music to help others.

Borczon started to play guitar, to emulate his older brother, who bought him his first guitar. At first, he learned to play "by ear," with no instruction. He played in Catholic Church folk masses, which were popular at that time. All of his early playing was on acoustic guitars, and he did not own an electric guitar until much later, after college. When he was a junior or sophomore in high school, for a short time he lived with "circus people" on a ranch, riding horses and taking others on trail rides. At the ranch, he joined his first acoustic band, playing popular songs by Crosby, Stills, and Nash; Cat Stevens; and other artists.

As Borczon continued to improve on the guitar, he began his first formal music training by taking classical guitar lessons at Slippery Rock University, where he was majoring in psychology. Up until then, he did not know how to read music. He had also never heard of music therapy.

He first heard about the field of music therapy through his music teachers at Slippery Rock. Music therapy appealed to him, and he decided to attend Slippery Rock for two years and then transfer to Duquesne University, which offered a degree in music therapy. The plan was to save on tuition since Slippery Rock was a less expensive, public university, and Duquesne was a more costly, private university.

However, after spending two spring breaks in Florida, the warm weather hooked him. When it came time for him to transfer, he opted for the music therapy program at Florida State University (FSU) in sunny Tallahassee. (Nowadays, he could have stayed at Slippery Rock for all of his college years, because it now has a successful music therapy program.)

FSU had high musical standards, and Borczon had to work hard to meet them. Simultaneous to working on his degree in music therapy, he completed a second degree in guitar performance.

Borczon completed a six-month music therapy internship at Sunland Center in Tallahassee, Florida, working with individuals with developmental disabilities. Following his internship, he was employed there as a Behavioral Specialist and Assistant Unit Director.

Wanting to continue his education, Borczon landed a teaching assistant position, teaching guitar at the University of Southern Louisiana in Lafayette, where he completed a master's degree in music performance.

Next, Borczon worked at the Parkland Pavilion Psychiatric Hospital in Baton Rouge, Louisiana, where he created the hospital's first music therapy program. He served both adult and adolescent mental health and substance abuse clients. Providing help to adolescents had been a goal for Borczon, due to his own difficult, aimless, fatherless, teenage years.

Talking about how music therapy training has changed over the past decades, Borczon laughs at the difference between what he was taught in school and what he now teaches his own students. He admits, back then, some of the necessary skills were not learned in the classroom. They were learned on the job. He gained crucial competencies as a therapist by coleading therapy sessions with social workers and psychiatrists.

For the remainder of his career, Borczon has been directing the music therapy degree program and teaching classical guitar at CSUN. His first ten years at CSUN were devoted to designing the music therapy curriculum and developing his program. The program started small and grew slowly. He estimates that he has trained approximately two hundred music therapy students, and limited total students at any given time to around thirty, counting freshmen, sophomores, juniors, and seniors. He has relied on several part-time adjunct faculty members to teach some of the course work.

It wasn't until the end of his first decade of teaching that Borczon reentered clinical work by contracting with local agencies. Some of his contracted music therapy work is described in his excellent book, *Music Therapy Group Vignettes* (1997, Barcelona Publishers).

We began to talk about hate music. Borczon had not heard of Get Some 88, but he had feelings about hate music and music therapy.

When asked about Dr. E. Thayer Gaston's early music therapy teaching that "music is derived from the tender emotions," Borczon countered with a quote from the Greek philosopher, Plato:

> "Music too, in so far that it uses audible sound, was bestowed upon us for the sake of harmony. And harmony, which has motions akin to the revolutions of the Soul within us, was given by the Muses to him who makes intelligent use of the arts, not as an aid to irrational pleasure, as is now supposed, but as an auxiliary to the inner revolution of the Soul, when it has lost its harmony, to assist in restoring it to order and concord with itself."

In other words, he explained that music is derived from all emotions and can be used not only for aesthetic, pleasurable, positive expression of feelings but also to reflect the state of our innermost feelings and thoughts. And if those internal feelings and thoughts involve negative emotions—such as depression, anger, fear, or hatred—that is okay. The music can still be used in therapeutic situations to help individuals heal.

I gave Borczon a scenario to consider, where a client is referred for music therapy and the initial music therapy assessment indicates that the client's preferred type of music is neo-Nazi, white power, racist music. I asked him how he would proceed.

Borczon's first comment, which is true for many therapeutic settings, was that therapists often have the right to refuse services to a client if they ethically believe that they cannot work with that person or cannot help them. There may be a conflict between the client's preferred music, which music therapists are trained to honor, and the facility or program's policies. Within reason, music censorship can occur in some therapeutic settings, especially when that music is considered to be interfering with the client's ability to make positive therapeutic gains. For example, listening to songs that advocate for drug use may be prohibited in a substance abuse or chemical dependency treatment facility.

Beyond any ethical concerns, consideration of program policies, and allowed censorship, Borczon stated that, in most cases, he would use hate music during music therapy sessions. He said that he would "have to" use the music to understand the person. He would accept the music as a "part of who they are" and would not place judgment. He would use the music to establish a trusting, therapeutic relationship with the client.

After listening to the music, he would verbally process what the music meant to the client. The goal would be to discover the reasons why the client prefers that type of music. What emotional responses did the music elicit? Did the music produce an effect on the client? Is the client okay with the music, or the lyrics? If yes, why? If no, why not? Did the music contribute to the reasons why the client came to treatment? If so, what changes would the client like to make, as a result of being in therapy? What are his/her individual treatment goals? Is the person aware of options beyond what is expressed through the hate music?

Switching to an example of working with a client who had committed rape, Borczon explained that he would have to accept that part of the person's past and try to move beyond that point in his life without judgment. He would not condone rape, but he would view that person's past behavior as a part of that person—not the whole person—but, possibly, the reason why that person was seeking therapy, help, and a chance to heal. He said that he would try to give the client "options for life" moving forward. "Personally," Borczon stated, "I could work with them."

Returning to the hate music scenario, Borczon emphasized that if the client's goal was to "become more hateful," then he would need to "step back." He explained that his goal is not to make a person more hateful but to "exist in harmony with the world," both the world within themselves and the world around them.

Borczon stated that he believes society favors people getting along with each other and being tolerant of others. If a client's goal for treatment was to reach self-actualization, both internally and externally, Borczon could work with the client. If the client's goal was to become more hateful, he would find a way to terminate his involvement with them.

Borczon recognized that the First Amendment of the US Constitution did not mention music. But he felt that it should, and does, absolutely apply to music. He also felt that amendments to the US Constitution probably had different meanings and connotations when they were first written. He opined, "They were meant for the time in which they were written." He said that some "tweaking" might be welcome to update the amendments and make them fit the current, more modern world. Borczon viewed free speech as a founding principle of our country, and that music as free speech also needs to be recognized in the same way—as a primary principle.

I asked Borczon questions about his book, *Music Therapy Group Vignettes,* and how some of his writing might apply to hate music. He had written about strong cultural archetypes that could be "universal and/or genetic." I wanted to know if he thought that some opinions, perceptions, and cultural ideas could be passed down genetically, through generations.

Borczon felt that there was evidence of archetypal human beliefs, found across geographic and cultural boundaries, and that some of them became recessive genes that could be traced. However, he shared, "Part of who we are is genetic, and part of who we are is environmental." And some of our archetypal belief systems have "morphed," depending on the environments that influence us. This creates a state of conflict in some of us because, on one hand, we want to act the way our genetics compel us to act and, on the other hand, we want to act the way our environment demands.

Applying this to hate music, Borczon theorized that if a person grew up in a location where slavery had existed, the Civil War took a toll, the singer Johnny Rebel was present, and earlier generations had negative reactions to those events, it was possible that some of those emotions were passed on genetically. Hate music could be a legitimate expression of the reaction to negative events.

In my mind, this seemed to match ideas expressed by Dr. Degruy, in her book, *Post Traumatic Slave Disorder.* Even though some events were experienced in the past several generations ago, there could be lasting effects on what individuals feel and believe. Trauma can affect future generations. Some people may like and believe hate music, even if the message of that music does not match the current situation. In some cases, that music might just reinforce an inaccurate perception of the current situation. Hate is all in the eyes of the beholder. Or as Taylor Swift sings, "Haters Gonna Hate."

We even talked about the Golden Rule, as it applied to using hate music in music therapy sessions. Many of us have learned the Golden Rule as, "Treat others the way you would like to be treated." In healthcare, which includes music therapy, the flipside might be more appropriate: "Treat others the way they would like to be treated." Put another way, health care professionals must understand the wants, needs, cultural beliefs, and preferences of their clients—and not impose their own ideas onto how those clients want to be treated.

Remember, this idea was also stressed by Meagan Morrow, the music therapist who treated Congresswoman Gabby Giffords. Borczon felt that the two approaches were saying the same thing: the focus always needs to be on the client. He asks his students to imagine what a client sees for the first time when they, as music therapists, walk into the room.

Borczon said, "Both the therapist and the client have expectations about how they want to be treated. A client who prefers hate music probably does not want to be argued with. He or she does not want to be lectured about their love of hate music, nor have it ignored. It's a part of them. The fact that they are in therapy indicates that either they, or some other party—their family, employer, the police, their church, their girlfriend/boyfriend, or some other entity—feel that something isn't working. Their preferred music is a starting point for understanding them, and exploring why they are in therapy, and what they would like to change."

Borczon told me that he sometimes prays before leading a therapy session, but that is usually to help him take attention off the day-to-day events in his life and to refocus on the needs of his clients. He did not feel that religion plays a big role in his music therapy practice.

Since hate music attacks different demographic groups, I asked Borczon about the diversity of his students as CSU. Borczon shared that he was currently serving on a committee to consider if a master's degree should be required as the entry-level degree to become a credentialed music therapist. One of the considerations of that committee was whether or not requiring the advanced degree would limit the number of minority students who could enter the field.

He described the makeup of his current student group as being approximately 55 percent white, with the remaining 45 percent comprising a mix of Hispanic, African American, Asian, Persian, one partial Native American, and others. He felt that some of those current students would not be able to afford a master's degree program, especially if the current job market did not offer higher wages for that degree. (Other fields, such as occupational therapy, physical therapy, and pharmacy have all started to require advanced degrees for some settings and jobs, and often those employment opportunities offer higher wages.)

Like other music therapists and music therapy faculty members such as Jim Borling, Borczon has often been involved with debriefing natural and manmade disasters. Borczon has been called on to help victims after the following events: the 1994 Northridge earthquake, the Oklahoma City bombing, the Columbine High School and San Diego school shootings, the San Diego fires, the 9/11 attacks on the World Trade Center/Pentagon/Shanksville, and Hurricane Katrina.

He has also consulted with other music therapists involved with disaster relief and has written about and spoken on the subject of uses of music therapy with trauma victims.

As Borczon approaches an age when many people start contemplating retirement, I asked him if he would miss teaching music therapy students. He said that even if he cuts back on his teaching load, he will want to keep teaching and providing music therapy services where needed.

But some of his hobbies will receive ongoing attention. He has had several surgeries on his hands for a variety of reasons and works to regain some of his guitar-playing skills. A longtime card player, Borczon has played in amateur and professional poker tournaments, sometimes winning, at least, small payouts. He has played four times in the annual World Series of Poker at the Rio All-Suites Hotel and Casino in Las Vegas. One year, he finished 138th out of three thousand entrants. In 2018 he finished eighty-first out of one thousand three hundred participants. He has increased his time on the golf course, and recently (September 8, 2018) won his first tournament at the Simi-Hills Golf Club.

The contrast between Borczon's life and career and the stories of musicians who sell their hate music recordings through Get Some 88 is dramatic. The latter group has been involved with criminal activity, violence, drug use, white supremacy, segregation, and spreading hate through music. Borczon's life has focused on the uses of music to help and heal; on tolerance, inclusiveness, and acceptance of others; and on being a good citizen. Ron's life has not been without challenges, including growing up without his father, but, in spite of them, his choices were more positive.

In my mind, I heard the advice of Randy Blazak saying, "Don't hate the haters." Although the contrast of this pairing of stories seemed obvious, I still needed to find a better understanding of why some people turn one way and others turn another. Specifically, I wanted to find out more about why some people became involved with hate music and stayed involved, but also why other people decided to leave those beliefs behind and make changes in their lives. My research continued. Since I live on the West Coast, I wanted to look for stories in other parts of the country, including events following Charlottesville.

Ron Borczon, California State University Northridge, Northridge, California. Used with written permission.

Chapter 12

Heritage Connection

Tina Haynes

A fter Charlottesville, I began to notice similar events in other parts of the country. I saw reactions to hate music appear in news reports coming from other states and cities. These next two stories focus on Tennessee. I think they illustrate, again, how hate music and music therapists often coexist, geographically. In Tennessee, hate music has been present in several ways, and music therapist Tina Haynes has provided music therapy to veterans for over thirty years.

Heritage Connection

A GROUP NAMED HERITAGE CONNECTION MADE IT TO the SPLC's 2017 list of national hate music groups. As I began to read about Heritage Connection, I found that they had performed several times in Tennessee. At the same time, an October 29, 2017, article in *USA Today* bore the headline, "White nationalists rally in 2 Tenn. cities." It was only two months since the well-covered events in Charlottesville. The *USA Today* story reported on what could have been similar incidents in Shelbyville and Murfreesboro.

I immediately thought of a music therapy colleague working in Murfreesboro, Tina Haynes. Wanting to get her reactions to the news report and interview her about her own story, I arranged to talk with Tina Haynes via phone. As we chatted, I became aware that I needed to read more about the state, to put any stories about either Heritage Connection or Haynes into context.

Tennessee has a long history of opposing sides and open debate. Considered as a whole, it seems ambivalent about racial issues, bordering on suffering from multiple personalities. It was the last state to secede from the Union during the Civil War and, except for Virginia, it provided the largest number of soldiers to the Confederate cause. However, it also supplied more Union soldiers than all of the combined other states in the entire Confederacy. It was the first state admitted back into the Union after General Lee surrendered at Appomattox, Virginia.

The war ended in 1865, but that doesn't mean that philosophical and political battles have not continued within the state. The years immediately after the war had been called Reconstruction, but opposing ideologies and ill feelings were, and are, still present. Buildings, homes, bridges, and roads may have been repaired but, in some quarters, the human foundations needed for rebuilding relationships seem a bit shaky.

The war was followed by disfranchising laws that discriminated against newly freed slaves and poor whites, most of them living in rural areas in the central or western parts of Tennessee, making it harder for them to cast votes. Those tax-paying citizens did not regain full, equal voting rights and representation until well into the twentieth century. Jim Crow laws also established segregation in the state.

Today, the state is divided into three "Grand Divisions"—East, Middle, and West. The three areas differ economically, culturally, geographically, legally, and, in some ways, politically. The Eastern section is sometimes referred to as "all-white East Tennessee." This is another indicator of some modern-day divisiveness within the state. Located in the center of the United States and bordering on eight other states, Tennessee can be viewed as a microcosm, or laboratory, reflecting some of the prevailing controversies and polarization across the nation.

It has some conservative "right" leanings in the eastern part of the state, and liberal "left" contingencies toward the west. Those political preferences exist along a continuum, and the three grand divisions can't be labeled as exclusive enclaves of any particular political thought.

Tennessee is home to the Great Smoky Mountains National Park, the most visited national park in the United States. Other national parks in the state represent several important historical events and places, including the Trail of Tears National Historic Trail, the Natchez Trace Parkway, the Shiloh National Cemetery, Fort Donelson National Battlefield, and the Andrew Johnson National Historic Site. As the names indicate, the state has a long and sometimes painful history of relationships with minority populations, including African Americans and Native American tribes. Today, the state is approximately 76 percent white, 21 percent black, 9 percent Hispanic, 2.6 percent Asian, and .2 percent Native American.

Tourism is a major source of revenue for Tennessee, placing it in the top ten states for both American and foreign visitors. The tourist industry brings billions of dollars into the state each year, from money spent on hotels, modes of travel, restaurants, taxes, concerts, museums, battlefields, etc. That money translates into the creation of over one hundred fifty thousand tourism-related jobs. Strong tourist promotional materials and campaigns drive the industry, but recent reports show the need to bring in more groups to feed the park system's budget.

Some of those tourists are attracting more attention than others. The state has fifty-four state parks and recently those parks have become a focus of controversy due to their use by racist groups to hold rallies and conferences. And hate music plays a role in some of those events.

A June 2017 headline in *Nashville Scene* announced, "White Supremacist Conference Returns to State Park." For the sixth year in a row, the American Renaissance Conference was slotted for Montgomery Bell State Park. Attendees were requested to dress professionally for the conference, apparently believing that the presence of KKK hoods would be a dead giveaway of the actual purpose of the conference. Speakers included immigrant-haters, an author who had written about the threat of African Americans to white Americans, another author who wrote about his clashes with Muslims, and a Holocaust denier and advocate for slavery.

In November 2017, a *USA Today* headline stated, "Are white nationalist groups meeting in state parks? Tennessee won't say." According to the story, the State of Tennessee was requesting a list of people and organizations who had been granted reservations to use state park meeting spaces, from its own Tennessee Department of Environment and Conservation, which oversees park reservations.

That request was denied. The reason provided was that sharing a list was not allowed by the recently passed House Bill 312, sponsored by State Representative David Hawk, a Republican. He denied allegations that the bill was meant to keep the presence of white supremacist groups under wraps and said that the bill intended to protect the personal information of guests at state-run hotels and campgrounds.

Another motivation seemed to be the income produced for the state park system, which had shown declining occupancy rates and revenues. Questions to Governor Bill Haslam about the controversy led his spokesperson to remind the public of the governor's statement, a month earlier, prior to a "White Lives Matter" rally, that white supremacists were "not welcome in Tennessee."

White nationalist, racist groups such as Stormfront, American Renaissance, The Southern National Congress, the League of the South, and the Knights of the Ku Klux Klan have been well represented at meetings, events, and conferences. Notable attendees at some of the white supremacist events have included David Duke, Thomas Robb, Stephen Don Black, Edward Reed Fields, William White Williams, Tom Pierce, Matthew Heimbach, William Flowers, James Edwards, and Sam Dickson—all known racists and leaders of various white supremacy organizations.

If they are not welcome, why are they choosing to hold their gatherings in Tennessee?

A second article, in the same issue of *USA Today,* by the same author, Natalie Allison, offered an explanation. She shared that in the previous seven years, fourteen white nationalist organizations had used Tennessee parks for their meetings—including at Norris Dam State Park, Cumberland Mountain State Park, Montgomery Bell State Park,

David Crockett State Park, and Fall Creek Falls State Park.

A spokesperson for Tennessee State Parks, Eric Ward responded, "Tennessee State Parks does not endorse hateful ideology in any form." He added that the state is "legally required to provide access." More than private meeting venues, the state parks could not deny the use of their facilities. They also provided park rangers, at taxpayer expense, to maintain security and keep conference attendees separate from anti-racist protesters and Antifa representatives, hoping to mitigate the risk of violence breaking out between the groups. Private venues have more leeway to deny use of their facilities and typically do not have in-house security forces.

Some of Tennessee's state parks provide brochures touting local attractions, but some exclusions seem to indicate racial bias.

For example, the Norris Dam State Park brochure fails to mention the cultural center in nearby Clinton, Tennessee, where a statue celebrates the twelve black students who, in 1956, were the first to attend an all-white school in the South, following the Civil War. After an explosion in 1958, the school was virtually destroyed. A white supremacist group, the National States Rights Party (NSRP) was suspected of the crime but never prosecuted. The NSRP was also suspected of numerous other crimes, for more than a decade, and has been very visible at the racist conferences in the Tennessee state parks.

Shrouded in secrecy, Tennessee does not always know, in advance, the beliefs, political leanings, and affiliations of various groups reserving state park facilities. Sometimes the reservations are made in the name of a family reunion group. Journalists are not always informed of or admitted to the meetings. Attendees are coached in the use of decoys, how to make undetected reservations, strategies for arranging alternate locations, ways to dress to avoid attention, tips for traveling incognito, and other tactics. There is recognition that counterprotesters could show up, so they keep details of the meetings to themselves. Dates and places are communicated via secret blogs, specific websites, mailings, word-of-mouth, and protected back channels.

It's not just Tennessee state parks that attract white supremacists. A *New York Times* article, in 2001 reported on a new music park in rural Tennessee, Skullbonia. Named after an old fighting practice—when bare fists apply blows to the head—the concert venue was openly racist. Confederate flags flew, and concert attendees could bring in their own coolers of beer and whiskey. KKK items were sold from booths, and concertgoers' T-shirts bore all kinds of white supremacist and white separatist images and messages.

The owner of the venue was caught between polarized groups in the area—the racist ideas of some in the community and local church members who disliked the open consumption of alcohol. A booth vendor, when asked if blacks were welcome at concerts, said, "I'd advise against it. It's not a good idea. They're liable to get beat up."

There were rumors of a history of lynchings in the area. The Skullbone Music Park website indicates that the park is still active and planned a "rockin' 2018." It now sponsors all-ages concerts, and coolers filled with alcohol are no longer allowed inside the venue.

In a divided state, some residents resist the presence of white power events. Somehow word leaks out, and community groups can host counter-events and respond to the racist ideology.

For example, in 2017, a conference titled, "Not in Our State: Oppose the Hate," was scheduled to coincide with the American Renaissance conference in Montgomery State Park. The organizers of the counterprotest described it as a "teach-in," adopting Supreme Court Louis Justice Brandeis's quote that, "sunlight is the best disinfectant." They hoped to shed light on racist ideologies, encouraging Tennesseans to support an environment of tolerance, inclusiveness, and acceptance.

Music is a major part of Tennessee's history and culture. Popular music genres—from rock n'roll, to the blues, to jazz, to rockabilly, to country, to rap, and on and on—are all represented. Well-known artists such as Dolly Parton, Elvis Presley, Chet Atkins, Aretha Franklin, Johnny Cash, Carl Perkins, Jerry Lee Lewis, Roy Orbison, Charlie Rich, John Lee Hooker, Junior Wells, Martina McBride, Taylor Swift, Kano, Three 6 Mafia, and Kings of Leon have ties to the state.

There are also several tourist attractions recognizing the role of music in the state: the Memphis Rock N' Soul Museum; the Country Music Hall of Fame and Museum, in Nashville; the Tina Turner Museum and Flagg Grove School, in Brownsville; and the International Rock-A-Billy Museum, in Jackson. Music is like air, and whether or not a musician is famous or successful, is beside the point. People live and breathe music in Tennessee. And as mentioned above, music is also found at the state's racist meetings.

Which brings us to the story of Heritage Connection, a musical group listed on the 2017 list of Music Hate Groups, published by the SPLC. The group started as a duo in 2003, when sisters Charity and Shelby Pendergraft were only ten and twelve years old. More recently, they have added their younger brother, Andrew, to some of their performances.

Raised in a Christian family, the girls are the grand-daughters of Reverend Thomas Robb, leader of the Knights Party, a racist organization originally called the Knights of the KKK, based in Arkansas. The principles of "love thy neighbor" and "love thy enemy" seem to be lost on these girls, possibly due to the influence of their mother, Rachel Pendergraft. Several of her speeches are found on YouTube.

The gist of the girls' message seems to be the preservation of the heritage of the white race. More specifically, the white, Christian race. Or, the Southern, white, Christian, Aryan race. Descendants of "superior" Aryan, white, European countries.

There are other clues to the real message and intent of Heritage Connection. Advertisements promoting some of their performances encourage attendees to "bring your Confederate flags." On websites about them, the phrases, "Love Your Heritage," "It's Time for an Aryan Awakening," "Uniting our Race Through Song" and "White Pride Worldwide," are prominently displayed. The duo almost exclusively performs at rallies, camps, conferences, and churches that feature other white supremacist presenters and speakers.

For example, for many years, the sisters have been featured performers at the annual European Heritage Festival in Pulaski, Tennessee. According to the SPLC, that festival has links to David Duke, the Council of Conservative Citizens, and *The Barnes Review*—organizations that have, both literally and figuratively, attacked blacks and Jews, opposed race-mixing, advocated for segregation and returning immigrants to other countries, insulted nonwhite races, and denied the Holocaust.

Hosting the European Heritage Festival does not sit well with the residents of Pulaski. Located in south-central Tennessee, close to the Louisiana border, the city is considered the birth of the KKK. The Confederate General, Nathan Bedford Forrest, is credited with being a national leader during the early years of the KKK and is honored by groups who gather there.

In 2010, the mayor of Pulaski told the SPLC, "There's never been a local person involved in these marches or rallies." Local businesses have closed during numerous events, in protest of the negative, racist content. Residents have also been encouraged to ignore the racist groups who flock to their town. Expressed in behavioral therapy language, ignoring unwanted behavior can lead to the extinction of that behavior. Believing that the outside groups are seeking attention and publicity, ignoring them has been mostly successful. At other times, outside media have been there to cover the meetings, undermining some of the efforts of the local population to remove attention.

The mayor of Pulaski also explained that laws prevent the prohibition of meetings in Pulaski, as long as the organizers comply with the expectations of their granted permits. This has been challenged in court, resulting in legal language that allows one lawful assembly in Pulaski per day. Under the US Constitution, citizens have that right to lawful assembly.

Let's consider the music of Heritage Connection. Here are the titles of the CDs they have released: *Aryan Awakening, Standing Our Ground, Rise to the Challenge, and Gospel in the Heartland: Songs of Our Folk*. Songs include "Living Nightmare," "Propagandized America," "Dying Fire," "Alien Flood," "Aryan Warrior," "Fairytale Love," "Dumb Boy," "Final Straw," and "Jacket of Grey." Video clips of performances of most of these songs can be found on YouTube.

The sisters play a variety of instruments, including guitar, violin, and drums. They write most of their own songs. The quality of their singing voices has been criticized but, in fairness, some of the video clips of their performances were poorly recorded and mixed. It's possible that their musicality is more evident during live performances.

The last song in the list above, "Jacket of Gray," was performed, but not written by, the Pendergraft sisters. It mourns the death of a sole Confederate soldier, defending Southern heritage. Was it just a song, honoring a hero and veteran of a war?

I thought of the soldiers who fought in the Civil War, on both sides. War is violent. People die. Is it worth it to die for states' rights? To preserve a culture and economy that depended on slavery? If I grew up in a Southern state that was part of the Confederacy, would I feel differently? If I were black and enslaved in the South, separated from my family, and denied human rights, would I also mourn the death of a Confederate soldier?

If I encountered that song in a music therapy session, what would I do? Would I use the song to help a client explore his or her thoughts, feelings, or values? Would I have the strength not to let my own biases cause me to censor the song?

I was again reminded of the First Amendment, and how it contributes to the sharing of ideas and forces us to think, which is a cornerstone of democracy. I was reminded of my training, professional standards of practice, and code of ethics.

As I listened to Heritage Connection sing their songs on YouTube, I noticed how different they were from other types of hate music. They weren't like Johnny Rebel. They weren't like Skrewdriver. They weren't neo-Nazi skinheads.

They were young, smiling, laughing girls. On some of their blogs, they complimented each other's appearance, calling each other "pretty."

That, they were, with long blonde hair and knee-length colorful dresses, but under the singers' exteriors, the music expressed hate. They put forward an innocent veneer of not hating anyone—just celebrating their heritage and wanting to preserve their Christian, white, Aryan race. They felt pride in what they were singing about. They were home-schooled, good girls. They found criticism hateful, and they refused to print any negative feedback that they had received. They labeled the ones who were speaking out against racism as hateful.

In a blog, one of the Pendergraft sisters clarified that she likes Spanish food but not Mexican food. She explained that Mexicans (i.e., nonwhites) ate lizards, rats, and root vegetables before Spanish explorers (i.e., whites) taught them how to make food edible. Had the Pendergrafts ever actually tasted Mexican food? Had they ever studied the history of Mexico? For that matter, had they ever eaten any food that wasn't assumed to be from a white, European culture? There was a lack of knowledge of some of the advanced civilizations that occupied parts of South America long before the Spaniards came. Or even of delicious, edible Mexican food that existed before European influences.

The word "brainwashed" entered my thinking, but was that fair? The Heritage Connection girls seem to have adopted, without question, the beliefs of their mother and grandfather. Now as married women, with children of their own, I wondered if they were passing down those beliefs to the next generation.

I wished I could talk to the Pendergraft siblings to better understand them. Had they considered other perspectives?

Had they questioned or rejected any of their family's apparent racism? Like other white supremacist musicians, as they grew into adulthood, had they formed friendships with people from other races and changed some of their own views? Have they come to realize that people are people, regardless of skin color, or nation of origin? As their children were born, did they notice that they were not born with prejudices against members of other races?

I also discovered that I could not order any of their CDs, so I had to rely on YouTube to consider their music. Except at their own appearances and performances, had they stopped selling their recordings to the general public? If so, was it because of the negative backlash? Was it because of a lack of sales? Was it because they were evolving?

Tina Haynes

I CAN'T REMEMBER WHEN I FIRST MET TINA HAYNES, BUT I'm pretty sure it was at a music therapy conference. Professional and articulate, she was respected by other music therapists in Tennessee and across the United States. She was also active and well known as a music therapist within the national Veterans Health Administration. Michael Clark, a friend of mine who directed the music therapy program at Tennessee Technological College, spoke highly of her. Another colleague of mine, Barb MacLean, had worked for years in the VA system and reminded me that Haynes would be a good person to talk to about what was happening in Tennessee.

Heritage Connection sang about a Confederate soldier killed in battle and Aryan warriors. Haynes had devoted her entire professional life to working with veterans who had served both in wars and in times of peace. I saw that as a possible connection between their two stories. Veterans of the Civil War and current-day veterans. Both in Tennessee. Heritage of the past, heritage of the present. Both the Heritage Connection siblings and Haynes seeing themselves as Christians.

I read about Haynes's background, reviewed her work history, and then arranged to speak with her. She had recently retired after working as a music therapist for thirty-five years at the Alvin C. York campus of the Tennessee Valley Healthcare System. Located in Murfreesboro, the facility offers medical, surgical, and psychiatric services to all US veterans, without discrimination. Haynes told me that not only was the patient population diverse, but that employees also represented a wide variety of ethnic groups, races, and national origins.

She remembered working with patients who were black, white, Hispanic, Native American, and Puerto Rican. Her clients were mostly men, but there were some women. Her staff coworkers came from all over the world and included blacks, Germans, Chinese, Vietnamese, whites, and Muslims—among other groups.

I began by asking Haynes her reaction to the October 29, 2017, *USA Today* article, which reported on rallies in two Tennessee towns. She shared that locals were opposed to the rallies and advised to stay away and not give outside organizers and participants any notice. Haynes agreed with the recommendations to remain at home and withhold attention but admitted that some groups of counterprotestors still gave the media plenty to observe and report. Some of both the protestors and counterprotestors arrived from other states. She wished that the news outlets had stayed away so that neither side received the publicity it craved.

The first rally, in nearby Shelbyville, was reportedly attended by two hundred white nationalists carrying a Confederate flag and chanting (that other form of hate music) for closed borders and deportations. Nearly four hundred counterprotestors played a recording of Martin Luther King's "I Have a Dream" speech to drown out a white nationalist presenter. While one side chanted, "White lives matter," the other side chanted, "Black lives matter," and "blood and soil." Members of several known white supremacist, racist organizations were seen in the group of protestors.

The second rally, in Haynes's town of Murfreesboro, was ignored by many locals. Black and white pastors in the town told their congregations that these types of events were not welcome. Some local businesses boarded up their windows and closed for the day.

The protestors who had participated in the earlier White Lives Matter rally, in Shelbyville, stated that they were now marching to protest the presence of Somali and Sudanese refugees settling in central Tennessee. A handful of coun-terprotestors carried black scarves and chanted "Go home," "refugees are welcome here," "this is what democracy looks like," "Nazis, go home," and "shame." Like chants of "air ball" at a basketball game, the group's chants attempted to humiliate, confront, and embarrass the opposing team.

I began asking Haynes questions about her personal story. She grew up just north of Charleston, West Virginia, and the beautiful vocal inflections of that region can still be heard in her voice. There were several large chemical plants in Charleston, and the industry drew a diverse group of chemical engineers and other workers. She also lived close to Guthrie Air Base, so there was a constant turnover of service members and their families.

Haynes shared that her schools were mostly white, not because of forced segregation or busing, but because she "just went to the schools closest to my house." She admitted that her neighborhood was predominantly white, but she remembered members of other groups being present. She recalled an Iranian student, befriending a black family, a black teacher, at least one "oriental" student, some Native Americans, and a strong, local Greek community. Her father and another father, from a black family, coached a baseball team together.

Her fondest childhood memory was her involvement at her church—a close-knit, country Methodist church. She participated in the youth group, which included some of her classmates from school. She remembered the church as a "wonderful, loving, nurturing, community," where families bonded "just like the little Baptist Church down the street."

Haynes became a devout Christian, but her characterizations of her faith reflected different interpretations and understandings than those of the Pendergraft siblings of Heritage Connection. Haynes said that she might not like the behavior of another person but, as a Christian, she would never hate or feel superior to that person.

Haynes felt that there were no major traumas or catastrophes in her childhood, but at some point, her parents divorced. At the age of six, Haynes begged her mother to take music lessons. After that, she claims she "never stopped." As early as the fourth grade, she joined the school band and marching band, playing the trumpet. Both her faith and her involvement with music started at a young age.

Haynes first heard about music therapy by reading an article in *Reader's Digest,* sometime in the 1960s, at the age of nine. She felt that God ordained that it was the right path for her. When she was fourteen, a friend started attending Ohio University and noticed that it offered a degree in music therapy. Following high school, Haynes took some time off, visiting an aunt and uncle in Phoenix, Arizona. She felt comfortable there, setting the stage for her later music therapy preparation.

However, since Ohio University was only about one hundred miles from her home, when it came time to start college, Haynes began her music therapy studies there, under the direction of Professor Brian Wilson. After her freshman year, she transferred to Arizona State University. She studied under Betty Isern Howery, a modern-day music therapy pioneer, and completed her bachelor's degree, graduating *magna cum laude,* under the Phoenix sun.

To complete her required six-month music therapy internship, Haynes began applying to programs that offered stipends. She wanted to focus on her training and not have to worry about locating a secondary job to support herself. She accepted a paid intern position in Nashville, and three months later she learned about a music therapy job in nearby Murfreesboro. She applied and was hired. She worked her entire thirty-five-year music therapy career at that facility.

Haynes worked with psychiatric patients, veterans suffering from PTSD, those with traumatic brain injuries, some with dementia, others with neurologic disorders, geriatric patients, substance abusers, and individuals with serious pain issues. She utilized a full spectrum of music therapy approaches including songwriting, improvisation, drumming, relaxation training, guided imagery, pain management, and teaching healthy leisure skills. Almost all of her services were provided to groups of patients. Due to her caseload and the sheer volume of patients, Haynes seldom had the time or luxury to provide treatment to single, individual patients.

As the only music therapist within the recreation division of the hospital, Haynes was at times frustrated with the size of her caseload. The total bed size of the facility fluctuated over time but, during her career, she served two, thirty-bed acute psychiatric units, four hundred fifty inpatients, two hundred fifty long-term care patients, and some outpatients. She felt spread thin, with no active voice in management.

Using a hypothetical situation, I asked Haynes what she would do if she encountered a patient who preferred hate music. Music therapists are trained to use their clients' preferred music and to assess individual tastes. She said that she would start by asking the patient what musical elements seemed the most important—was it the lyrics? the instrumentation? the rhythm? the volume? From there, she would process the feedback, but also identify other music with those elements that the patient might like. By honoring the patient's music, she could begin to build a trusting, therapeutic connection.

A friend from Arizona, Suzanne Oliver, told her about a distance learning training program in Neurologic Music Therapy offered by Colorado State University. Haynes applied and was accepted since she was already a board-certified music therapist. This established a connection with Colorado State, which is where she later pursued a master's degree in music therapy.

I asked Haynes about music censorship at her facility. She said that there was no policy on music censorship. She shared that most of the patients did not bring their own music with them to treatment, although several had personal CD players. The facility contained a music library that allowed patients to check out music but did not contain any hate music. As iPods, iPhones, and other listening devices entered the market, patients were allowed to make more choices and download their own preferred music.

When asked to share a success story, she thought of a female patient who received guitar lessons as a part of her treatment. Following discharge, the patient reported that whenever she caught herself not practicing or playing her guitar, it was a sign that her severe depression was returning, and that she needed help. She used guitar-playing to monitor her own symptoms.

Haynes has contributed to the field of music therapy through professional service on various assemblies, boards, and committees of music therapy associations. She was proud of her eight years of service to the National Exam Committee of the Certification Board for Music Therapists, including one year as chair. She has also published articles and documents, including contributing to a status report on music therapy with military operations for the AMTA.

She served as a reviewer for practice guidelines for six different psychiatric diagnoses, which were developed by the American Psychiatric Association in 2000 (they have been updated since then). She also gave several presentations to the Planetree organization, a national chain of facilities that places a strong emphasis on incorporating the arts into healthcare.

Remarkably—believing in a lifetime of learning—Haynes recently completed her master's degree in music therapy, after retiring.

Tina Haynes, Murfreesboro, Tennessee.
Used with written permission.

Chapter 13

Behold Barbarity

Sandi Holten

Almost like a follow-up to his father's song, "Gotta Serve Somebody," Jakob Dylan's song "Evil is Alive and Well," recognizes that some people choose a path of negativity and hatred.

Behold Barbarity Records and Distro

Behold Barbarity Records and Distro, based in Plymouth, Minnesota, appeared on the SPLC list of hate music outfits. The company was somewhat unknown to locals but gained some attention following Charlottesville.

The Minnesota winters are brutal and cold enough, but researching Behold Barbarity sent a deep chill down my spine. One website described Behold Barbarity this way:

> "Behold Barbarity was created to further the distri-
> bution of perverse and blasphemous black death
> doom war sludge thrash speed extreme metal

and other violence from all over this f**ked up planet!!! This label/distro located in the United States specializes in SATANIC BLASPHEMIES and HATE. "Political correctness" and trends have no place here!"

But Behold Barbarity's website saw itself differently, as believing in free speech. It reported that it was opposed to censorship.

As with other hate music websites, merchandise had a prominent place at the Behold Barbarity page. There were "Don't Deliver Us From Evil," "No Lives Matter," "Muslims Are No Friends of Mine," and "I Won't Coexist," T-shirts; "Blasphemy" tank tops; and an anti-Semitic T-shirt with the German phrase, "Die juden sind unser ungluck" on the front, which translates to, "The Jews are our misfortune." On the back was a star of David, with a "no" symbol—a bar through a circle—on top of it.

The music available through Behold Barbarity was equally concerning. A band named Organized Resistance presented an album titled *Day of the Rope.* Aryan Blood offered their album, *Through Struggle to Victory.* A tape titled *Gathering of the Putrid Demons* was hawked by the band Anal Vomit. Goatmoon was represented by its album, *Hard Evidence—Illegal Live Activities 2009.*

I contacted friends and relatives in Minneapolis, but none of them had heard of this company. It had been operating under the radar of the majority of the general public. That seemed to change following the events on August 11 and 12, 2017, in Charlottesville, Virginia.

Minnesota had seen a recent increase in hate crimes and acts of hate. The state had documented fourteen anti-Muslim incidents in the past year. A Muslim mosque had suffered an inexplicable explosion. The Jewish Community Relations Council of Minnesota and the Dakotas tallied thirty-three anti-Semitic incidents over the previous two years. Fliers were found in diverse places, including the University of Minnesota campus and Fargo, North Dakota, directing: "real Christians, drive out your parasite class." Alt-right supporters were seen flashing Nazi salutes, and counterprotestors confronted them, sometimes with violence.

A story on Minnesota Public Radio reported, "Racist skinhead and neo-Nazi groups have a statewide presence, and they're just two of 10 active hate groups in the state." SPLC confirmed this, showing ten Minnesota groups on its master US Hate Map. There appeared to be more lone actors in these situations, but the point was made that extremists often gain or strengthen their views through interactions with others—sometimes through organizations and sometimes by sharing music.

Daniel Koehler, a German counterterrorism researcher and a fellow in the George Washington University Program on Extremism, had consulted with groups in Minnesota. He has worked with both jihadist and neo-Nazi extremists and their families. He talked about both groups. "Of course the content and goals can differ," he said, "but both groups are convinced they are the victim of an existential threat posed by an evil and superior enemy who needs to be fought and destroyed in that final battle of good versus bad."

Following Charlottesville, it came to light that Behold Barbarity Records and Distro was owned by Aaron Wayne Davis, a fast-rising intellectual property attorney with the law firm Patterson Thuente in Minneapolis. He had previously worked as a music promoter, representing more than a dozen record companies. Before deletions, the law firm's website said this about Davis:

> "Aaron Davis is a key member of Patterson Thuente's litigation team and also leads the firm's arts and entertainment practice. Aaron's practice focuses primarily on litigation of intellectual property disputes. He has assisted clients with disputes regarding patents, copyrights, trademarks, entertainment contracts, rights of publicity, trade secrets, trade dress and other business torts."

By all accounts, he was viewed as a highly experienced and capable attorney and had won several lawsuits, some with large monetary settlements.

Upon learning that Davis was the owner of Behold Barbarity Records and Distro, the law firm promptly fired him. This sparked a nationwide discussion of whether or not neo-Nazis, white supremacists, or others perceived as discriminatory, can, or should, be fired. It is a gray area, and laws differ by geographic location. Employers must consider the effects of extreme ideas on their business, its image, and its remaining workforce. Some employees have been fired for participating in discriminatory behaviors and events.

I asked my brother-in-law, a former reporter for the *Minneapolis Star Tribune*, to drive by Behold Barbarity and let me know his observations. He and his wife went to an address they found on the internet but found an Applebee's Grill and Bar at that location. I asked them if maybe Behold Barbarity was being run out of a back room at the restaurant.

My brother-in-law joked. "No, I don't think so, but the bartender looked a bit suspicious."

Behold Barbarity's artists spew hate in all directions. An article on the website for Digital Music News gave the following examples: A song by The Raunchous Brothers advocated for killing gays. A song by Goatmoon attacked blacks. The Greek Band, Der Stormer, had lyrics that railed against Jews.

I turned to YouTube to see if I could sample some of the music for sale at Behold Barbarity. I scanned the list of albums and CDs available for sale. A group named Segas Findere offered albums with titles such as *Bound by Hatred, DeSSemitize, Massacre Supremacista, Never Stop the Hate, Machine of Jewicide, United by White Terror Propoganda,* and *Bound by Hatred.* The band, Angelust, offered *Pussy Annihilation,* which included a song by the same name. Three bands—Lords of Depression, Infernal Sacrament, and Tetragrammacide—offered a combined album titled *Atomic Regurgitation from Three Mouths of Homicidal Hate.* Hohl, from their album, *Blackmass/Ritual Holocaust,* put forward the songs "Sacrificing the Flesh of the Untermensch" and "Sickness Unto Death."

The music was described as Black Metal, Death Metal, and Noise. The latter label seemed to be the best fit. The music was loud, aggressive, and angry, with lyrics that were almost completely undecipherable. My initial reaction was, "Who buys this music?" immediately followed by, "What subgroup of the general population is attracted to this music?"

Other metal bands in Minnesota have been active against Behold Barbarity. They have tried to shut down festivals sponsored by Davis, and even tried to hack into his company's online payment system to wreak havoc. One metal head was quoted as saying, "We'd prefer they didn't exist. We would like these people to be more emotionally intelligent, to understand other cultures and essentially let everybody be."

Another metal fan was quoted in the publication *City Pages* as saying, "No, I'm not willing to cede any territory to these ideas. I don't want to see any one venue become a white power venue again. Not everyone remembers how hard everyone fought to get these f**kers out of town. I don't want to see that happen again."

Sandi Holten

SANDI HOLTEN, A BOARD-CERTIFIED MUSIC THERAPIST, works at the Park Nicollet's Struthers Parkinson's Center, previously housed inside Methodist Hospital in St. Louis Park, Minnesota, but now located in a free-standing facility in nearby Golden Valley. She lives and works near where Behold Barbarity Records and Distro operates. When I contacted her, she shared that she was not aware that a hate music company was in the area. Her story is one of pure coexistence in the same geographic location—another example that hate music and music therapy can be present in the same environment, often unaware of each other. The juxtaposition of hate and healing.

According to the Parkinson's Disease Foundation, close to a million US inhabitants suffer from Parkinson's disease (PD). This exceeds the combined totals of individuals afflicted with multiple sclerosis, muscular dystrophy, and Lou Gehrig's disease. Not counting people who have the disease but have gone undetected, newly diagnosed cases can be as high as sixty thousand annually. There have been studies assessing the prevalence of PD according to gender, race, age, geographic location, and other characteristics, but results seem to vary and come from studies that have only included limited, sometimes unique samples. It appears that males are diagnosed with PD more often than females.

Readers may know somebody who has PD. If so, they may have noticed that the person exhibits visible shaking, called tremors, when that person is otherwise inactive. While that is a visible symptom, other indications remain less obvious.

Individuals with PD sometimes appear stuck when trying to walk, referred to as Bradykinesia. They may be hard to understand due to low voice tone or garbled speech. Talking can also become more complicated because of drooling or difficulty swallowing. Physically, they might appear stiff, have a stooped posture, or find it hard to maintain balance. All of these symptoms make it challenging for a person to competently perform normal daily motor tasks.

Nonmotor symptoms of PD can include depression, social isolation, anxiety, constipation, poor impulse controls, pain, psychotic thinking, hallucinations, cognitive deterioration, inability to sleep, sexual difficulties, and urinary dysfunction. Between motor and nonmotor issues, it is obvious that individuals with PD require treatment and support, including use of strong medications administered routinely and regularly. The disease passes through five identifiable stages, growing progressively worse.

While the prevalence of PD with different demographic groups appears inconclusive, it is entirely possible that some hate musicians, like members of the general population, may eventually be diagnosed with the disease and require therapy—maybe even music therapy. It is less likely that music therapists will ever require the services of hate musicians unless they are recovered from living lives of hate. Perhaps, in the future, music therapists and "formers" might find ways to collaborate to help others adjust to changes in their life after hate.

Music therapy is provided to individuals with PD, in collaboration with an interdisciplinary, physician-led treatment team. Studies of the brain have led to a greater understanding of the complexities of PD, and how music might be used to assist those stricken by the disease. Research has shown that some music stimulates levels of dopamine and serotonin, which are decreased in persons with PD.

Music, especially rhythm, can help with organizing and coordinating movement. Singing, or even tapping one's hand in rhythm while speaking, can help with breath support for speech and better coordination of muscles around the mouth and tongue. Slower music can assist with calming overactive body systems and lead to relaxation, sometimes promoting sleep. Even improvising music and writing songs can help PD patients express their feelings, connect with others, and improve their quality of life.

I've known Sandi Holten since working in Minnesota, but that was long ago. I recently attended a presentation of hers at a music therapy conference. I contacted her to ask if she could share her story with me, especially how she became involved with music therapy and PD patients. I also wanted to learn how she felt about coexisting in a location where a hate music company sold products promoting hate.

Holten was born right where she currently works in Golden Valley, Minnesota.

She was the youngest of four children, all given names that start with the letter "S."

She shared that her mother said if she ever had a fifth child she would have named the baby "Stop." Her father was a blue-collar, union electrician, and her mother had a variety of jobs, in spite of some serious health problems.

Holten remembers a happy childhood with loving parents who strongly valued education and reading. Somehow they managed to purchase a full set of *Collier's Encyclopedia*, which was used by all siblings to study and complete their schoolwork and minimized the need for some trips to the local library.

Coming from an intact, loving family was not always the case for some children who grew up to become hate musicians. Some, but not all, came from broken homes, had abusive parents, felt ignored or neglected, were victims of bullying, or lived in environments where drugs or alcohol were present. That is not to say that all children who became music therapists came from totally problem-free families.

However, my research indicated that strong family relationships usually directed some children away from hatred and guided them to make more positive choices in their lives. Starting families, or reestablishing ties with their families of origin, often contributed to former hate musicians successfully deciding to exit from extremist groups.

"From the get-go," Holten remembers being musical. She was always singing, sometimes to her stuffed animals. She remembers seeing the play *Sound of Music* when she was four years old. Sandi's parents were not musicians, but they loved music. Their 33 1/3 rpm record collection was eclectic, including Nat King Cole, operas, musicals, country music, and other genres. Holten recalls hearing the sounds of the rock group Steppenwolf rising from her brothers' record player in the house's basement.

Holten first heard about music therapy during her senior year in high school while attending a "college night" informational event. She thought, "I love music, and I love psychology, so I think this could be a good match for me." She enrolled at Augsburg College in Minneapolis, completing a Bachelor of Science degree in music therapy in four years. She was greatly influenced by her major professor, Roberta Metzler (now, Kagin), who directed the program.

Next, she completed her required internship at Golden Valley Health Center under the supervision of Dolores Fleming and Mindy Barnes Hoke. She worked primarily with adult psychiatric patients and adolescents with addiction issues. She felt that every music therapist who she worked with at GVHC helped to shape and form her. Holten was the last music therapist to work at Golden Valley Health Center before it closed. She was there for nine-and-a-half years. She had a few, short-term jobs after that, but she has worked at Struthers Parkinson's Center since 1996.

I asked Holten about her mentors as a music therapist. Beyond her internship, one music therapist who influenced her was Dawn McDougal Miller. Dawn, who Holten describes as a "job creator" in the Minneapolis/St. Paul area, was the one who told her and others about possible employment opportunities and actual job openings in the Twin Cities. Holten credits Dawn with helping her learn about her current job at Struthers.

Rose Wichmann, Holten's boss at Struthers, has supported her growth as a therapist for over twenty years. Holten also recognized Michael and Corene Thaut, the doctors who established the Academy for Neurologic Music Therapy at Colorado State University, as inspiring and influencing her through their training program in methods of neurologic music therapy. She was in the first group to complete "Fellowship" training from that organization—an advanced certification—and serves on its advisory council.

Suzanne Oliver, founder and executive director of Neurologic Music Therapy Services of Arizona, was another therapist who provided inspiration. Holten's work with Parkinson's patients was also highly impacted by others who work in home settings, because of their emphasis on holistic health care.

Mentoring, during their careers, is a prevalent feature for many music therapists. Consider that mentoring also plays a role in the hate music community. Some musicians, like Wade Michael Page, have played in multiple bands. And the recruitment of new members to extremist groups can often involve older family members, existing members, and events to teach new members about what to believe—"the cause."

Holten said that she looks at diversity with a "cultural curiosity," trying to use music therapy interventions that are sensitive to her patients' backgrounds and make sense to them. A person's faith is one consideration, as is age. As a Christian, she believes that her work is a calling, and that she is there as the "hands of Jesus Christ." Her faith is important to her and what she does, but she is clear that she does not evangelize or put her religion "out there" to clients.

Holten talks about how the treatment for PD has improved over the past decades. Her job provides her with ongoing continuing education and supported her in pursuing both her certification as a Neurologic Music Therapist and attending PD excellence conferences. She was also a founding faculty member on the Allied Team Training group for the National Parkinson Foundation, hearing presentations from others but also providing training about music therapy. She has published a book chapter on the uses of music with PD patients.

I asked Holten about her reaction to learning about Behold Barbarity Records and Distro. Trying not to judge, she said that she found the company "disturbing." She saw the company as using music to, in her words, "perpetuate what I feel is the absolute opposite of health and well-being."

She continued. "After years of working with adolescents, whose music, some of it, was pretty violent and hate-filled as well. It's important. If I ever had the opportunity to work with somebody who this was their music, I feel like I would need to explore and try to understand it more, listen to it, which I wouldn't want to do. But I feel like I needed to do that, without judgment, because, if I'm seeing them in a therapeutic setting, then there needs to be changes in their life, obviously, and I need to understand where they're coming from. That's their culture. It would be very difficult."

Her response reflected the code of ethics, professional standards of practice, and nondiscrimination policy of the AMTA. Those expressed values are also present in the domains tested by the Certification Board for Music Therapists.

For the next set of stories, I turned to the eastern side of the United States. The SPLC included several hate music groups there. I was to learn that hate music is found in all geographic locations.

Sandi Holten, Struthers Parkinson's Center, Golden Valley, Minnesota. Used with written permission.

Chapter 14

EAST COAST HATE MUSIC

RICK SOSHENSKY

Since I have spent most of my life on the West Coast, I wanted to expand and explore the hate music groups that the SPLC had identified on the East Coast. These two stories share what I found out.

I matched the hate music stories with the story of a music therapist coexisting in their midst. By the time I finished a draft of this book, the three SPLC West Coast hate music groups had been removed from their list, but there remained numerous hate music entities in many eastern states. Of course, people living on the West Coast still had hate music in their communities—mostly supplied by local bands and musicians.

East Coast Hate Music

THE EAST COAST OF THE UNITED STATES IS NOT EXEMPT FROM hate music. On its 2017 list of hate music groups, the SPLC included five groups on the eastern side of the United States:

Poker Face, in Allentown, Pennsylvania; Wolf Tyr Productions, in Holbrook, New York; Micetrap Distribution in Maple Shade Township, New Jersey; United Riot Records in New York, New York; and Label 56 in Nottingham, Maryland. Since Charlottesville, several of them have shut down. I will share what I found out about each of them, ending with the main focus on Label 56 because it is reported to be surviving and thriving.

Poker Face is a band, centered on singer/songwriter Paul Topete. Other band members have come and gone since the band originally formed in 1994. Its music has been called racist by the SPLC. The leader of the band, Topete challenged the SPLC to cite any of the band's lyrics to back up that claim. It could not. He countered that the SPLC is "...trying to create race tensions. They're not trying to create race solutions." In his eyes, the band was being criticized for being "white, conservative, and Christian." He admitted that his band strongly opposes illegal aliens, but says its members are fully in favor of legal immigration. He pointed out that his father was a legal immigrant from Mexico.

The ADL has also criticized Poker Face. It labeled Topete an anti-Semite due to his ongoing relationships with other Jew-haters, antigovernment militias, Holocaust-deniers, and assorted conspiracy theorists. The band has also been criticized for posting racist and sometimes anti-Semitic information on the forum of its website and other white supremacist sites.

Again, Topete pushed back, calling the ADL's accusations "a clear case of slander and libel." He said that the postings accounted for only 3 percent of the content on its forum, that those posts were written by other authors, and that they were available on the Poker Face website because the group believes in the "free exchange of ideas."

His other defense was that he did not deny the existence of the Holocaust, but has stated that only ninety-seven thousand people died, as opposed to the documented number of six million-plus. It made me wonder if a lower number of murdered individuals somehow made the Holocaust less horrible. A YouTube video of an interview with Topete was titled, "Was Hitler Really the Bad Guy?"

Topete also stated that he was interested in exposing Jews who have committed crimes against their own race or the United States. He has opined, in an interview, that 60 percent of all undocumented crimes in the United States were carried out by Jews. He stated that it was "not beyond the scope of reasonable doubt" that Israel was involved in the 9/11 airplane attacks on the World Trade Center, the Pentagon, and in Pennsylvania.

Remarkably, Topete advertised for a "gutsy lawyer" to sue the ADL, in a publication of the American Free Press, a known racist organization. The same issue also ran an advertisement for the National Alliance, which stated that it was "the only organization in the U.S. for White folks only."

In 2005, the band played at the state convention of the Libertarian Party of New Jersey, on the campus of Rutgers University. However, the following year they were canceled from that event, due to pressure applied by a group called the One People's Party, which objected to some of the postings on Poker Face's website. The Libertarian Party tried to defend the band, stating, "Nothing in their music says anything about racism or anti-Semitism," but Poker Face was still prevented from performing.

Poker Face has been around for over twenty years, playing to all ages, all races, and all religions, up and down the Eastern Seaboard. Devout believers in the Constitution and their First Amendment rights, they usually perform at venues that are described as "patriotic." They play at right-wing political rallies, including those of Senator Ron Paul, and have been politically associated with the Tea Party. They are good musicians—better than some other bands that have been labeled as hate mongers. They do not fit the mold of groups like stereotypical neo-Nazi skinhead bands. The lyrics to their songs are neither overtly racist, nor anti-Semitic. They focus on peace and freedom.

It appears that they have been labeled as a hate music group primarily due to the politics, statements, and associations of Topete. However, those reasons are not overtly reflected in Poker Face's music. A representative from the SPLC told me that the band is on their hate music list because of their involvement with right-wing, extremist festivals.

Wolftyr Productions is a Nationalist Socialist Black Metal record label, based in Holbrook, New York. The owner of Wolftyr is Paul Guhring, who has also used the names Paul Tyrian and Bobby Dokken. According to the New York City Antifa chapter, Guhring has been associated with such bands as Witchblood, Grafvolluth, Kama Rupa, Blood and Sun, BELIEVER.LAW, Graveland, Hate Forest, Goatmoon, M8L8TH, Grand Belial's Key, Heathen Hammer, and Slavecrushing Tyrant, among others—either singing with them, promoting their concerts, contributing recordings to their tribute albums, selling their records and CDs, hawking their merchandise, or otherwise supporting them.

In Patchogue, Long Island, some locals went to a record shop in the corner of an antique store, after seeing a flyer advertising the availability of "underground metal" vinyl recordings. What they found was primarily a collection of music by bands advocating for anarchist, anti-Semite, fascist, white separatist, and white supremacist ideologies. Some photos of the represented bands, found on the internet, included Nazi symbols, some band members giving "Heil Hitler" salutes, and still others dressed in the garb of neo-Nazi skinheads.

The locals who visited the record store were quoted as saying, "There were scatterings of bands that weren't associated, but the vast majority was the very sketchy Nazi-related stuff. It was disgusting." They also said that many of the recordings and merchandise items sold at the store were from peripheral neo-Nazi bands or other groups that were not a part of mainstream metal circles.

One of the men who had established the store was none other than Guhring, who offered a defense that many of the symbols found on the album/CD artwork, websites, and merchandise in the record store came from esoteric pagan ideologies. He said that just because the Nazis adopted those symbols did not necessarily mean that the bands were neo-Nazis, or followers of Adolf Hitler.

Another of Guhring's activities includes involvement with Heathen Circle, dedicated to promoting the heritage of white Europeans and their descendants. Heathen Circle publishes a magazine that includes praise for fascists, white supremacist musicians, and racist gangs.

Following local media coverage of the record store in Patchogue, Guhring and his business partners took down their Facebook sites, took the record label offline, and closed the shop. They said they had no upcoming concerts scheduled and no new business plans. James Skidmore, the president of the Greater Patchogue Chamber of Commerce, said, "We've worked hard to get away from that. We want the message clear that hate is not welcome in Patchogue. Even just a small pop-up. A little bit of cancer is still cancer."

Next, I read about Micetrap Distribution, founded and apparently run solely by Steve Wiegand. Micetrap Distribution's website includes the following language:

> "Micetrap Distribution has quickly established itself as one of the most reliable, fastest, and lowest priced sources for underground music, videos, books and flags in the world. Although some of the items available on this site contain violent or racist themes, Micetrap Distribution is merely supplying a service and in no way condones illegal activities or the acting out of the lyrics contained on these compact discs. The album and song titles, artwork, pictures and lyrics are the intellectual properties of the various bands and do not necessarily represent the personal views of Micetrap Distribution.
>
> "All materials are completely legal in the United States and it is entirely your choice as to whether or not you want to purchase them. If you are offended or opposed to anything contained on my website, close your browser immediately. Simply put, these items are made available for those that seek them. Rather than attacking ideologies and legal merchandise, I suggest that my opponents refocus their attention onto real issues that plague our society; rape and sexual abuse, murder, drugs, thefts, assault and other illegal activities."

I guess Wiegand didn't understand that the music and other merchandise he sold were often used to recruit members to white supremacy organizations and that believers in that cause sometimes were involved in all of the behaviors listed above.

A business statement on Micetrap's website reads: "Micetrap Distribution , LLC. supplies an always expanding selection of quality items with the lowest prices, quickest shipping and best customer service possible." Wiegand, again, puts forward a rosy picture of a company that prides itself on meeting market demands in a quality way. A company profile on Zoom info shows Micetrap revenues of 2.5 million dollars, but it is unclear if that is an annual total or for some other period.

In spite of the racist products that Micetrap sells, Wiegand has had many conflicts with other factions of the hate music industry. His competitors have claimed that he sells bootleg copies of the music, videos, and T-shirt art of some bands. One competing business owner claimed that Wiegand bought the rights to several internet domains to prevent other groups from registering those names. An example was Volksfront.net, which Wiegand purchased as a way to prevent a skinhead group of the same name from owning that domain.

He has also been accused of hacking other white supremacist websites or sending viruses to their computers. In a court case involving another white supremacist, Wiegand provided videotape, which was used to show that person was a felon in possession of a gun. Wiegand dismisses these stories as part of a "record label war," and claims that other companies are just trying to hurt his sales. However, his reputation has caused him to be "persona non grata" among other hate music industry businesses and insiders.

Wiegand began his foray into hate in 1996, when he founded the website White Pride Network. He started Micetrap Distribution in 1998 and it quickly grew into a major hate music source. For a time, he also ran the operations of 14 Word Press, since its founder was in a high-security prison in Colorado, serving one hundred fifty years for two murders, racketeering, and other crimes.

For those unfamiliar with the "14 Words" of the white supremacist/white separatist/white nationalist cause, they are: "We must secure the existence of our people and a future for white children." Those fourteen words are often followed by an additional fourteen words: "Because the beauty of the White Aryan woman must not perish from the earth." Between the publications of 14 Word Press and the sales of records and other merchandise by Micetrap Distribution, Wiegand provided the goods to recruit hundreds, if not thousands, of new members to the racist movement. After negative publicity, he eventually sold his interest in 14 Words Press.

The music that Micetrap Distribution sells includes such titles and artists as:"Hitler Was Right (More Dead Jews)" by Ethnic Cleansing, "Gays Have Gotta Go" by Midtown Bootboys, "Keep the Hate Alive" by Racist Redneck Rebels, "Bulldozer of Semitic Destruction" by Warbutcher, "Freezer Full of N****r Heads" by Grinded Nig, "Too White For You" and "Racially Motivated Violence" by Angry Aryans, "The White Race Will Prevail" by Race War, "Der Ewige Jude" (English translation: The Eternal Jew) by Volkszorn, and the entire catalogs of the groups Skrewdriver and Aggravated Assault

Devin Burghart, who works for the Institute for Research and Education on Human Rights, is quoted as saying that Wiegand's Micetrap Distribution had sold products representing the most "hard-core, violent and racist music in the entire industry." However, the company's Facebook page included a cartoon stating, "Stop Interfering with My Freedom of Speech."

In 2004, Wiegand lost his job managing a gas station, when local newspapers wrote stories about Micetrap Distribution. He sued his employer for wrongful termination. During the trial, he claimed his First Amendment rights were being violated, again stated that it was legal for him to sell his products, and said that he found some of the records and merchandise that he stocked to be "funny." The judge did not agree. He lost the lawsuit but continued to run Micetrap Distribution.

By 2017, following the events at Charlottesville, Wiegand finally shut down his business. In announcing the closure, he was quoted as saying:

> "...at the point a Jewish community center is concerned or the guy down the street and his kids are worried, in this world with how charged up it is and all the violence, it's time to end it."
>
> "All of this violence going on, I don't want to contribute to it. I don't want to be connected to it. I don't want to be labeled as somebody that is a part of it. I don't have any inner peace."
>
> "I can't keep saying, 'I'm not a bad person, I'm not a bad person,' when I keep selling this stuff."
>
> After saying that he wanted to find his "own self peace" again, he added, "I am going out on my own terms while sales are increasing at a rapid pace, simply to pursue a happier, less stressful life that also spares my friends and the neighborhood I love."

United Riot Records, founded in 2003, is still operating. It is currently based in New York City and operated by the controversial 211 Bootboys, a multiracial skinhead group. A description of the 211 Bootboys on the United Riot Records website states that there has never been a "color policy" limiting membership in the "social club." Some sources report that 211 allegedly refers to the California law enforcement code for robbery.

Another publication theorized that 211 refers to the first two letters of the alphabet and stand for "Brotherhood of Aryan Alliance." Still other sources question whether the 211 Bootboys are related to a prison gang with the same name based in the Colorado prison system. That gang is also sometimes referred to as the Aryan Alliance, or the Brotherhood of Aryan Alliance.

Controversy follows the record company because United Riot has been criticized by antiracist, anticommunist, and antifascist groups for the type of music it promotes, the bands it supports, its nonmusic-related behaviors, and the audience it attracts. The record company responded to the criticism on its website:

> "Our label UNITED RIOT RECORDS is an underground music label. The label has been run by several people of color over the years since 2003. We have also released music by all genders and races and continue to do so. This is straight from the Labels mouth, REAL NEWS. Anything else is completely fake. We will continue to bring you music of all forms and thank you for the support."
>
> "Dozens of slander articles throughout the years from journalists who work hand-in-hand with

Antifa have attempted to brand 211 as a bunch of street thug, drug dealing, Nazi's. In reality, the crew is a non-profit social club, made up of predominantly working class veterans, of all races, who emphasize country, family, free speech, and like to play music on the side."

United Riot Records schedules concerts mostly in the New York City and Washington, DC, areas, and has been accused of scheduling bands that promote nationalism and Islamophobia in their song lyrics. For years, the 211 Bootboys and United Riot Records have been involved with an annual New York City Oi! Fest. A wide range of fans has attended those music festivals, but there is a strong element from the violent skinhead movement.

Bands that have performed in recent NYC Oi! Fests included Offensive Weapon, Close Shave, Queensbury Rules, and the Firm. Those bands have also performed in other countries on the same bills as bands associated with far-right, extremist, nationalist, Blood and Honour, white supremacy, and neo-Nazi movements.

Some of the bands that United Records supports and promotes in concerts include: Offensive Weapon, Battle Cry, Lonewolf, Brute Force, Combate 49, Embattled, the Sentinels, Banged Up, Queensbury Rules, American Eagle, Skinfull, Frontline Soldiers, Sexual Suicide, Cheech, Chesty Malone, Mongo, Close Shave, Tattooed Mother F**kers, Total Annihilation, and The Slice 'Em Ups. The music of these groups includes the genres of punk, Oi!, hardcore, metal, rock 'n' roll, and even ska. The label claims that it is interested in all classifications of music.

However, many of the label's sponsored concerts are

promoted secretively, sometimes through posters or other forms of communication, which are targeted to their known skinhead audience. Due to efforts of antiracism and antifascism organizations to shut down some of the concerts, marketing efforts have been carefully targeted to certain interested groups and individuals. In some cases, the venue names are even excluded from posters, flyers, and other promotional materials. Makes you wonder how the bands develop an audience, but they do.

In early 2017, members of the 211 Bootboys were implicated in an assault on two brothers inside and outside a New York City bar, Clockwork. Stories reported that six or seven men, wearing 211 patches, attacked the twin brothers, because an Antifa sticker on one of brothers' phones angered them. The victims received serious head wounds, requiring a trip to the hospital for treatment.

While several of the East Coast bands and record companies experienced negative publicity, shaming, legal issues, and business struggles after Charlottesville, one company appeared to achieve continued business growth and profits—Label 56. Run by Richard Haught Jr., a founding member of the Maryland Skinheads, Label 56 was founded in 2005 and is located in a section of Baltimore, Maryland.

The strategies that it has employed to gain market share and minimize a negative backlash include avoiding media attention, expanding its music catalog, developing relationships with East Coast skinhead groups, establishing ties with international hate music circles, sponsoring concerts, producing a periodic online radio show, hosting a blog on its website, and taking an aggressive stand against Antifa tactics.

The record company practices what it calls "identity politics." Avoiding the terms "white supremacist," "white nationalist," "neo-Nazi," and other labels that draw a negative reaction from the general public, the company sometimes refers to itself as "pro-European." A blog posting on its website stated, "Unfortunately, the age of political correctness and social justice says that it's wrong to have an identity that isn't minority or immigrant."

The label also defends its First Amendment right to free speech in the United States. The host of a Label 56 podcast said, "America is the only country that has next-to-zero restrictions on freedom of speech." In Europe, where anti-hate speech laws are more restrictive, the label has released censored versions of the songs of some of its artists.

Despite its "pro-European" self-image, the merchandise that Label 56 sells, and the music it promotes, run the gamut from far-right extremism to the obviously racist. It sells Rock Against Communism patches, Confederate flags, racist podcasts and videos, and speeches by white supremacist author William Pierce. It also sells music CDs by such groups as Bound for Glory, Jason Augustus, Absolute Terror, Final War, 96 Brigade, Spirit of the Patriot, Force Fed Hate, The Skumfederates, and End Apathy, one of the bands of Sikh temple shooter Wade Michael Page.

Again, downplaying the racist, discriminatory content of many of the recordings it releases, Label 56 has adopted the slogan, "Independent Music for Independent Minds." On its website, it states, "We want you to enjoy music for what it is and not because some radio station says you should. So have a look around our website and check out the mp3's. Hopefully you will find something you enjoy. Many of the CD's we stock are limited and international releases by independent labels and bands, so if you see something you are interested in grab it up, it may not be here tomorrow."

Label 56 artists have been labeled as purveyors of hate music by the SPLC, the ADL, various Antifa chapters, Google, Yahoo, iTunes, Amazon, and One People's Project.

Rick Soshensky

Music Therapy, in the United States, has some of its earliest roots on the East Coast. In 1779, an article titled "Music Physically Considered" was published by an anonymous author in *Columbian Magazine*. The article—based, in part, by practices in Europe—discussed uses of music to regulate emotions and influence a person's physical condition. It also advocated for using music practitioners who had received adequate training. Those ideas are still relevant today.

A second article, also by an unnamed author, appeared in 1796. Titled "Remarkable Cure of a Fever by Music," the writer shared the case of a music teacher whose fever was allegedly decreased and then eliminated by listening to music. Both of these articles were anecdotal and would be challenged in today's more scientific environment, but they showed that consideration was being given to pairing music with medicine.

Starting in the nineteenth century, writings about music as a healing medium appeared in books, music publications, medical journals, newspapers, and graduate school theses and dissertations. Solomon, Davis, and Heller produced an extensive bibliography of some of those early sources in 2002. Their document, published by the AMTA, presented a list of early music therapy writings that spread over forty-two pages.

Authors included medical doctors, psychiatrists, psychologists, college faculty members, students, and others.

Topics ranged from uses of music with special populations to applications of music in specific geographic locations or institutions and research articles exploring the effects of music on different domains. The historical literature demonstrated that a variety of writers from numerous disciplines were recognizing and applying music to help individuals or groups maintain or improve emotional, physical, cognitive, spiritual, and even vocational health. Today, new historical music therapy-related references are still being discovered, adding to the original Solomon, Davis, and Heller bibliography.

Influenced by Dr. Benjamin Rush—a physician/psychiatrist teaching at the University of Pennsylvania—two medical students wrote early nineteenth century dissertations about the uses of music to treat diseases. The first, *An Inaugural Essay on the Influence of Music in the Cure of Diseases*, was written by Edwin Atlee in 1804. Samuel Matthews wrote the second dissertation, *On the Effects of Music in Curing and Palliating Diseases,* two years later, in 1806.

As the nineteenth century progressed, writings about the uses of music in institutions for the blind, deaf, and mentally ill appeared. Mostly written by independent, unconnected authors, the literature gained little widespread public attention or traction in moving music therapy forward as a discipline or profession.

In the early years of the twentieth century, the first glimpses of efforts to establish music therapy as an organized field of study and practice began to appear, led primarily by several women.

The first was Eva Vescelius, who founded the Therapeutic Society in New York City in 1903. There is evidence that she gave a brief, twelve-minute presentation on "Musical

Vibration in the Healing of the Sick" at the second meeting of the International Metaphysical League in New York City, in 1900.

Together with her two sisters, Vescelius studied voice and performed in many parts of the world. Their concerts included appearances at hospitals and asylums. Vescelius wrote and spoke about music therapy. One of her publications, in addition to several articles, was a booklet titled *Music in Health*. Her activities related to music therapy ran from 1900 to 1917 and laid some of the groundwork for future music therapy associations. However, without the scientific rigor found today, the results of her work were sometimes untested and not validated through research.

Overlapping with Vescelius was the work of a nurse, Isa Maud Ilsen. She was familiar with the work of Vescelius and applied some of the same ideas to work with hospitalized soldiers during and after World War I. She became the director of Hospital Music in Reconstruction Hospitals for the Red Cross—using music with war veterans experiencing medical and surgical needs. By 1919, she was offering music therapy lectures at Columbia University in New York City. This was the first known incidence of music therapy courses being regularly taught at a college or university in the United States.

In 1926, Ilsen founded the National Association for Music in Hospitals. One of the main functions of the organization was to familiarize musicians with procedures used in healthcare facilities so that they would be supported, rather than resisted. Ilsen had articulated rules for musicians to work in hospitals in 1919, requiring them to:

1. obtain permission of the physician in charge,

2. establish rapport with the chief nurse and assistants,

3. wear clothing that was bright and cheerful,

4. avoid somber music,

5. avoid use of the trumpet, cello or portable organ, and

6. use tact and common sense.

When Ilsen formed her National Association for Music in Hospitals, the *New York Times* published an announcement that scholarships were available for musicians who wanted to work in hospitals. The money for the scholarships had been raised by a group of supportive women, and it increased the number of musicians being trained as music therapists. However, a professional credential was not yet available.

Another early music therapy pioneer was Harriet Ayer Seymour, who also overlapped with both Vescelius and Ilsen. She had received musical training in both New York City and Germany. With advanced piano skills, she taught at New York's Institute of Music Art—later renamed the Julliard School of Music.

Seymour's relationship to music therapy spanned from 1915 to 1944. During World War I, she provided music services to hospitalized soldiers. In 1920, she published an article titled "What Music Can Do for You." By 1924, she had founded the Seymour School of Musical Reeducation, where she offered classes about music therapy and produced a journal.

Seymour was active in several organizations that promoted the use of music within hospitals, both as entertainment and as a therapeutic modality. Examples of those organizations include the Music Committee of the New York State Charities Aid Association and the Federal Music Project of the Works Progress Administration.

Success followed. In March 1938, the *New York Times* reported that musicians were working in seven New York City hospitals and two women's prisons and that six thousand five hundred individuals were receiving music treatments. In many of these early cases, music therapy was provided by volunteers, or through part-time employment. Music therapy was not yet recognized as a viable full-time occupation.

Seymour founded the National Foundation for Music Therapy (NFMT) in 1941, which offered music therapy classes until 1944. With a strong focus on treating World War II veterans, the NFMT claimed to have trained over five hundred musicians to work in New York City hospitals and other clinical settings. At the end of her music therapy career and her life, Seymour published a music therapy clinical practice guideline titled *An Instruction Course in the Use and Practice of Musical Therapy*. It may have been the first publication to detail music therapy approaches and methods with a variety of populations.

One hundred miles north of New York City, in the same region of the country as some of the hate music groups described above, lies the smaller city of Kingston, New York—population, close to twenty-four thousand. Recent history began with Dutch immigrants. However, there is some evidence of local inhabitants before the Dutch, notably Native American Indians of the Esopus tribe. Given the current polarization in our culture, about immigrants—especially illegal immigrants—it's interesting to consider this example (of many) of how European immigrants assumed control of land that was once the home to others.

Kingston has become a strong supporter of the arts. The Kingston Arts Commission's mission statement is "…to strengthen the local economy by attracting and promoting artists, arts venues, and arts entrepreneurs; encouraging cultural tourism; creating opportunities for training and employment in a range of creative fields; and enhancing quality of life amenities that will make Kingston a more attractive City in which to live. By so doing, the City of Kingston will gain greater regional and national recognition."

Kingston is where Rick Soshensky, a music therapist, established the Hudson Valley Creative Arts Therapy Studio. The studio offers music therapy, art therapy, creative writing, filmmaking, dance therapy, and drama therapy services to individuals, groups, and communities that have experienced disabilities. Soshensky and volunteer students serve clients of all ages who have encountered mental illness, developmental and intellectual disabilities, disorders along the autism spectrum, substance abuse, emotional and behavioral problems, traumatic brain injuries, physical disabilities, spinal cord injuries, neurological disorders, HIV/ AIDS, dementia, and other medical issues.

I first met Soshensky when I invited him to participate in an institute titled, "Uses of Music and Music Therapy in the Prevention and Treatment of Chemical Dependency," as part of the 2003 national conference of the AMTA, in Minneapolis. I had read Soshensky's 2001 article, "Music Therapy and Addiction," published in the professional journal, *Music Therapy Perspectives*. The institute included a panel of seven practitioners—six from the United States and one from Canada—who had incorporated music into the prevention or recovery programs of addicts and alcoholics. The institute was well attended and contributed to the growing discussion of how music can be used to help people who misuse, abuse, or are addicted to drugs or alcohol.

As I read about the East Coast music groups described above, I thought of Soshensky. Outside of that 2003 institute, I knew very little about Soshensky's story. What I had known, the years had taken away. I contacted Soshensky, explained the gist of the book I was working on, and opened communication. After some emails, some online research, and a telephone call, Soshensky agreed to an interview.

Soshensky told me that he grew up in New York—first in Queens, and then in Long Island. He felt that he had good parents and was loved. He felt safe. His parents gave him a lot of freedom and did not micromanage him, so they didn't always know his whereabouts. He got into trouble one time when he had a flat tire in a location where he was not supposed to be.

Soshensky shared that his parents and other members of his family were major influences in shaping his beliefs and values. He said that he tries to treat his children the same way.

Soshensky remembered growing up in the "Woodstock generation" and the pop music "youth" culture of the sixties and seventies. He attended a large festival at Watkins Glen but preferred up-close, smaller music venues.

Describing his boyhood neighborhood as white and Christian, Soshensky said he still struggled with some things. He encountered some bullying and shaming, possibly because of his ethnic-sounding last name. When asked about his family history, Soshensky shared that his grandparents were European immigrants and that he had Jewish ancestors on both his father's and mother's side of the family—some from Russia, and others from Austria.

His father was a mapmaker for the US Army Air Force during World War II. He served at the Battle of the Bulge in Belgium and saw plenty of action. Soshensky believes that he was traumatized by the experience. One of his father's poignant memories occurred during an evening walk. While walking, he met another soldier, an infantryman, and the two of them came upon a glass room built around a grand piano. As bombs dropped around them, and with little regard for losing their lives, they played music together all night. Soshensky described this as the "opposite" of hate music. It was just two humans connecting through music.

During his twenties and thirties, Soshensky gigged as a singer/songwriter. He had fantasies of becoming the next Bruce Springsteen or Tom Petty. He loved root music, Pete Seeger, the Beatles, Bob Dylan, Jimi Hendrix, and other pop music performers of the day. He worked hard at performing and songwriting, playing both locally and around the world.

After trying to become a rock star for over fifteen years, questions started popping up: "What's my future?" "Am I good enough?" "What else could I be doing?" "Am I destined to become an aging bar-and-wedding singer?" "Will I be somebody, some day?" He began to feel angst and scared regarding the prospects of his career choice. Like some former hate musicians, he began reconsidering what he wanted to do with his life.

While in his mid-thirties, Soshensky's father told him about the field of music therapy, which he had heard about on TV, telling him, "I know this is for you." Soshensky started to explore the field, and "found the New York music therapy crowd." He said that as soon as he "took the plunge" and started to pursue music therapy, his musical self-doubts went away.

He shared, "I was good at it. Other people recognized me for being good at it. I was at home." He said that all the skills that he had honed and developed as a gigging musician could then be used in sessions with clients.

Soshensky jumped into the field with enthusiasm. He already had a bachelor's degree in psychology from the State University of New York at Buffalo, but he followed that with a master's degree in music therapy from New York University. He studied at the famed Nordoff-Robbins (NR) Center for Music Therapy, becoming one of the first guitarists to receive certification as an NR Music Therapist. Before Soshensky's studies at the NR Center, the school's methods had been primarily piano-based. Soshensky completed an internship at Metropolitan Hospital in New York City.

As his career progressed, Soshensky earned credentials as a certified music therapist with the American Association for Music Therapy, a board-certified music therapist through the national Certification Board for Music Therapists, a certified brain injury specialist through the American Academy for the Certification of Brain Injury Specialists, and a licensed creative arts therapist in the State of New York.

Soshensky has been an exemplary representative for the field of music therapy. He has published numerous articles, book chapters, and book reviews. Readers are encouraged to view his many videos on YouTube (search for "Rick Soshensky") to see him in action with his clients. He is also writing a book about his studio practice, so readers are encouraged to watch for its publication.

He has taught at the State University of New York at New Paltz and Molloy College and says that he has talked about hate music in his classes, stressing that underlying impulses can be expressed through music. In addition to teaching, he has spoken at a variety of universities, clinical facilities, on internet features, and at professional seminars and conferences. His work has been featured in print, on the radio, and on web-based interviews and profiles.

In 2007, Rick received an Innovative Practice Award from the New York State Health Facilities Association and, in 2008—2009, *Therapy Times Magazine* included him on a list of the "Most Influential Clinicians, Researchers, and Leaders in the Therapy Industry."

During his twenty-five years as a music therapist, Soshensky has worked at the Center for Nursing and Rehabilitation, the South Brooklyn Health Center, the King County Hospital Center, Jacobi Medical Center, Heartsong Inc., and Hudson Valley Creative Arts Therapy Services Inc.—all in New York. Let's just say that he found his calling.

Reviewing Soshensky's places of employment, accomplishments, and recognition is one thing. Talking to Soshensky about his clients and hearing his passion for helping others is another. We Skyped and talked about his ideas for using music to help others. And we talked about hate music.

For Soshensky, the goal in therapy is to find a way to play music with a variety of clients, to facilitate some type of nonmusical personal growth for them. His studio has no policy regarding music censorship, but he has experienced administrative censorship at other organizations where he has worked. He prefers to channel strong negative emotions or behaviors into the music.

Recognizing that there are all kinds of songs—some even considered to be anti-social—he said, "All expression is valid." Soshensky said that he would never stop a client from expressing what they were feeling. He explained that the strength of a therapeutic relationship could foster communication, demonstrate understanding through listening, and validate a person's reality. He added, "There's a difference between singing it and doing it." However, he does not support allowing members of a therapy group to introduce or play music that would be harmful to another group member.

Soshensky was not familiar with the hate music groups from his area of the country listed above, but he is now. He shared that he has encountered clients who chose to express pain, anger, and other negative emotions. He finished our Skype chat by saying that music is based on reconciling shadow impulses of life with spirituality—between the "devil on one shoulder, and the angel on the other."

Soshensky concluded, "There's nothing wrong with happy music, but more music deals with pain." A different perspective than Dr. Gaston's claim that all "music is derived from the tender emotions." Soshensky, as a music therapist, favors music based on a healing intent.

Rick Soshensky, Hudson Valley Creative Arts Therapy Studio, Kingston, New York. Used with written permission.

Rick Soshensky. Used with written permission.

Chapter 15

WOMEN AND HATE

DAUGHTERS OF HARRIET

"Keep Ya Head Up" is a song written by Tupac Shakur in 1993 (Interscope Records). The late rap artist challenged the negative treatment of women and advocated for positive change.

Women in Extremism/Prussian Blue/ Kt8/Misogynist Music

IN THIS SET OF STORIES, I WILL TALK ABOUT THREE MAIN things. Following a brief introduction about women in extremist organizations, I will share a couple of examples of hate musicians who are women. Second, I will explore hate music directed at women—misogynist music. And third, I will share the story of five female music therapists who have formed an ensemble to use songs and chants to spread positive, loving, peaceful messages.

Author Michael Kimmel, in his book *Healing from Hate: How Young Men Get Into - And Out Of—Violent Extrem-*

ism, (2018, University of California Press) repeatedly makes the point that the reason so many males join extremist groups is due to gender issues. Young men are looking for a way to prove their manhood and be a part of something that they consider to be important. They have felt powerless, are angry at their situation, and looking to place blame.

Some of what I read portrayed the women in extremist movements as supporting the men in their lives by serving two, conflicting roles: either whore or Madonna. Providing sex, or being angelic and raising white children, or both. This is sometimes labeled as "tradwives," meaning that women want a traditional, primary role of having and raising children. Tradwives recognize the biological differences between men and women and feel that their roles should also be distinctly different. They view the feminist movement as women trying to assume traditional male roles.

Some women who have been active in the white nationalist movement have been criticized by men for assuming roles that rightfully should belong to men. In some ways, it's like, "Join us in the movement, but know your place." The white nationalist movement and some forms of hate music are rife with misogyny. However, for some women in hate movements, there is also a strong antifeminist flavor. For those women, the emphasis reflected sentiments expressed in the song "Stand by Your Man," a hit for Tammy Wynette in 1968.

Women have served numerous roles in the white supremacy movement and other hate organizations. They have prepared the food for and served as hostesses for KKK meetings and picnics. During the height of KKK prominence, they donned hoods just like their male counterparts. They have advocated for the protection of Civil War monuments that stand as reminders of slavery.

They police educational systems, selecting what textbooks can be used, and how to present history—or homeschooling their children. Men imprisoned for racial violence are supported by them. They have recruited for militia groups. Some women have denied the Holocaust and have supported anti-immigrant organizations. Conspiracy theories have been created and promoted by them. Even as some women advocated for women to have the right to vote, their advocacy was only for white women to gain that right. It's obvious that although the number of women in hate organizations is less than male members, they have maintained active involvement for a long time.

We hear a lot about white supremacy, but there are also men and women who advocate for male supremacy.

Women who have participated in discriminatory politics have been largely ignored or forgotten due to the male dominance of right-wing organizations. However, one example I found is Cornelia Dabney Tucker.

Tucker was instrumental in supporting Senator James Eastland's efforts to fight against civil rights progress. She fought against the appointment of the first black Supreme Court justice, resisted school integration, and led other protests. Although her involvement is not as well-known as those of her male counterparts, she is an example of the female side of white power politics.

As Elizabeth Gillespie McRae wrote in her article "The Women Behind White Power" (2018, *The New York Times)*: "White women have made white supremacy a much more formidable and long-lasting force in American society, sustaining it at both the local and national levels."

Some men joined hate movements, in part, due to the social aspects and access to women and sex. Other men found the movement made them feel more "like a man," protecting the women in their lives, as long as the women sometimes accepted quiet, subservient roles. The white power movement also includes a splinter group of men labeled "incels," short for involuntary celibates—men who feel that women have unjustly denied them sex. They feel that women owe them sex and it's their right to demand it or take it by force.

I mentioned Author Michael Kimmel's book, *Healing from Hate: How Young Men Get Into—And Out Of—Violent Extremism* above. As indicated by the book's title, the main focus of his research was on men. However, he also wrote passages about the "women of the right." Some entered extremist movements through established organizations, such as the KKK and Hammerskin Nation (a network of white power skinhead groups), even though those groups are traditionally men-only. They wanted to be housewives and raise their white children, like past generations. In some cases, that was not possible, due to the economy forcing them to work outside the home.

Some passionately shared the ideologies of men in the movement, but eventually left "the cause" after being treated as less than equals, or solely as sex objects by the men. Some left because they disagreed with violence as a tactic. Parts of the "alt-right" movement view the role of women as nurturing and men as protectors and risk-takers. Nurturers don't see their role as participating in protest rallies. Other women have been turned off by men talking about "legitimate rape," and women being denied a voice in the movement. However, after Charlottesville—where the "unite the right" protestors were mostly men—there have been more efforts to involve women in hate groups.

Kimmel estimated that about 25 percent of the white supremacist movement is female. Another author, George Hawley—who wrote *Making Sense of the Alt-Right* (Columbia University Press, 2017)—estimates that female participation is lower, around 20 percent. This is almost the opposite of the field of music therapy, which is predominantly female.

In his book, Kimmel shares the findings of research done by sociologist Kathleen Blee, who interviewed almost three dozen women involved in right-wing extremist groups. She found that the demographics of the women closely matched those of the men—lower- and middle-class and educated; more than a third of them with postsecondary degrees, or in college. In contrast to the men, however, none of the interviewed women had been abused as girls.

In the following passage, Kimmel summarizes what seems to attract women to extremist groups:

"What brings women in? The same mundane reasons that bring people to all sorts of intense identity-oriented politics: a need to belong to something larger than themselves, the collapse of traditional familial or communal forms of identity. By contrast with the Swedes, only a handful of the American women followed a man into the racist world. Many were not especially racist when they entered and developed their ideology after they joined. Others simply drifted into the deviant subculture. One's friend liked skinhead fashion; another thought it would be fun to hang out with the fringe groups."

As noted in the previous chapter, The fourteen-word motto of the white supremacist movement is: "We must secure the existence of our people and a future for white children." That phrase is followed with: "Because the beauty of the White Aryan woman must not perish from the earth". The focus is primarily on the future of children and secondarily on admiration for "the beauty" of women.

As I read books and articles written by and about hate musicians—including those about women—issues of parenting and gender relationships were evident. In some cases, parents played an active role in teaching their children to be hateful. In other instances, a child's experience of parental abandonment or abuse produced an angry reaction to the world, which sometimes made young children and young adults ripe for recruitment by extremist hate groups.

As the second part of the white power motto above illustrates, there is an emphasis on "the beauty" of the White Aryan woman, with little or no statement of recognition for the strengths, intellect, or skills of women. Some men were recruited to hate groups *by* women. And some men left hate groups due to the influence of women who lovingly confronted, or tired of their racist, violent beliefs.

The birth of children also presented challenges. Some haters could see the pure innocence of young children and chose not to teach them to hate, while others seized the opportunity to fill their children's minds with their hate-filled beliefs. The relationships between hate groups, men, women, and children are varied and complex.

In a previous story, I shared information about Heritage Connection, two young women who have been active in the white power music movement. In their story, it was easy to see the influence of their grandfather, a KKK member, and their mother, who also accepts white supremacist beliefs. There is a long history of women being involved in the

KKK, dating back to the nineteenth century. The Heritage Connection girls were "spoon-fed" the beliefs of their older family members.

Now, let me introduce you to another pair of blue-eyed, blonde, female hate musicians.

The folk-pop duo, Prussian Blue, was one of the biggest selling music groups for Resistance Records back in the early 2000s. The band was comprised of twins Lynx and Lamb Gaede. The sisters started singing and playing music at age nine. They began their recording career in 2004, when they were only eleven years old. They were encouraged and supported by the National Alliance, a far-right organization. Their recording and stage name—Prussian Blue—reportedly refers to the color of the residue from Zyklon B, the gas used in the murderous gas chambers in World War II Nazi concentration camps. The girls sometimes performed at Holocaust-denial conferences and have downplayed the realities of the Holocaust. They have defended Adolf Hitler. They pointed out that Jews have been persecuted or "prosecuted" for centuries, and conclude that there must be good reason for that.

Driven by a white supremacist "stage mother," the girls recorded covers of white power bands, including Skrewdriver. They also wrote original songs, such as "Aryan Man Awake," "Skinhead Boy," and "Hate for Hate." Raised in Bakersfield, California, they adopted their mother's racist ideologies before they were old enough to know any better. As quoted by the SPLC, their mother later put it this way: "What young, red-blooded American boy isn't going to find two blonde twins, sixteen years old, singing about white pride and pride in your race…very appealing?"

Their mother, April Gaede, is open and proud about being a white nationalist. Married three times and the victim of husbands who allegedly used drugs and victimized her with domestic abuse, she was raised to accept racist and sometimes misogynist philosophies. She has been active in the neo-Nazi National Alliance, and later, the National Vanguard. She criticized other races, calling them "annoying," "dirty and messy," and perpetrators of violence and rape against whites. She made it clear that she is opposed to diversity, multiculturalism, and feminism.

One of her efforts included an attempt to launch a white nationalist dating service. She wanted to match white Aryan men with white Aryan women, to fill the world with pure, white Aryan children. For long periods, she homeschooled her two daughters, using pre-civil rights era textbooks and a curriculum of her design. Maybe April inherited her belief system from her father, Bill Gaede. He reportedly displayed a swastika on his belt buckle, painted one on his truck, and even used the symbol to brand his cattle.

April's twin daughters, Lynx and Lamb, were the darlings of the white power music scene, contributing to the fortunes of Resistance Records, which sold their two CDs. Following a story about them on the ABC show *Primetime,* they were approached by other programs and forums, including *Dr. Phil, Gentlemen's Quarterly, Newsweek, Good Morning America,* the *Los Angeles Times, Maury Povich, Teen People, Vice* magazine and others. They even received media coverage in England. They toured in the United States and in Europe. Their fifteen minutes of fame didn't last long. As their teen years progressed, the media attention subsided, and their support from the white supremacist music industry faded.

According to numerous news reports, the girls now live in Montana, either with or near their mother, who moved there to get away from the increasing diversity in Bakersfield. They may be married (their last names have changed), and they have forsaken their previous hateful beliefs. Neither of their Facebook pages mention Prussian Blue. They claim that they have now adopted a liberal, hippie philosophy of life.

Lamb Gaede has been quoted as explaining, "I was just spouting a lot of knowledge that I had no idea what I was saying." They are quoted in a publication of the SPLC as now saying, "I love diversity," and "It makes me proud of humanity every day that we have so many different places and people."

They attribute their change of heart to medical marijuana, which they have used to combat serious, legitimate medical issues. In one article, it was reported that they said their favorite musician was Barney, the purple dinosaur. Quite a change from singing Skrewdriver and RAHOWA covers.

They have been out of the limelight since 2006, but, at that time, their mother didn't buy their conversion. She claimed that they were just saying what people wanted to hear, to gain popularity at school and reduce the negative responses they were receiving. She claims that they were just "using the Jew (*sic*) media to make bank as usual. If they had done anything else they would not have gotten any attention." They have not promoted a new album since 2006. They have expressed that they are trying to keep a low profile because, "There are dangerous people in White Nationalism that don't give a f**k, and they would do awful things to people who they think betrayed the movement."

I guess we will have to wait and see what their future holds and whether or not their change of heart is genuine. Even if it is, like other former hate musicians, their hate music remains. Their recordings have been banned by Spotify, but I was able to listen to them on YouTube.

———

I ALSO READ ABOUT ANOTHER WOMAN WHO SEEMS TO be involved with white power hate music, a singer for the band KT8, in Orange County, Southern California. In an interview posted on the website of the Nationalist Women's Front, she talks about singing Skrewdriver covers, being influenced by her grandparents, and being proud to show her children photos of her performing at white power venues while pregnant with them. She offered this advice to other white women in the white power movement:

> "...don't buy into the media narrative. It's all bulls**t. Our core beliefs are not as unpopular as the media and trolls would have you believe. We are everywhere. You are not alone. You are not wrong. There is a huge push right now to eradicate traditional values, push multiculturalism and demonize whites. Because they have a huge platform to spread their message, it can seem factual and intimidating. Don't let it get to you. Push forward with a purpose. You can have the beautiful, righteous life of your dreams without compromise."

I respectfully disagree, but she also states, "I have no interest in writing or playing for people who are not like minded." Seems that considering the opinions of others, or researching and analyzing controversial issues, is not something that she welcomes.

Should children who are so deeply influenced by their parents and grandparents (or others) be cut some slack? Should they be forgiven for past (or current) transgressions and shown compassion, grace, and understanding? Should people be allowed to change, grow up, and form their own opinions? Can they change?

I was reminded of the biblical passage, "He that is without sin among you, let him cast the first stone" (John 8:7). Don't we all have past behaviors and ideas that we regret? As a music therapist, with a career that has lasted over forty years, I emphatically answered "Yes" to my own questions. I have witnessed, firsthand, recoveries and dramatic changes in people, when offered information, care, kindness, love, acceptance, support, therapy, and other forms of help. In some cases, it has required inpatient treatment, or relocation, to remove them from toxic environments. In other cases, medication has helped.

For others, as William Sears, one of my first music therapy professors said, "Life is therapy." I was also reminded of the First Amendment, guaranteeing us all the right to free speech. What the Gaede sisters sang about in the past, and *KT8* still sings about in the present, might be offensive to many but inspiring to others. It is legal, even if currently censored by many digital music outlets.

We know that women participate in extremist groups, right-wing groups, and hate music groups, but what about music that expresses hatred toward women—misogynist music?

As a man, it makes me uncomfortable to try to represent a female perspective on hate music. Funny I should say that now, because I am not African American, Jewish, disabled, gay, or part of other minority groups talked about in this book. But there's something about trying to represent the perspective of women that makes me feel more guarded.

I disagree with hate music, whether it is by a woman or a man, or directed at any demographic group. Like other forms of hate music, some misogynist music embarrasses me. More than that, it sickens and horrifies me. Maybe it's the sensitivity I learned from all of my female relatives, co-workers, and friends. Maybe it's the heightened awareness brought about by the "Me Too" movement.

On August 4, 2019, Connor Betts killed nine people and wounded seventeen others in Dayton, Ohio, including his sister. He was killed by police to end the incident. In the aftermath, it was revealed that he was the lead singer in a misogynistic metal band named Menstrual Munchies, which had released albums titled "6 Ways of Female Butchery," "Sexual Abuse of a Teenage Corpse," and "Preteen Daughter P$$sy Slaughter."

Following the incident, details emerged that Betts had drugs in his system, had been acting strange, and was described by the member of another band as being "sick in the head." Betts's band released songs about rape, murder, necrophilia, and other gruesome acts against women—a musical genre called "pornogrind." Add pornogrind to the growing list of hate music categories.

It is an understatement that there is a large body of songs that are disrespectful, insulting, mean, degrading, and hateful toward women—most of it written by men. One of John Lennon's songs was titled "Woman is the N****r of the World" and admonishes listeners to think about the plight of women and take appropriate action.

To appreciate the depth of misogynist music and try to understand it, I first did a keyword search on the website,

Lyrics.com. The site, one of many such searchable song sites, allowed me to see the number of songs and albums that included lyrics that most people would find offensive. These types of lyrics are "in the tails" of a normal distribution curve, but some have permeated "common cause" variation. Some of the keywords are so awful, that I am reluctant to share them here, except to make the point that hate music directed at women is widespread.

Here are the search words, followed by the number of songs and albums that came up: b**ch (29,188 songs; 92 albums), whore (4,268 songs; 15 albums), slut (1,584 songs; 8 albums), rape (1,655 songs; 100 albums), talk too much (49,590 songs), "f**k her" (13,417 songs); c**t (847 songs). Granted, as I scanned through the lists, there were many duplicates or covers of the same song, but that did not greatly diminish the sheer number of misogynist songs. And these were just songs containing derogatory language. From my perspective, I can't think of a similar body of songs or lyrics that expresses such disrespect or hatred toward men.

To get more specific, consider some of the song titles I found: "Let's Hear it for Violence Towards Women" (Boyd Rice), "Smack My B**ch Up" (The Prodigy), "B**ch Suck Dick" (Tyler, The Creator), "B**ch, You Ain't S**t" (The Game), "Gold Digging Whore" (Steel Panther), "Gutter Slut" (Violence), "F**k Her Gently" (Tenacious D), "Domestic Violence" (RZA), "All Women Are Bad" (The Cramps), "Talk Dirty" (Jason Derulo), "You Talk Too Much" (Clarence Carter), "It's a Man's World" (James Brown), "One Less B**ch" (N.W.A).

These are just a small sampling of misogynist songs. Why do songwriters choose these topics? These words?

Have these thoughts? Don't these singers have mothers, wives, daughters, and female friends and neighbors? What are they thinking?

One of the most hateful was the first song listed above, "Let's Hear it for Violence Towards Women," from Boyd Rice's album *Hatesville*. The cover of the CD features a drawing that includes a woman with a low-cut top and a very short skirt, holding a gun. The song is a spoken word rant, over a techno-musical background. The lyrics state that women should be relegated to only two roles: to provide sex, and to be beaten.

The song is wrong on so many levels. All levels. It makes me angry that I bought the CD and listened to it. I can only imagine the reaction if my female friends and relatives heard this song. When listening to it on headphones, I forgot to turn off the external speakers. Hearing it, my wife immediately charged into the room and asked me to turn it off.

Of equal concern is how it could enter the consciousness of a young boy or man and influence their views of women. How many adolescent boys, upon hearing this song, now think it is okay to assault a woman? Is it meant to make us think? Did Boyd Rice write it in jest, as satire, or as a misguided attempt at humor? Is the song an expression of his real perception of women? Should this type of song be protected free speech?

Rice admits to being a misogynist. When asked, "Why?" during an interview for *Misanthrope,* he responded, "Just a lot of experience with women. I don't think women deserve the same rights as men. I don't think women are on an equal footing with men. I think they're totally different creatures. I think the world operated better when they had less say over the way things went, had less control."

He shared that he does not like to argue with a woman, but when a woman again asked, "Why?' he said, "Because you overreact, you get all emotional, and fly into a tizzy."

Rice wrote a nonmusical piece titled *Revolt Against Penis Envy, or R.A.P.E.* He presented arguments in favor of men's natural superiority to women, and wrote, "Rape is the act by which fear and pain are united in love. It is the triumph of harmony through oppression. Rape teaches balance, the natural balance of man=above/woman=below. This balance is a lesson which woman must learn, and only man can teach her." When this writing was challenged, he stated that it was meant as "tongue in cheek," but admitted, "I think all the stuff I said was basically true."

Violence toward women is a public health issue, influenced by hate music. The World Health Organization estimates that 1-in-3 women worldwide have experienced either physical and/or sexual intimate partner violence or nonpartner sexual violence. Male intimate partners account for approximately 38 percent of murders of women. As John Lennon encouraged us, we must think about it and make changes.

Are less obvious misogynist songs less hateful? Should Bob Dylan be singing "Just Like a Woman" trying to define womanhood? What about the Beatles' song "Run for Your Life," threatening to end a girl's life if she is caught with another man? Should Rod Stewart be singing about taking a girl's virginity in "Tonight's the Night"? What message is Billy Joel giving to young men when he tries to convince a Catholic girl to give up her virginity in his song, "Only the Good Die Young." Is Robin Thicke's song, "Blurred Lines" respectful to women when he labels them with derogatory terms and claims that he knows what they are thinking?

Misogynist music is somewhat unique in the hate music universe, because it crosses all musical genres, and cultural, political, and spiritual lines. It demonstrates all of the common characteristics of hate music: an expression of hate, dominance, superiority; use of taboo language; false stereotypes; lawlessness; and lack of empathy or remorse.

It is also found in more mainstream music. Other examples include: "Every Breath You Take" (The Police), "Delia's Gone" (Johnny Cash), and "Diane" (Hüsker Dü); bluegrass songs like "Little Sadie," "Bank of the Ohio," "Poor Ellen Smith," and "Down in the Willow Garden;" and even classical compositions like Aaron Copeland's "I Bought Me a Cat."

In country music, "bro-country" songs include references to "hot girls," "partying," and "chasin' every girl that wasn't fast enough." Country songs frequently focus on the physical attributes of women, more than any other characteristic. Examples include Luke Bryan's "Blood Brothers" and Florida Georgia Line's "Get Your Shine On," which is about a group of men requesting a woman to dance for them (not with them).

I found an article titled "The 15 Most Misogynist Lines in Rap History." The lines are too obscene to cite here but were contained in songs by Big L, Snoop Dog, Jasper Dolphin, Jay Z, Bizarre, Lil Wayne, Eminem, Cam'Ron, Fredo Santana, Chief Keef, Jadakiss, and Danny Brown—some very well-known and successful rap/hip-hop musicians. The songs contain themes of using women as sex objects, beating them, gang-raping them, choking them, and killing them.

Uzochi P. Nwoko, a writer for *The Crimson*, wrote an article, "Alleviating the Effects of Misogyny in Rap and Hip Hop Music":

"...a reevaluation is certainly warranted, and not just for rap. Misogyny manifests itself widely across genres from rock 'n' roll to country music. Instead of censorship, consumers of rap and hip-hop who will ultimately become the genre's creators should be cognizant of the messages that they subconsciously integrate into their thoughts, actions and vocabulary. Words are powerful, and consistent auditory exposure to an ideal can have concrete effects on people's mentality....In a bid to make America a more socially equitable place, rap and hip hop consumers should try to optimize the positive effects and minimize the misogyny in the music they listen to."

Some of this reevaluation is happening in certain categories of music, but not fast enough. One profession that continues to assess the harmful effects of music and utilize music for conflict resolution, healing, and positivity is music therapy.

Daughters Of Harriet

THE AMTA ESTIMATES THAT ITS MEMBERSHIP IS APPROXimately 87 percent female. It is difficult to give a similar estimate for the field of hate music but, as mentioned above, a large number of hate music groups are male. Even with a few women included, hate music has been described as a male, testosterone-driven phenomenon.

I've heard some defenders of hate music say, "It's just music. It's not hurting anyone." Nothing could be further from the truth. Let's review some examples:

November 12, 1988—Kenneth Murray Mieske and friends, members of the East Side White Pride skinhead gang, and heavily involved in the Portland, Oregon, Death Metal music scene, murder Ethiopian student Mulugeta Seraw with a baseball bat.

January 8, 2011—Jared Lee Loughner, a fan of the song "Bodies (Let the Bodies Hit the Floor)" and Mayhem Fest, shoots nineteen people in Tucson, Arizona, killing six. One surviving victim was Congresswoman Gabby Giffords.

August 6, 2012—Wade Michael Page, musician with at least eight white power bands, kills six people at a Sikh temple in Wisconsin.

June 17, 2015—Dylann Roof, whose music-listening included the neo-Nazi skinhead band White American Youth (much to the distress of lead singer, Christian Picciolini, now a founder of the organization, Life After Hate), shoots and kills nine people at the Emanuel African Methodist Episcopal Church in Charleston, South Carolina.

April 2019—Holden Matthews, describing himself as a "metal (music) fan to the bone," is charged with three counts of arson in the burning of three historically black churches in Louisiana.

August 4, 2019—Connor Betts murders nine people and wounds seventeen others in a shooting rampage in Dayton, Ohio. He is heavily involved with pornogrind, the misogynist music genre.

It has been estimated that 98 percent of mass shooters are men, with a high percentage of them also being suicidal and many of them influenced by music.

With gender playing a critical role in hate music and the profession of music therapy being largely female, I looked for an example of a female musical group that presented a contrasting story to hate music.

Daughters of Harriet (DoH) is a quintet of singers named after Harriet Ayer Seymour, one of the twentieth-century music therapy pioneers mentioned in Chapter 14. Some haters and hate musicians want to honor their heritage. The same is true for music therapists.

There are five members in the DoH: Jodi Winnwalker, from Portland, Oregon; Lisa Jackert, from Long Beach, California; Barbara Dunn, from Whidbey Island, Washington; Maureen Hearns, from Logan, Utah; and Robin Rio, formerly from Arizona, but currently in Virginia. They have eleven college degrees among them—not only in music therapy, but also in social work, psychology, and interdisciplinary studies.

I interviewed Jodi Winnwalker to compare her business, Earthtones, to Soleimoon Recordings, one of the organizations labeled as a hate music group by the SPLC. Both companies were based in Portland, Oregon. Soleilmoon Recordings, owned by Charles Powne, represents over one hundred twenty artists, now mostly through mail order. Out of those hundred-plus artists, it appears that only two resulted in Soleilmoon being labeled by the SPLC as pedaling hate music: Death in June and NON (a Boyd Rice project).

Powne defended himself and his company in an article published by *Willamette Weekly*. He shared that he refused to sell recordings by Skrewdriver, because they were so blatantly racist. Powne also said that he was an "endorser" of the SPLC and was surprised that the SPLC had labeled his company a source of hate music.

He was quoted as saying, "The solution to bad speech is not to shut it down, but to overcome it with more speech." A supporter of the First Amendment, he reported that he has been selling Death in June recordings for more than twelve years and was not pleased with the current, negative attention. He believes that he is just a good businessman, serving the wants and needs of some of his customers. A capitalist. His website indicates that he has dropped Death in June and NON from his catalog of offerings. The SPLC, in return, dropped Soleilmoon from its hate music map.

For full disclosure, I admit that I am a long-time supporter of the SPLC. That organization is one of the groups that has tracked and fought hate, taught tolerance, and helped people who have been victimized—by taking legal actions. Founded in 1971, it has an almost fifty-year track record of doing good. However, like all of us, it is not perfect, and its labeling a company as hate music can damage that business—some intentional, some unintentional.

Its cofounder, Morris Dees, was fired in April 2019, which led to other key leaders resigning. The scope of the organization's problems was somewhat vague, but reports mentioned a toxic internal environment that included a lack of diversity in its workforce, decisions made predominantly by white leaders, and sexual harassment. An interim director was appointed, who immediately hired an external consultant to help define the issues. The organization is committed to addressing its internal challenges while continuing its important work. We are all imperfect.

A Buzzfile company profile for Charles Powne says that his business began in 1984, although his business may include more than Soleilmoon Recordings. That same profile indicates that his business may have three employees and generates approximately $290,000 per year. Powne told the *Willamette Weekly* newspaper that Soleilmoon accounts for $100,000 of that total. Business is good.

Today, Earthtones has twenty-four employees, some part-time and some full-time. There are thirteen music therapists, a few horticulture therapists, an art therapist, an accountant, an administrative assistant, and music therapy and horticultural therapy interns. The organizational chart for Earthtones continues to grow and evolve as the business adjusts to the changing healthcare environment. The company has an annual budget of approximately $420,000. Similar to Soleilmoon Recordings, Earthtones is a for-profit company.

The second member of DoH is Lisa Jackert. I contacted Jackert, originally, because she was located close to another outfit on the SPLC list of hate music groups, Hate Crime Streetwear Productions. Like Soleilmoon Recordings in Portland, Hate Crime Streetwear—listed as being in Anaheim, California—has also been eliminated from the SPLC list, another indication that the hate music industry is constantly changing, and that efforts to confront companies that sell hate music have been successful.

In some ways, Jackert's music therapy career has been similar to other music therapists. After receiving her initial college degree, she completed a music therapy internship at St. Mary's Hospital in St. Louis, Missouri. As she gained experience, she earned a master's degree in psychology, as well as specialized training in treating individuals suffering from dementia and Alzheimer's disease, therapy supervision, crisis prevention, guided imagery, and cognitive-behavioral therapy. Continuing education is a requirement to maintain her credentials.

Jackert has worked at numerous clinical locations in Southern California, including both inpatient and outpatient settings. For fifteen years she has worked full-time at Community Hospital of Long Beach, which borders Orange County. She also works at several part-time positions, including running her own private practice, Music Therapy Services of Long Beach. Almost all of her clinical work has been with adults, primarily with mental health issues. Shortly after telling me about her work at the hospital in Long Beach, Jackert learned that the hospital was closing, and she was being laid off. She has continued to work through contracts with several other local hospitals and organizations.

Jackert performs in the Southern California area, in a musical duo named Feter and Lisa.

I asked Jackert about the proximity of Hate Crime Streetwear Productions to where she lives and works. She was not familiar with that company and had not heard any of the music by the artists in its catalog. We began to explore her experience with hate music, or how she might deal with it in her work.

Jackert told me that, to her knowledge, she has never had a client who was the victim of a hate crime. However, she has worked with clients who have been raped or have experienced domestic violence. She has worked with clients of many races, although she admits that some of her services are provided to Caucasians because sometimes they are more apt to have good health care insurance. (When she works with inpatients at her hospital, patients can have private insurance or no insurance at all. In the outpatient section, services are limited to patients who either have private insurance or Medicare Part B coverage.) Even though the numbers have been less, blacks, Hispanics, and Muslims have all been treated by her at her hospital.

The third member of DoH is Robin Rio. She has sung all of her life. In her youth, her family sang madrigals together, and now she continues that practice by singing with her husband and children. Until recently, Rio was a tenured music therapy professor at Arizona State University, but she now lives in Virginia—offering close support to family members.

Rio's professional work includes publications and presentations about working with individuals who are suffering from dementia, uses of music with homeless adults, music therapy with youth offenders, services to patients on oncology units, and process-oriented music therapy. She has been professionally active in the AMTA, holding a regional office, serving on committees and boards, and on the editorial board for *Music Therapy Perspectives*, a national, professional, peer-reviewed journal. She is the co-founder of Strength-Based Improvisation Training, which teaches an advanced practice methodology to experienced music therapists. She has published a book, *Connecting through Music with People with Dementia: A Guide for Caregivers* (Jessica Kingsley, 2009) .

On an international level, Rio has taught in the graduate music therapy program at Universidade Lusiada in

Lisbon, Portugal, and has given presentations at world music therapy conferences in Oxford, England, and Seoul, South Korea.

Rio has also sung and recorded with the groups Synaptic Soul, Cappella Sonora, and Bartholomew Faire.

Beginning in 1976 and for the following thirty years, the fourth member of DoH, Dr. Maureen Hearns, was a school-teacher. Over the last fourteen years, she has been on the faculty at Utah State University in Logan, Utah, where she is currently an associate professor and academic program director for the music therapy program.

Hearns has been an active participant in the music therapy profession. She has presented at local, national, and international conferences. She is a past-president of the Western Region of the AMTA and has also served the Association for Music Imagery and on the board of directors for the Certification Board for Music Therapists. Hearns has conducted research related to the self-care of music thera-pists and how it affects their professional and personal lives, as well as research on music therapy with females who have encountered domestic violence, and mother-child bonding in families where domestic violence was present. She has given presentations and authored publications, including a book chapter on ethical practices in music therapy clinical supervision.

In addition to singing with DoH, Hearns has a twenty-year history of performing, traveling, and recording inter-nationally with the Mormon Tabernacle Choir. She has used music in personal ways—creating sacred spaces, establish-ing a sense of community, forming and improving relation-ships, and enhancing a feeling of closeness to nature. She has even used music with her pets and animals.

The final member to join the DoH was Dr. Barbara Dunn, whose doctoral work focused on the use of music in conflict transformation. Dunn studied how music could be used in conflict mediation within communities, which is highly relevant to hate music and to help decrease polarity and hatred within our current national environment.

Since 1984, Dunn has provided music therapy services in the state of Washington. She has a private psychotherapy and music therapy practice but also provides both music therapy and social work services in several healthcare settings, including Whidbey General Hospital, Music Works Northwest, Bailey-Boushay House, and Providence Medical Center. She works with a variety of clientele and patient populations, including those with medical issues, physical disabilities, psychiatric issues, AIDs, and other conditions.

Like the other four members of DoH, Dunn has given numerous presentations and has published a book chapter, a monthly column in *Victory Review Magazine,* and the book, *More Than A Song: Exploring the Healing Art of Music Therapy* (University Book Store Press, 2012). Her doctorate dissertation is also available through ProQuest (publication no. AAT 3342508).

Music therapy students must declare a major instrument and, in her case, it was voice since singing is one of her passions. In addition to the concerts and recordings with her four colleagues, Dunn also performs and records as a solo artist, and with others, and has released two CDs of original songs: *More Than a Song,* a companion recording to her book of the same title, and *The Sparrow Takes Flight.*

In an interview with Dunn, I asked her if she would ever perform on stage with a hate music group or solo hate musician. She said that if the message was hateful, she would not want to participate. However, she is interested in using music to mediate and resolve conflicts. Might it prove productive for musicians with different viewpoints to participate in musical call-and-response sessions, musical debates, or sharing together through song? Could making instrumental music together be a starting point? Might some understanding be gained, ideologies challenged, or perspectives broadened? Something to consider.

The five women evolved into a singing group gradually, over several years, mostly through contact at music therapy conferences. By attending each other's professional presentations, chatting at conference events, and discussing their individual experiences and activities, they discovered that they all shared an interest in chants. In their *Daughters of Harriet Songbook,* they define a chant as: "A vocal meditation based on two or three simple melody lines that allow variations on rhythm, harmony, and expression. Through this improvisatory exploration a contagious sense of unity and well-being is created."

Rio and Jackert first got the ball rolling—or the chants a-chanting—at a regional music therapy conference in Hawaii in 2007. They offered a five-hour training based on traditions of therapy, worship, ethnomusicology, and songwriting. Hearns attended that session and was an active participant. Winnwalker was also present at that conference and invited attendees to sing with her when she accepted a regional award.

Following the awards ceremony, these four women brainstormed about how to create singing experiences that would be similar to drum circles, but combine words and music, and emphasize "musical forms that provide deep expressions of our inner experience."

Following the conference, Jackert suggested Dunn as the fifth music therapist who would be interested in this new endeavor. The vocal quintet led their first chant circle at a national music therapy conference in Louisville, Kentucky, in 2007. That chant circle was part of an educational, concurrent session at the conference—meaning that only certain conference attendees signed up. Part didactic lecture, part demonstration, and part experiential, the session taught traditional chants and dances from several cultures.

Based on the response to that initial session, music therapy conferences since then have offered time slots for chant circles, so that all conference attendees can attend and participate. It seems natural that music therapy conferences—which include business meetings, committee and council meetings, presentations on evidence-based practices, demonstrations of methods and techniques, research reports and research poster sessions, information on how to document and track treatment outcomes, and information about different client populations—should also include some live music, either as a part of those other agenda items, or as stand-alone events.

The DoH have met that need. Collectively, the five women have recorded two CDs of original chants and produced a book, *Daughters of Harriet Songbook: You are a Song...From the Heart.*

The DoH, Prussian Blue, and KT8 all either have Facebook pages or links to other information about them. You can hear some of their music either there or on YouTube. There is a contrast between the groups, in musical styles, names of songs, themes in their lyrics, and the ability to understand the lyrics.

I listened to KT8's song, "My Name is Hate," from their album *Kill Baby Kill*. The song paid homage to hate. I could not understand the words, but they were easy to find through a web search. I also listened to the CDs by the DoH. Their chant titles indicated beliefs and themes that were opposites from KT8. Examples include: "We are Here to Care for Each Other," "Let Love Surround You," "While Love Remains," "Lighten My Spirit, and "Precious Life." It was easy to understand their lyrics on first listening.

All of these female groups have fans and supporters. They have not been accused of doing anything illegal. They practice freedom of speech. They believe passionately in their causes. But two of the groups promote discrimination and hate, while the other group promotes love.

Daughters of Harriet—from left to right: Dr. Maureen Hearns, Jodi Winnwalker, Lisa Jackert, Robin Rio, Dr. Barbara Dunn. Used with written permission.

Chapter 16

Recapitulation and Coda

H ate music exists and influences the spread of hatred in the world. Whether it is white power music, rockabilly country songs, chants, national anthem verses, rap, country, jazz, fashwave, Jamaican murder music, pornogrind, or any other musical genre, hate music is out there. The common characteristics are evident: direct statements of hate, encouragement of violence, use of frowned-upon language, perpetuation of negative or false stereotypes, criminality, and lack of empathy or remorse. It blames targeted groups for the ills of society, assuming a victim stance. It discriminates against minorities and advocates for maintaining the status quo for those in power. Due to its presence and continued influence, it can be considered a public health issue.

In the hate music halves of my paired stories, there are details about individuals, bands, record companies, and distributors. These stories are representative of hate music but not the whole picture. The hate music industry is continuously changing, and apparently growing. Currently, the 2020 SPLC list of hate groups includes twelve entities labeled as hate music groups. These organizations are primarily distributors or sponsors of music rallies or festivals.

The actual number of performers or bands is estimated, by the ADL, at over one hundred fifty.

Like hate music, music therapy continues to grow. In the United States today, there are over 3,900 members of the AMTA, including roughly 2,300 professional members, 1,000 undergraduate students, 455 graduate students, and 150 members in other categories (e.g. associate, retired, inactive, life, honorary life, affiliate, and patron). The AMTA estimates that, in 2016, music therapy services were provided to approximately 1.6 million clients, in over 96,000 facilities in the nation.

The Certification Board for Music Therapists reports that there are currently approximately eight thousand board-certified music therapists. In the United States, there are over seventy colleges and universities that offer bachelor's degrees in music therapy, thirty-nine that offer master's degrees, and nine that offer doctorate programs.

Hate music is not new. Historic sheet music archives verified that music had been used for many hateful reasons in the past, passing ideologies, thoughts, and feelings across generations.

Hate music exists along a continuum from the least hateful to the most hateful. But even the least hateful—those micro-aggressions—cause harm to innocent people. While frustration, anger, and hatred might legitimately be felt and expressed toward individual bad actors in the world, we must be careful not to blame entire demographic groups. Unfortunately, in 2019, one song ended with a line that claimed we have now been freed to express hatred.

Minorities are not the only targets of hate music. There are also antiwhite songs demonstrating hatred toward white men and women. Examples include songs like "Kill

Whitey" by Menace Clan and "Kill D'White People" by Apache. Jihadist rap music advocates for the murder of infidels. Gangsta rap glorifies criminal behavior. Even the police, whose role is to serve and protect, are attacked by songs such as "Cop Killer," co-written by Ice-T and Ernie C, and "F**k the Police" by N.W.A.

There are valid reasons for groups to feel "left out" and angry. People perceive that the economy works against them. They are opposed to affirmative action because it benefits others—even if it is an attempt to "level the playing field" and provide equality and fairness. Groups are upset that ongoing education is either unavailable to them or, when available, leaves them in debt. Unemployment makes people feel helpless and entitled to jobs held by individuals outside of their demographic. Declining industries result in job losses and make it difficult for some to maintain financial solvency. COVID-19 has turned our world upside down.

To quote Randy Blazak, "Some people are freaking out over the current environment." Perceived societal hardships lead to frustration, anger, and hatred—emotions that we have all felt. Those feelings have also led to hate music.

The themes of hate music are varied. Some hate music advocates for complete separation of races for the safety of all, or to prevent "white genocide." Religious groups are debased, criticized, and attacked—often by members of other religions. Some songs advocate for a racial holy war. Women were sung about in gross terms, sexualized, name-called, and treated with disrespect. Individuals with disabilities are threatened with being pushed down stairs in their wheelchairs or described as undeserving of life. A whole category of murder music advocates for the killing of gays and is defended by religious interpretations. Immigrants are blamed for all of the ills of society, sometimes based on limited bad actors.

Finally, hate music attacks the Jewish "ZOG," or Zionist Organized Government. The belief is that Jews conspire to control the government, financial institutions, and the media. It seems that the only group that has avoided being a target of hate music is white males—the main group in the United States that has maintained a life of privilege and power. My group. A life that I have taken for granted too often.

There are ironies and inconsistencies in some of the thinking expressed in hate music. When one segment of the population criticizes another group for abusing "safety net" or "entitlement" programs, that very segment also participates in those programs. Hate musicians stand by their right to free speech but attack journalists and religious groups, ignoring the constitutional rights of freedom of the press and freedom of religion. Immigrants are demonized by individuals who were immigrants themselves or descended from immigrants.

There were many rationalizations and excuses for hate music. First Amendment rights were often cited. For older songs and compositions, songwriters and composers claimed the zeitgeist defense, that things were different when they wrote their compositions. Others tried to explain their music as satire, humor, or attempts at being comical. In some cases, creators of hate music said that they were just reflecting back what they were seeing in society, trying to get us to think. Some writers of hate music said that their works did not voice their own beliefs, but expressed the viewpoints of characters, either actual or fictional. At times, hatred was presented as a form of self-defense, to protect against white genocide. Finally, some purveyors of hate music claimed a capitalist argument, that they were just meeting the demands of customers. Regardless of the excuses and defenses, the fact remains that hate music has staying power, reinforces victimology, blames others for perceived injustices in the world, and has led to hurting innocent people.

Articles and books describe the causes and beliefs of haters and hate musicians as corrupt, unfounded, immoral, debunked, pseudoscience, misinformed, false, rooted in ignorance, lies, and discredited. In therapy, these inconsistencies in thought are sometimes referred to as "thinking errors" or "cognitive distortions." Even Don Black, the founder of Stormfront, had worried that his site was attracting the wrong type of people.

On the music therapy side of my paired stories, I chose music therapists for a variety of reasons. Felice Wolmut and Vally Weigl were Jewish musicians who survived extreme hatred during the Holocaust. Deforia Lane descended from slaves, and her ancestors and family members experienced racism. Maegan Morrow, Jim Borling, and Ron Borczon used music to help people recover from disasters, including victims of hate crimes. Russell Hilliard and Spencer Hardy represented the LGBTQ+ community and have experienced negative judgments by others.

Lisa Jackert, Tina Haynes, Sandi Holten, Jodi Winnwalker, and Rick Soshensky coexist in parts of the country where hate music is present. Some of these therapists created and directed new businesses, becoming job creators for others. Olga Samsonova-Jellison, Felice Wolmut, and Vally Weigl were all immigrants—Samsonova-Jellison, voluntarily, and the other two involuntarily. Samsonova-Jellison now uses music to help other immigrants and refugees.

Alice and Joe Parente and Celeste Keith have devoted their work to emphasizing abilities over disabilities. The music therapists in my stories provide treatment services to a variety of populations, including mentally ill, medically fragile, couples with fertility issues, veterans, Parkinson's patients, the terminally ill, and those with other special needs.

Music therapist examples encountered difficulties and challenges of their own. They have been discriminated against. Circumstances have forced them to endure great hardships and grief, including the loss of family members and changes in geographic locations. One battled addiction. Two experienced pregnancies out of wedlock and another struggled with infertility. While the music therapy profession continues to improve in its use of well-researched, evidence-based practices, there is always a need for additional, well-designed studies. There are occasional detractors and dissatisfied consumers.

None of these music therapists support white genocide. None of them participate in the control of government, financial institutions, or the media. None of them are race traitors. They are just common, ordinary human beings. They appreciate their rights as citizens to enjoy life, liberty, and the pursuit of happiness. They use music to improve the quality of life of others. They are innocent and, as members of specific groups, unjustly targeted by hate music.

How are hate music and music therapy alike? How are they different?

Both groups have long histories. They are not new, recent fads. Hate has always existed. Humans have also used music to maintain, restore, or improve domains of health, long into the distant past.

Fiscal pressures affect both groups. For haters, they often believe that others hurt the economy or have damaged their personal financial situations. Those affected by changes in the economy look for others to blame and hate. Claiming superiority, they feel entitled to jobs ahead of others. Music therapists must constantly be aware of the economics of healthcare and have been affected by hospital closures, cuts to special education budgets, reduction of forces by healthcare companies, or situational layoffs.

Where hate groups must constantly struggle to survive financially, music therapists must deal with creating jobs, maintaining existing positions, securing payment for their services, or qualifying for insurance and other third-party reimbursement. They can also sometimes blame others—including healthcare corporations, administrators, managers, and politicians—for poor and fiscally irresponsible decisions affecting the healthcare system.

Hate music has expressed hatred toward others, encouraging the use of violence up to and including murder. It demonstrates pride in negativity, a flaunting of disrespect for political correctness, and a lack of compassion, empathy, remorse or decency. Just like the title of a Skrewdriver song, the psychiatric diagnostic manual would label some hate music as antisocial. On the flip side, music therapists use music to help improve lives, including the development of positive social skills.

Hate musicians have no formal, openly shared, agreed-upon policies prohibiting discrimination, codes of ethics, or standards of practice. Many racists devote themselves to the fourteen-word motto: "We must secure the existence of our people and a future for white children." The profession of music therapy has a nondiscrimination policy, a code of ethics, and Professional Standards of Practice. Here are excerpts from those documents:

> "The American Music Therapy Association (AMTA) is committed to a policy of non-discrimination and equal opportunity; fairness, justice, and respect for all persons. AMTA works to ensure that the association, AMTA academic programs and internships, and settings in which music therapists work are safe and welcoming regardless of actual or perceived characteristics, including race ethnicity, color, religion, ancestry, age, national origin, immigration status, socioeconomic status, marital status, language, ability, gender, gender identity, gender expression, sexual orientation, developmental level, health status, or any other personal identity, distinguishing characteristic, or disabilities." (AMTA Non-Discrimination Policy)
>
> "Provide quality client care regardless of the client's race, religion, age, sex, sexual orientation, gender identity or gender expression, ethnic or national origin, disability, health status, socioeconomic status, marital status, or political affiliation." (AMTA Code of Ethics, February 1, 2019)
>
> "Interact with the client in an authentic, ethical, and culturally competent manner that respects privacy, dignity, and human rights." (The Certification Board for Music Therapists, board certification domains)

The two groups differ in gender makeup. Approximately 87 percent of credentialed music therapists are female.

Accurate information about hate music groups is difficult to obtain or predict, but young white men appear to be the largest percentage.

The most striking difference between music therapy and hate music is how the two use music. In the early music therapy textbook, *Music in Therapy* (The Macmillan Company,1968) Dr. William Sears presented theories that he labeled "Processes in Music Therapy." His writing provided an initial framework for the uses of music in therapeutic settings. The next page shows Sears' outline of those functions in the left column, compared to observations about hate music in the right column. Both fields recognize the powers of music.

As I have repeatedly emphasized, hate music is a public health issue. The field of public health emphasizes that prevention of problems can be more efficient and effective than treating them, even when treatment is available.

To prevent hate music, root causes and contributing factors must be considered. Quality improvement professionals use a variety of methods to identify root causes of problems. A fishbone diagram, also called an Ishikawa or cause-and-effect diagram, can be used to brainstorm contributing factors to hate music. I developed Diagram 1, shown on page 364.

PROCESSES IN MUSIC THERAPY	HATE MUSIC
EXPERIENCE WITHIN STRUCTURE	
Music demands time-oriented behavior.	Some haters spend their time listening to hate music.
Music demands reality-oriented behavior.	Some hate music is based on "alternative facts," which have been disputed, disproven, and debunked.
Music demands immediately and continuously objectified behavior.	Some hate music demands making other demographic groups the object of hate.
Music permits ability-ordered behavior.	Some hate music is "ableist" music, attacking "other-abled" and disabled individuals.
Music permits ordering of behavior according to physical response levels.	Some hate music encourages movement or dancing, often resulting in mosh pits and violent responses to others.
Music permits ordering of behavior according to psychological response levels.	Hate music allows behaviors that provide psychological release, including the expression of anger, blame, and victimization.
Music evokes affectively ordered behavior.	Hate music expresses feelings that are not based on "the tender emotions."
Music provokes sensory-elaborated behavior.	Hate music is often experienced under the influence of alcohol or drugs.
Music demands increased sensory usage and discrimination.	Hate music evokes strong negative responses. Listeners often describe feelings of power over others.
Music may elicit extramusical ideas and associations	Hate music encourages discrimination, racism, violence, substance abuse, and other negative ideas and associations.
Music provides for self-expression.	Hate music is protected free speech and is legal, except for certain restrictions.
EXPERIENCE IN SELF-ORGANIZATION	
Music provides compensatory endeavors for the handicapped individual.	Hate music has expressed hatred toward individuals with handicaps.
Music provides opportunities for socially acceptable reward and non-reward.	Hate music is often antisocial and frowned upon by society. However, it has been normalized and rewarded in fringe groups and present in some mainstream music.
Music provides for the enhancement of pride in self.	Hate music reinforces ideas such as "white pride, worldwide," and is a source of pride within hate groups.
Music provides for successful experiences	Hate music sometimes elicits a false sense of increase in self-esteem.
Music provides for feeling needed by others.	Hate music is used as a recruitment tool for hate groups and to raise funds for the operation of those groups.
Music provides for enhancement of esteem by others.	Knowing hate music provides an "in" into hate groups. Members of hate groups have expressed feeling empowered.

PROCESSES IN MUSIC THERAPY	HATE MUSIC
EXPERIENCE IN RELATING TO OTHERS	
Music provides means by which self-expression is socially acceptable.	Hate music is considered socially acceptable within hate organizations but not to the general public.
Music provides opportunity for individual choice of response in groups.	Members of hate groups allow responses to hate music to be acceptable when they assemble.
Music provides opportunities for acceptance of responsibility to self and others.	Hate music reinforces loyalty between members of hate groups but disloyalty to non-group members.
Music provides for developing self-directed behavior.	Giving up hate music could aid in recovering from hate.
Music provides for developing other-directed behavior.	Some hate music encourages violence toward others, discrimination, and negative behaviors toward others.
Music enhances verbal and nonverbal social interaction and communication.	Hate music is prevalent in the social environments and communication mechanisms of hate groups.
Music provides for experiencing cooperation and competition in socially acceptable forms.	Most hate music is socially unacceptable, except within hate groups. It is considered to be generally extreme but is also found in mainstream music.
Music provides entertainment and recreation necessary in the general therapeutic environment.	Hate music goes beyond entertainment. Its use in therapeutic settings can be positive or negative.
Music provides for learning realistic social skills and personal behavior patterns acceptable in institutional and community peer groups.	Opposition to hate music can be considered a reason for exclusion from hate groups and their selective communities.

*Left column from Sears, William W., "Processes in Music Therapy," published in Gaston E Thayer(ed), *Music in Therapy*, The Macmillan Company, New York, 1968, pp 30-44.

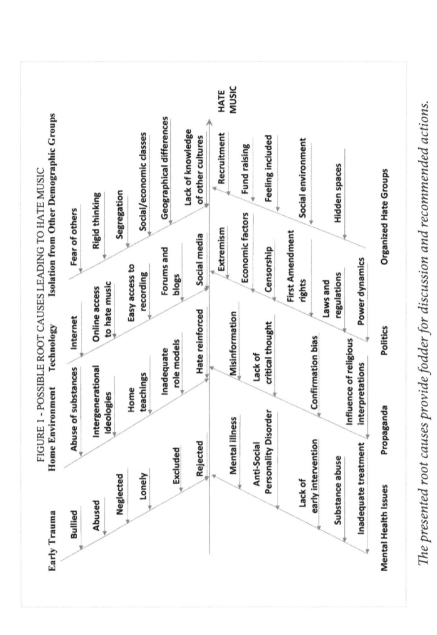

The presented root causes provide fodder for discussion and recommended actions.

Address Childhood and Adolescent Trauma

In Chapter 1, I stated that this is an anti-hate book, but it is not an anti-person book. Many hate musicians experienced traumatic events early in their lives. As previously described, they felt marginalized. Some came from broken homes or dysfunctional families. Domestic abuse, and/or excessive drinking or drugging were sometimes present. Some of them felt like failures.

For men, it was a feeling of emasculation. They were seeking a place to belong and be accepted—to live up to societal pressures to "become a man." Both males and females wanted to be involved in something that they viewed as important. They were interested in the economy, politics, and activism. They were angry and looking for others to blame for perceived injustices in life.

To prevent recruitment by hate groups, a countermeasure is to identify those who are vulnerable and involve them early in non-hate activities. Quick identification and intervention are essential. Make them feel welcomed and included. Participating in musical performance ensembles is an excellent option, but not the only one.

This book has focused on music therapy, but there is a plethora of other music vocations, both amateur and professional. Songwriters, composers, recording engineers, church choir directors, orchestra directors, music teachers, dancers, etc. can all help identify and engage troubled individuals. Members of any other vocation or avocation can do the same. Teachers, coaches, hobbyists, clergy members, therapists, artists, and others must be on the lookout for traumatized, disenfranchised youth. Spot them, reach out to them, and involve them.

My research convinced me that it is wrong to characterize all members of hate music groups as ogres—antisocial, sociopathic, psychopathic, evil, mentally ill, chemically dependent, lower class, uneducated, or morally corrupt—even if those descriptors fit some of them. To hate them is to re-traumatize them and is a major barrier to helping them change. To reach generalizations about them as a group is to do exactly what we ask them not to do.

That is not to excuse their spreading of hatred and violence in the world. It is still hard for their victims to forgive them, and we must support the victims. Is grace, love, and forgiveness even possible? To me, it just seems hypocritical to hate haters back. We all hate to some degree but, taken to a violent extreme—being outside normal variation—spreading hate in the world is usually destructive and unproductive. It may be viewed as benefiting one group, but the whole of humanity suffers. Many haters eventually realize this for themselves, while some need to be convinced.

Some hate musicians grow out of their beliefs. They mature, learn, and change. Some are lovingly confronted by spouses or other family members who have not given up on them. For those who have children, they see the innocence in their children's eyes and choose to break the cycle of hatred that was passed on to them. For others, they recognize the falsehoods and hypocrisy of their causes through self-study and experience. They make a friend who is gay. They have a family member who is disabled. They get married. They find an occupation. Life is therapy.

Tim Zaal—the former neo-Nazi punk who almost killed a gay kid—elaborated on the transformation that led to his involvement with the Museum of Tolerance in Los Angeles:

"I had a child and something shifted. One day I was with my son in a grocery store and he said, 'Look daddy, there's a big black n****r.' I realized it didn't make me feel good or powerful. I was shamed. The violence wasn't working anymore. Slowly I removed myself from that lifestyle. I still had a very closed mind-set, but then I started to mix with and trust people from different backgrounds and ethnicities. These were people I once would have perceived as enemies who now accepted me for who I was. Their tolerance in a way re-humanized me."

Address Mental Illness and Use/Misuse of Substances

WE MUST SUPPORT THE DEVELOPMENT AND USE OF INDI-cated mental health and substance abuse treatment services. There is some evidence that mass murderers such as Dylann Roof, Connor Betts, Wade Michael Page, Chris Harper-Mercer, and Jared Lee Loughner spent time listening to or producing hate music but also had mental illness issues. Their behaviors were noticed by others. Why weren't they receiving needed services?

Individuals who suffer from mental illness often have co-morbidities or confounding conditions. In relation to hate music, misuse or abuse of substances is often present. The organization Life After Hate (LAH) has been successful helping people exit from hate groups, because its staffers include "formers"—previous haters who have disavowed those beliefs. In my work with addicts and alcoholics, I have seen a similar phenomenon: those entering recovery trust those who have succeeded in their own recovery programs.

LAH has adopted a recovery philosophy that is similar to the 12 Steps of Alcoholics Anonymous.

There are some similarities between individuals who are trying to give up drugs or alcohol, and those who are trying to give up hate. Sometimes, to succeed, they need to give up both. Stories about hate musicians described heavy alcohol consumption and drug use. More evidence of the hypocrisy of some hate movements. Once individuals have broken from their past ideologies and behaviors, they must learn how to deal with backsliding and how to prevent relapse. This is often a long process, with setbacks along the way. Their lives are threatened, and some are labeled as "race traitors."

TABLE 2 presents some behaviors that relate to those who are struggling with addictions. When applied to haters and hate musicians, these same strategies could help them recover and avoid relapse. Music is a potent tool to illustrate and teach recovery principles, form new associations, reframe cognitive distortions, and reinforce new behaviors. Giving up hate should include giving up hate music, and that music can be replaced with music of hope. As a first line of this book stated, it may be painful to have a swastika tattoo removed from your neck, but it may be equally painful to give up your preferred music.

TABLE 2
*Relapse prevention behaviors**

NON-RELAPSERS	RELAPSERS
1. Have developed a repertoire of coping skills: decision-making, cognitive restructuring, refuting, stress reduction, communication, assertiveness, feeling expression	1. Either don't have or don't use coping skills
2. Have a high degree of self-efficacy; believe in self; attribute lapses to the situation	2. Don't believe in self; attribute lapses to self-failure
3. Attend and involve themselves in a recovery program; get a sponsor; ask for help; work the program	3. Don't work a program; try to do it alone
4. Positive attitude; handle depression; have a "can do" attitude; commit to change	4. Negative attitude; tendency to be depressed; pessimistic; "can't do" or "won't do" mindset; lack commitment
5. Goal is abstinence	5. Goal is controlled use
6. Bounce back from lapses; a lapse is a one-time event	6. Turn lapses into relapses
7. Proximal focus; "one day at a time"	7. Distal focus; are overwhelmed by maintenance for long periods
8. Marital and family cohesion; healthy relationships	8. Marital, family, and relationship discord
9. Have a developed support system beyond recovery program	9. Limited network
10. Avoid or reframe old cues; establish new cues and associations	10. Respond to old cues
11. Attend aftercare	11. Drop out of aftercare
12. Reward themselves for successful change	12. Punish themselves for failure; don't give themselves credit for success
13. Participate in a program of physical self-care (exercise, sleep, nutrition)	13. Sedentary; don't exercise; poor eating habits; poor sleeping habits
14. Have a spiritual life; attend church	14. No sense of spirituality; do not attend church
15. Employed	15. Unemployed
16. Talk focused on behavior changes	16. Talk focused on drug/alcohol "war" stories; retelling stories about drinking/drugging

*From Ficken, Ted, "Music Therapy with Chemically Dependent Clients: A Relapse Prevention Model," in *Music Therapy and Addictions (Aldridge, David and Fachner, Jörg, editors),* Jessica Kingsley Publishers, London, 2010, page 110. Used with written permission.

Interrupt the Cycle of Familial, Intergenerational Hate

It may be intrusive and difficult to deal with what happens in the homes of hating families, but there are some possible actions. We must be aware of those around us. If we notice parents abusing, neglecting, or abandoning their children, we must report our observations to appropriate authorities. We must offer support to victims of hate and hate crimes.

If we hear children making hateful and racist statements, we must question where they are learning those ideas. Perhaps we need more regulations on home-schooling, with more oversight of curriculum. We can also role model a more inclusive environment and present opposing viewpoints in respectful ways. We can invite both parents and children to participate in non-hateful activities, groups, clubs, and communities. As mentioned above, feeling included may be all it takes for them to reconsider the hate in their lives.

Consider New Information

Propaganda must be understood and confronted. Yes, there is fake news, which is why we should gather information from a multitude of sources and then apply critical and analytic thought to evaluate what we see and hear. Journalists have ethical standards they are trained to follow. Don't watch the same news program each night. Instead, rotate between numerous sites and sources to learn different perspectives. Read contrasting books, especially those that disagree with your current opinions. Conduct fact-checking. Challenge your own biases, as well as the biases of others.

It may be enlightening to play "point/counterpoint" with yourself, or others. Make lists of pros and cons about issues. Understand the complexities. Become better informed. As Bob Dylan wrote, "Know your song well before you start singing."

If we have adopted the beliefs of our parents, our social group, our church, or even a hate group, we must step back and ask questions. We may confirm those beliefs, but it won't hurt to challenge them and, in some cases, refute them with new information.

We should support freedom of religion, but there are clear examples of intersections between hate music and various religions. There are anti-Semitic songs, Jihadist rap songs, and songs claiming religious superiority. In the first several months of 2019, there were attacks on two mosques in New Zealand, the burning of multiple black churches in Louisiana, mass casualty events at Catholic Churches in Sri Lanka, and shootings at a synagogue in San Diego. These examples are recent, but there have been many other cases of hate being brought to places of worship.

Does hate music contribute? Did hate music play a role in radicalizing the white nationalist in New Zealand? Most people I know go to their place of worship to practice their faith, and to denounce evil. I think that religious leaders can, and should, play a role in limiting hatred in the world. We should demand this.

Support Technology Standards and
Regulations Opposed to Discrimination

THERE HAVE BEEN COUNTERMEASURES TRYING TO LIMIT THE availability of hate music over the internet. The following companies have taken steps to identify and eliminate hate music from their sites: GoDaddy, Google, Apple, Spotify, Facebook, Reddit, Instagram, Rainbo Records, BandCamp, SoundCloud, Deezer, CD Baby, and Amazon. However, with the thousands of songs available on these and other music retail and streaming sites, it is often difficult to screen and remove all hate music. Some sites depend on their customers and listeners to self-identify offensive and objectionable music. Others have tried to use algorithms to search the lyrics of songs that they carry, to locate songs that contain specific words associated with hate, racism, criminality, or violence.

I wrote to several online music retailers to find out how they handle hate music. Do they refuse to carry it? Do they rely on their customers to identify it? Do they support free speech, with no exceptions? I wrote to iTunes, eMusic, Napster, Rhapsody, Tidal, Symphonic, MondoTunes, iMusician, TopSpin, and TuneCore. Of those, only TuneCore responded. The following language was included in the Terms and Conditions for using its service:

> "The Site and Services may be used and accessed solely for lawful purposes.
>
> You agree to abide by all applicable local, state, national and foreign laws, treatises and regulations in connection with our use of the Site and Services, including, without limitation, applicable common law, all relevant statutes, and the rules and regula-

tions of the Office of Foreign Assets Control of the U.S. Department of the Treasury."

And… agreement to not:

"…upload, submit, post, email, or otherwise transmit, via the Site or Services, and Recordings or other materials that are, in the sole opinion of Company, unlawful, harmful, threatening, obscene, harassing, defamatory or hateful or that contain objects or symbols of hate, invade the privacy of any third party, contain nudity (including, without limitation, any pornography, erotica, child pornography or child erotica) are deceptive, threatening, abusive, inciting of unlawful action, defamatory, libelous, vulgar or violent or constitute hate speech or are otherwise objectionable."

We should report observed hate music to our preferred music download sites and support them in establishing similar anti-hate language in their service's Terms and Conditions.

Be Politically Involved

I SUPPORT THE FIRST AMENDMENT AND DISAGREE WITH most censorship when it comes to hate music. Listening to hate music, for purposes related to this book, helped me understand the beliefs and perspectives of others. I was not persuaded to like and support hate music, but now I am better informed. It is important to protect all voices, even if we disagree with what they are saying.

We should all support organizations that use music to spread love and positivity in the world. I have mentioned several in this book, but here is a partial list, with some additions: Krip Hop Nation, Musicians Without Borders, empower Music & Arts (including Posi Music), Turn it Down, The Playing for Change Foundation, Hungry for Music, MusiCares (a Grammy organization), Process Theatre, and the AMTA. I am sure there are others. Imagine a clearinghouse to communicate between these organizations and coordinate positive legal, political, and musical actions.

Music can have a strong impact in many domains—cultural, political, cognitive, physical, social, spiritual, etc. It has been used by politicians in their election campaigns. It can be so influential, both in good ways and in bad ways, that censorship of music has often been attempted. For example, in Nazi Germany, surrounding World War II, music by certain, non-Aryan composers and musicians was prohibited.

Joseph Goebbels set rules for the use of music and required Germans to only use Aryan music that either promoted German nationalism or glorified Adolf Hitler. A negative use of music included using it to give comfort and hope to Jewish people being transferred to concentration camps, followed by use of music at those camps to humiliate, deceive, and torture. The music of Richard Wagner had such high prominence in Nazi Germany that, after the war, his music was not allowed to be performed in Israel for thirty-three years. Dictators the world over have censored music to influence and control their subjects and citizens.

Censorship can take several forms and can be driven by issues related to morality, racial concerns, value gaps between groups and generations, and fear. Individuals can exercise censorship by refusing to purchase music released by certain artists, by not buying tickets to see specific acts, or by destroying previously enjoyed music. Retailers can refuse to carry or sell music by controversial musicians, but this could infringe on the free speech rights of those musicians to express themselves.

The Federal Communications Commission can also sanction some music activities, such as canceling a performance because a band's music or name, invokes anti-religious sentiments. A radio or television station could be fined for playing a song that is judged to be indecent or obscene. In contrast to this, MTV, when it first arrived on the music scene, was criticized for not presenting black artists, another form of censorship. That changed for the first time when MTV began showing music videos by Michael Jackson. In 1955, the Juvenile Delinquency and Crime Commission in Houston, Texas, banned more than thirty songs, with heavy representation by black musicians.

Government involvement in censorship is sometimes perceived as interfering with First Amendment protections. The wives of several prominent politicians and businessmen created the Parents Music Resource Center (PMRC) in 1985. The founders included Tipper Gore, wife of Senator and Vice President Al Gore; Susan Baker, wife of Treasury Secretary James Baker; Sally Nevius, wife of former Washington City Council Chairman, John Nevius; and Pam Howar, wife of Washington realtor Raymond Howar.

The group pressured the recording industry to adopt a rating system. It also pressured radio and television companies to not broadcast some objectionable songs, recommended that record companies publish song lyrics on albums, advocated for parental warning stickers on records and CDs, encouraged keeping music with explicit covers under the counters at retail outlets, suggested reassessing concert contracts for artists who performed songs that expressed violence or drug use and successfully lobbied for the removal of some rock music and publications from some businesses, to avoid their negative influence on children.

Hearings about parental advisory stickers were held in Congress, with opposing viewpoints expressed by both musicians, representatives of the PMRC, and others. One witness, Dr. Joe Stuessy, testified that heavy metal music "had as one of its central elements the element of hatred." The PMRC published a list titled, "The Filthy Fifteen," which included songs that were deemed as promoting sexual activity, violence, drug use, or occult practices. Interestingly, none of the songs on the list represented hate music, despite neo-Nazi Skinhead music being present at that time.

Even before the congressional hearings concluded, the Recording Industry Association of America, agreed to place parental advisory stickers on some recordings. The actions taken by the PMRC were viewed by many musicians as violating First Amendment rights, and the organization and its leaders experienced a strong backlash, in the form of anti-BMRC and anti-Tipper Gore messages in the lyrics of some songs and protests at concerts. In the United States, the government attempted another form of censorship when a proposed law in 2006, which did not pass, tried to limit the government's funding of certain arts projects, including music. The law would have prevented funding of "material which denigrates the objects or beliefs of the adherents of a particular religion or nonreligion, or which denigrates, debases, or reviles a person, group, or class of citizens on the basis of race, creed, sex, handicap, age, or national origin."

What did pass was language that directed the National Endowment for the Arts (NEA), a government-supported agency, to consider, in its reviews of grant applications, "general standards of decency and respect for the diverse beliefs and values of the American public." Notice that the language asked for consideration, without requiring compliance.

The Supreme Court also endorsed the NEA's use of advisory committees comprised of members from "diverse geographic, ethnic, and aesthetic backgrounds." In the musical world, where market demands and profiteers sometimes drive popular music, the NEA has been viewed as a counterbalance, to allow greater freedom in music expression and a protector of First Amendment rights.

In the 1989 Supreme Court case named *Ward v. Rock Against Racism,* the court ruled, "music, as a form of expression and communication, is protected under the First Amendment." The court added, "Music is one of the oldest forms of human expression. From Plato's discourse in the Republic to the totalitarian state in our own times, rulers have known its capacity to appeal to the intellect and to the emotions, and have censored music compositions to serve the needs of the state."

Music therapists are not exempt from music censorship in their work. Kendall Joplin and Abbey Dvorak, from the University of Kansas, surveyed forty-two board-certified music therapists working in behavioral health settings. The researchers were interested in whether or not the respondents censored music and, if so, what musical or other factors led to that censorship. They defined censorship in music therapy as "music therapists refraining from using or redirecting clients away from using certain lyrics, themes, songs, or genres of music before (i.e. therapist planning), during (i.e. therapist facilitating), and/or after (i.e., censoring clients' music or verbalizations after they have been stated) expression."

The survey results showed that the majority of music therapists censored music, depending on the music's themes, lyrics, or genres. Reasons for the censorship included the reactions of clients, reactions of other therapy group members, observed discomfort or emotional distress, or an attempt to avoid a negative impact on the therapeutic relationship between a client and the music therapist.

Twenty-five percent of the respondents also stated that their personal biases influenced their decisions to use or not use certain music. These biases included their own religious or philosophical beliefs, discomfort with the musical content, or their clinical assessment that the client would not benefit from using certain music.

At many clinical sites, facility policies may prohibit the use of some music. For example, songs that touch on drug use might be prohibited in a substance abuse rehabilitation program. The study did not include specific questions related to censoring hate music, although some of the stated reasons for censorship included the uses of profanity, derogatory labels, and name-calling, references to violence, or misogyny.

It might be possible to address hate music without censorship. In his book, *The Cure for Hate,* Tony McAleer, a co-founder of Life After Hate (LAH), described a project that LAH participates in with an organization named Possible. The joint project, We Counter Hate, uses Artificial Intelligence to identify Twitter posts that are designated as egregious hate speech. An LAH representative verifies that the flagged tweets are hate speech, and then a reply is connected to the post, stating that if the post is left up or retweeted, a donation will be made to a nonprofit organization combating hate. Results showed a 48 percent reduction in retweets and an 18 percent self-deletion rate by the tweet authors. Could this same approach be applied to hate music on the internet?

Since politics can be seen as a possible root cause of hate music, a recommended action is to vote for candidates who are not supported by hate groups.

Learn About Your Culture and the Cultures of Others

BOTH CURRENT AND FORMER MEMBERS OF HATE GROUPS, including hate musicians, have been interviewed by researchers. Findings indicated that many of them had very limited exposure to, or contact with, the groups that they hated.

Anti-Semitic musicians did not know any Jews. Antiblack musicians could not name any African American friends. Antiwhite musicians did not hang around with white people. Some misogynists had limited experiences with women. Anti-LGBTQ+ musicians isolated themselves from members of the gay community. Musicians against individuals with cognitive, sensory, or physical differences did not personally know anyone with disabilities. And while some members of hate groups advocate for segregation or separation, one successful approach to decreasing hate between groups is to bring them together to get to know each other.

Consider some recovering haters. Christian Picciolini discovered that he liked customers that he met at his record store, despite his previous hatred of them. Frank Meeink, who is white, was invited to join a black Bible study group in prison. Following his release, he was hired by a Jewish businessman who shared his love of ice hockey and treated him with respect. He, too, discovered that he had hated those groups for no good reason.

TJ Leyden, after discovering the falsehood of his hatred against others, became a national speaker for the Simon Wiesenthal Center—a Jewish organization. Bryon Widner survived extensive surgery to have his hateful, violent, racist tattoos removed and now speaks at anti-racism conferences.

Another story supported the need to expose ourselves to other cultures. It conveyed how a black blues musician named Daryl Davis set about meeting with white supremacists, one-on-one, to create change. Davis had been the only black musician in a country band, playing gigs at venues serving mostly white customers. After one lounge performance, a white audience member complimented his music. Davis joined the man at his table for a drink—Davis choosing cranberry juice. The man shared that it was the first time he had sat down to have a drink with a black man. When asked why, it was shared that he was a member of the KKK.

From that single encounter, Davis was inspired to sit down with additional KKK members, sometimes in dangerous situations. Initially, the KKK members were willing to answer Davis's questions but never asked for his opinion. Eventually, a change occurred, and his interviewees became his interviewers. He now claims that, through civil conversation, many of the KKK members have left that organization, even giving Davis their hoods and robes. He was criticized by some black friends for "sitting down with the enemy," but his approach was very effective. By bringing people together for polite, respectful conversation, change was possible.

The story of Derek Black—as told in Eli Saslow's book *Rising out of Hatred: The Awakening of a Former White Nationalist* (Doubleday, 2018)—provided additional evidence that people grow, learn, and change. Derek is the only son of Don Black, a well-known leader of the white nationalist movement and a founder of the Stormfront website and forum.

Derek, who was homeschooled, followed in his father's footsteps and became a leading advocate and spokesperson for the white nationalist cause. But when he went away to college, he made friends from different races and was confronted by fellow students about his beliefs. According to Saslow's book, Derek kept an open mind, studied history, considered research and counterarguments, listened to the viewpoints of others, and finally, with great courage and personal cost, denounced his previous beliefs. His story proved that education and civil discourse could be a strategy for dealing with hate.

I found another example of a white nationalist musician who decided to give up those beliefs. Felix Benneckenstein was recruited into a far-right extremist group at the age of thirteen, in Germany. He liked the music, he played guitar, and he wrote convincing white nationalist, neo-Nazi anthems. But he had nagging doubts. He has a brother with Down syndrome, and what the Nazis did to disabled individuals bothered him. After conflicts between neo-Nazi groups, he found himself in jail.

He is quoted as saying, "To realize that everything you've done to yourself and others in the past years was built on lies is a bitter moment." He left the white nationalist movement and now works to help others in Germany leave hate behind through an organization named EXIT.

One recommended action is to visit museums and historical sites that are reminders of the damage done by extremism and hatred. For example, Derek Black and Tony McAleer traveled to European concentration camps and studied the truth about the Holocaust. I also visited Bergen-Belsen concentration camp, where Anne Frank died. The experience was informative, gut-wrenching, and emotionally moving.

In Washington, DC, visit the Holocaust Museum, the African American Museum, the Native American Museum, and others. In Montgomery, Alabama, visit the Legacy Museum: From Enslavement to Mass Incarceration. Among other things, the museum documents the history of lynchings in our country. There are countless museums and historical sites in the United States that tell the true stories of the negative effects of hatred. We must continually educate ourselves.

Take Action if You Observe Hate Groups in Your Environment

RESEARCH SHEDS SOME LIGHT ON HOW INDIVIDUALS GET into extremist hate groups, but also how they sometimes change and exit those groups. Some members of hate groups are dedicated to the ideology of a group, while others were attracted for other reasons, or solely because they wanted to be a part of any group—with, at least initially, less devotion to a particular cause.

Some are recruited through organizations, such as the KKK, neo-Nazi skinhead groups, websites like Stormfront or VDARE, or other lurking, extremist groups. Others were encouraged to join by family members, older friends, or members of the opposite sex. Hate music was often used as a recruitment and retention tool, to convince members to serve "the cause," as well as a way to raise funds for hate-related activities. If you observe hate music in your community, share your observations with authorities, the press, and anti-hate groups.

There are organizations devoted to preventing the growth of hate groups and helping individuals exit from those situations. Both the SPLC and the ADL track and confront hate groups. Become members and support them, both through donations and via communication. Supporting exit organizations is also a must. Examples include Exit USA—Life After Hate (LAH), The Forgiveness Project, Not in Our Town, Leaving the World of Hate—Homeland Security, Hate Group Disengagement—Los Angeles County, Serve2Unite (Arno Michaelis' organization), StrHateTalk (TJ Leyden's consulting firm), and One People's Project.

In particular, the LAH organization provides services to individuals wanting to leave hate behind. LAH was formed by former haters, including Christian Picciolini, TJ Leyden, Arno Michaelis, Tony McAleer, Angela King, and Frank Meeink—most of whom have written books about their journeys, including the influence of hate music in the hate movement. LAH also offers help to women via leaders like Angela King, who serves as LAH's program director.

Interestingly, the Trump administration, shortly after taking office, discontinued a $400,000 grant to LAH, which had been awarded during the Obama presidency. The money was quickly replaced and exceeded by a crowdfunding effort, including a $50,000 donation from quarterback

Colin Kaepernick and over $200,000 raised by efforts of TV personality Samantha Bee.

Hate groups use a variety of methods to raise money for themselves or their causes. Some form associations or clubs that require the payment of membership fees or reoccurring dues—all with levels that increase for additional benefits, such as subscriptions to publications. Websites are established, asking for voluntary donations. Hate merchandise is sold, including Confederate flags, belt buckles, patches, hats, jewelry, tattoo templates, banners, weapons, and clothing.

To purchase items, credit cards have been accepted in the past, but now many credit card services, such as Apple Pay, have denied or canceled the availability of those methods to hate groups. More frequently, cash, certified checks, or mail orders are required. Other methods of fund-raising have included donations from wealthy benefactors, which is rare; crowdfunding or crowdsourcing, which has been used mostly to raise small amounts of money, often for one-time projects; Bitcoin or other cryptocurrencies; and criminal activity, including the selling of drugs.

Selling hate music has been a major source of funds for hate organizations. One preventive measure is to interrupt their ability to sustain their finances and, instead, to offer financial support to anti-hate groups. Recognizing music as a funding source, even an anti-hate group like the SPLC had a group of musicians produce and record an album to raise funds for itself.

In the story about Behold Barbarity Records and Distro in Minnesota, I mentioned Daniel Koehler at the German Institute on Radicalization and De-Radicalization Studies (also on the faculty at George Washington University, where I teach). Koehler provided several references about the uses of music by violent extremist groups and how music is used in the radicalization process. He stated that there are "literally libraries full of" research on that topic. He also said that he was not aware of research of music used in de-radicalization. Perhaps it is time for that approach.

I read about hate music as a tool exploited by mostly far-right extremists, but what about far-left extremists? I found no evidence that Antifa groups were using music as a way to present their beliefs. Antifa should consider the power of music, as a replacement for its uses of violence.

I thought about Project Schoolyard, conducted by Panzerfaust Records. If they could distribute CDs of hate music to "create racists" in middle schools and high schools, a countermeasure would be to distribute CDs of songs offering alternatives. Imagine some of the best songwriters in the world coming together to write tunes addressing all of the bones on the fishbone diagram of possible root causes.

Tony McAleer, a LAH founder, wrote about his recovery in his book *The Cure for Hate*. He argued that you can't change people by arguing with them and appealing to their intellect. He advocated for appealing to their heart. Music is an excellent medium for this purpose. I would love to see LAH and the AMTA conduct a joint project to develop anti-hate measures, with special music resources for use in therapeutic settings.

I look forward to learning more about hate music and how to address it. In closing, now that I have learned more about hate music by listening to countless examples, I feel the need to remind us all of alternative messages. Here are some pro-love songs to add to your playlist: "All You Need is Love" (Beatles), "Love is the Answer" (Todd Rundgren), "Shower the People" (James Taylor), "What the World Needs

Now" (Jackie DeShannon), "Get Together" (Youngbloods),
"Work Together" (Wilbert Harrison), "I Believe in Music"
(Mac Davis), "Music is Love" (David Crosby), "Love and
Mercy" (Brian Wilson).

What would you add?

REFERENCES

Abhat, Divya (2017, March 10). Inside the Heads of People Who Don't Like Music. *The Atlantic*. Retrieved March 10, 2018 from https://www.the-atlantic.com/health/archive/2017/03/please-don't-stop-the-music-i-don't-really-mind/519099

AboutDisability.com *(n.d.)*. Disability in Popular Song. *AboutDisability.com*. Retrieved February 11, 2018 from http://www.aboutdisability.com/archive/song.html

About Soleilmoon. *Soleilmoon.com*. Retrieved October 29, 2018 from https://www.soleilmoon.com/about/

About Hate Crimes. *The U.S. Department of Justice*. Retrieved December 1, 2017 from https://www.justice.gov/crt/hate-crime-laws

About Heritage Connection. *Heritage Connection Band.com*. Retrieved April 9, 2017 from http://www.heritageconnectionband.com/About.htm

About Maegan Morrow (n.d.). Retrieved July 30, 2017, from http://maegan-morrow.com/about/

Abreu, Daniel (2016, May 21). Dancehall's Proliferation of Homophobia. *Medium.com*. Retrieved April 10, 2019 from https://medium.com/writ-ings-on-whatever-i-wanted/dancehalls-proliferation-of-homophobia-a4c4f88d2f2f

'Advance Australia Fair' and 'The White Australia Policy' (2014, September 26) *National Unity Government*. Retrieved March 11, 2018 from http://nationalunitygovernment.org/content/was-advance-australia-fair-writ-ten-white-people

Afternoon Lulz in the Classifieds: Gutsy Lawyer Wanted! (2010, July 10) *The Lamp*. Retrieved May 12, 2018 from https://ladylibertyslamp.wordpress.com/2010/07/10/afternoon-lulz-in-the-classifieds-gutsy-lawyer-wanted/

Aigen, Kenneth, DA, LCAT, MT-BC and Hunter, Bryan, Ph.D., LCAT, MT-BC. The Creation of the American Music Therapy Association: Two Personal Perspectives, in *Music Therapy Perspectives*, 2018, Volume 26, Number 2, Oxford University Press

Acker, Lizzy. (2019, January 9). Jeremy Christian's vocabulary and related ideas, explained. *The Oregonian*. Retrieved July 4, 2020 from https://www.oregonlive.com/portland/2017/06/jeremy_christians_vocabulary_a.html

Alberta Street History. *Alberta Main Street.org*. Retrieved October 29, 2017 from http://albertamainst.org/about/history/

Aldridge, David and Fachner, Jörg. Music Therapy and Addictions. *Jessica Kingsley Publishers*, London, UK, 2010

Allison, Natalie (2017, November19). Are white nationalist groups meeting in state parks? Tennessee won't say. *USA Today*. Retrieved January 20, 2018 from https://www.usatoday.com/story/news/nation-now/2017/11/19/white-nationalist-groups-meeting-state-parks-tennessee-wont-say/879469001/

Allison, Natalie (2017, November 19). Why white nationalists are descending on Tennessee's state parks. *USA Today*. Retrieved January 20, 2018 from https://www.tennessean.com/story/news/2017/11/19/forced-out-private-venues-white-nationalists-descending-tennessee-state-parks/830444001/

American Music Therapy Association. *Music therapy.org* retrieved from https://www.musictherapy.org (includes personal emails from Jane Creagan, Director of Professional Programs)

American Music Therapy Association (2017, November 16-19). A Mindful Approach to Music Therapy (2017 annual conference program). Write-up about Deforia Lane, page 6.

Andersen, Eric. Eyes of the Immigrant (lyrics). *Flashlyrics.com*. Retrieved December 15, 2018 from https://www.flashlyrics.com/lyrics/eric-andersen/eyes-of-the-immigrant-00

Andrews, Travis M (2017, August 23). Yes, neo-Nazis have rock bands, too. They've been around for decades. *Washington Post*. Retrieved August 23, 2017 from https://www.washingtonpost.com/news/morning-mix/wp/2017/08/23/yes-neo-nazis-have-rock-bands-too-theyve-been-around-for-decades/?noredirect=on&utm_term=.9c98e9f14937

Angry White Men (January 5, 2019.) White Nationalist YouTuber 'Philosophicat' Made a Neo-Folk Album with the Founder of a Skinhead Band. *Angry White Men.org*. Retrieved February 12, 2019 from https://angrywhitemen.org/2019/01/05/white-nationalist-youtuber-philosophicat-made-a-neo-folk-album-with-the-founder-of-a-skinhead-band/

Anti Defamation League (n.d.). Deadly Shooting at the Tree of Life Synagogue. Retrieved December 1, 2018 from https://www.adl.org/education/educator-resources/lesson-plans/deadly-shooting-at-the-tree-of-life-synagogue

Anti Defamation League (n.d.). A Brief History of the Disability Rights Movement.. Retrieved March 5, 2019 from https://www.adl.org/education/resources/backgrounders/disability-rights-movement

Anti Defamation League (2009) What Can We Do About Hate? Retrieved August 17, 2018 from https://www.adl.org/media/2269/download

Anti Defamation League (n.d.). ADL Troubled by B.o.B Rap Lyrics Promoting Anti-Semitic Conspiracy and Invoking Holocaust Denier by Name. Retrieved September 17, 2017 from https://www.adl.org/news/press-releases/adl-troubled-by-bob-rap-lyrics-promoting-anti-semitic-conspiracy-and-invoking

Anti Defamation League (n.d..) Bigots Who Rock: an ADL List of Hate Music Groups. Retrieved March 3, 2017 from http://archive.is/UIbA5

Anti Defamation League (2013, January 8). Deafening Hate: The Revival of Resistance Records. Retrieved February 15, 2019 from https://www.adl.org/news/article/deafening-hate-the-revival-of-resistance-records

Anti Defamation League (2017). Funding Hate: How White Supremacists Raise Their Money. Retrieved April 27, 2019 from https://www.adl.org/resources/reports/funding-hate-how-white-supremacists-raise-their-money

Anti Defamation League (2017, February 21). Google Deletes White Supremacist App From Play Store. Retrieved (n.d.). from https://www.adl.org/blog/google-deletes-white-supremacist-app-from-play-store

Anti Defamation League (n.d.). Volksfront.. Retrieved January 20, 2018 from https://www.adl.org/resources/profiles/volksfront

Anti Defamation League (n.d.). Hate on DisplayTM Hate Symbols Database. Retrieved August 20, 2018 from https://www.adl.org/education-and-resources/resource-knowledge-base/hate-symbols

Anti Defamation League (2013, February 12). Hate Rock online: New Tools for Racists and Anti-Semites. Retrieved (n.d.). from https://www.adl.org/news/article/hate-rock-online-new-tool-for-racists-and-anti-semites

Anti Defamation League (2012, August 8). Hate with a Beat: White Power Music. Retrieved September 17, 2017 from https://www.cnn.com/2012/08/08/opinion/nasatir-white-power-bands/index.html

Anti Defamation League (2014, November 24). Music Videos Enhance Violent Anti-Jewish Messages Online. Retrieved September 17, 2017 from https://www.adl.org/blog/music-videos-enhance-violent-anti-jewish-messages-online

Anti Defamation League (2009, December 17). Neo-Nazi Tries to Reach Youth through Music Downloads. Retrieved September 17, 2017 from https://www.adl.org/news/article/neo-nazi-tries-to-reach-youth-through-music-downloads

Anti Defamation League (n.d.). Rock Against Communism.. Retrieved October 30, 2017 from https://www.adl.org/education/references/hate-symbols/rock-against-communism

Anti Defamation League (n.d). Skrewdriver. Retrieved October 28, 2018 from https://www.adl.org/education/references/hate-symbols/skrewdriver

Anti Defamation League (n.d.). The Sounds of Hate: The White Power Music Scene in the United States in 2012. Retrieved October 28, 2018 from https://www.adl.org/sites/default/files/documents/assets/pdf/combating-hate/Sounds-of-Hate-White-Power-Music-Scene-2012.pdf

Anti Defamation League (n.d.). Deadly Shooting at the Tree of Life Synagogue. Retrieved December 1, 2018 from https://www.adl.org/education/educator-resources/lesson-plans/deadly-shooting-at-the-tree-of-life-synagogue

Anti-Fascist News (2017, March 19). Neo-Nazi Concert to Be Held at Joppatowne VFW March 25. Retrieved (n.d.). from https://antifascistnews.net/2017/03/19/neo-nazi-concert-to-be-held-at-joppatowne-vfw-march-25th/

Antifa Philadelphia (2015, January 30). Neo-Nazi Steven Wiegand of Micetrap Distribution Exposed. Philly Antifa Blogs. Retrieved (n.d.). from https://phillyantifa.noblogs.org/post/2015/01/30/neo-nazi-stevem-wiegand-of-micetrap-distribution-exposed/

Arellano, Gustavo (2013, November 13). The 10 Best Songs About Illegal Immigration. *OC Weekly*. Retrieved December 12, 2018 from https://ocweekly.com/the-10-best-songs-about-illegal-immigration-6578391/

Aron, Nina Renata (2017, August 23). This 'White Power' band has been the soundtrack of racist punk for 40 years. *Timeline*. Retrieved September 30, 2017 from https://timeline.com/skrewdriver-white-power-skinhead-70a54a99ee77

Ascend Recovery (n.d.). Introduction to Music Therapy. *ascendrecovery.com*. Retrieved July 29, 2017 from https://www.ascendrecovery.com/ebook-introduction-experiential-therapy/music-therapy/

Associated Press (2016, December 9). I'm a recovering neo-Nazi. Retrieved March 5, 2019 from https://nypost.com/2016/12/09/im-a-recovering-neo-nazi/

Barkham, Patrick (2014, July 16). La Bestia: the hit song the US border agency made to scare off immigrants. *The Guardian*. Retrieved November 26, 2018 from https://www.theguardian.com/world/shortcuts/2014/jul/16/la-bestia-song-commissioned-us-border-control-stop-immigration

BBC News (2018, January 10). 'Holocaust revisionist' on trial for anti-Semitic songs.. Retrieved February 2, 2018 from https://www.bbc.com/news/uk-england-derbyshire-42637888

Beirich, Heidi (2013, November 20) Volksfront: The Leadership. *Southern Poverty Law Center.* Retrieved August 21, 2018 from https://www.splcenter.org/fighting-hate/intelligence-report/2013/volksfront-leadership-0

Beirich, Heidi and Potok, Mark (2012, August 5). Alleged Sikh Templer Shooter Former Member of Skinhead Band. *Southern Poverty Law Center.* Retrieved March 20, 2018 from https://www.splc.org/news/2012/08/06/alleged-sikh-temple-shooter-former-member-skinhead-band

Berenbaum, Michael (n.d.). T4 Program: Nazi Policy. *Encyclopedia Britannica.* Retrieved March 5, 2019 from https://www.britannica.com/event/T4-Program

Billet, Alexander (2012, August 16). The music of racist hate. *Socialist Worker. org.* Retrieved (n.d.). from https://socialistworker.org/2012/08/16/music-of-racist-hate

Blabbermouth.net (n.d.). Rammstein Sues Germany for Placing Album On Restricted List. Retrieved July 9, 2018 from http://www.blabbermouth.net/news/rammstein-sues-germany-for-placing-album-on-restricted-list/

Blazak, Randy. Personal meeting February 9, 2018. Twenty-three personal emails exchanged between November 26, 2017 and January 22, 2019.

Bleiker, Carla (2017, August 16) Germany's national anthem: A song with a tricky past. *DW Akademie.* Retrieved March 11, 2018 from http://www.dw.com/en/germanys-national-anthem-a-song-with-a-tricky-past/a-40102655

Borczon, Ron. Personal interviews November 4, 2017 and January 27, 2018. Ron also sent emails August 5, 2017; September 7, 2017; September 22, 2017; October 20, 2017; November 3, 2017; January 23, 2018; September 22, 2018; January 30, 2019. Ron also sent other materials.

Borling, Jim. Personal interview October 25, 2017. Personal emails July 2, 2017; August 7, 2017; September 7, 2017; October 19, 2017; December 16, 2018; December 21, 2018; January 30, 2019.

Bowman, Emma and Stewart, Ian (2017, August 20). The Women Behind the 'Alt-Right'. *National Public Radio.* Retrieved March 2, 2019 from https://www.npr.org/2017/08/20/544134546/the-women-behind-the-alt-right

*Brainz.org.(*The Editors*)* (n.d.). 20 Most Misogynistic Songs Ever. Retrieved March 11, 2019 from https://www.brainz.org/20-most-misogynistic-songs-ever/

Brand, Juliane (n.d.). Karl Weigl: A Biographical Overview. *The Karl Weigl Foundation*. Retrieved November 8, 2018 from http://www.karlweigl. org/?page_id=132

Brief Timeline on Censored Music (n.d.). *American Civil Liberties Union*. Retrieved March 6, 2017 from https://www.aclu.org/other/brief-timeline-censored-music

Brufke, Juliegrace (2019, March 7). House passes anti-hate measure amid Dem tensions. *TheHill.com*. Retrieved March 9, 2019 from https://thehill. com/homenews/house/433085-house-passes-anti-hate-measure-after-tensions-flare

Burke, Caitlin (2018, January 15). How One Black Blues Musician Convinced Dozens of KKK Members to Quit. *CBN News*. Retrieved February 19, 2019 from https://www1.cbn.com/cbnnews/us/2016/july/how-one-black-blues-musician-changed-25-members-of-the-kkk

California State University Northridge home page (n.d.). Accessed Sept. 1, 2018 at http://www.csun.edu/academic/

Campbell, Andi (2018, May 4). A Long Island Record Shop Selling Neo-Nazi Merch Gets Das Boot. *Huffington Post*. Retrieved May 10, 2018 from https://www.huffingtonpost.com/entry/long-island-record-shop-neo-nazi-merchandise_us_5ae9bdaee4b022f71a03dd5a

Campbell, Eric (2017, July 21). One love, one hate, one hope: Tackling homophobia in Jamaica. *ABC News*. Retrieved April 10, 2019 from https://www.abc.net.au/news/2017-07-22/homophobia-in-jamaican-music-one-love-one-hate-one-hope/8711620

Capitalist Kids (2017, July 6). Anti-Immigrant Song. *Brassneck Records*. Retrieved November 16, 2018 from https://brassneckrecords.bandcamp. com/track/anti-immmigrant-song-2

Carpenter, Megan (2009, August 6). White Pride Pendergrafts Are The New Prussian Blue. *Jezebel*. Retrieved April 4, 2018 from https://jezebel. com/5331692/white-pride-pendergrafts-are-the-new-prussian-blue

Carpenter, Zoe (2015, June 23) A History of Hate Rock From Johnny Rebel to Dylann Roof. *The Nation*. Retrieved March 20, 2018 from https://www.the-nation.com/article/a-history-of-hate-rock-from-johnny-rebel-to-dylann-roof/

CBS News (2018, July 1) Right-wing activists Patriot Prayer, antifa clash at Portland protests.

CBS News. Retrieved July 1, 2018 from https://www.cbsnews.com/news/defend-pdx-patroit-prayer-portland-clash-today-2018-06-30/

Certification Board for Music Therapists website. https://www.cbmt.org

Chambers, Brianna (2027, August 17). Spotify pulls white supremacist music from the service. *cmgdigital.com*. Retrieved October 7, 2018 from https://sso.cmgdigital.com/static/server.html?origin=https%3A%2F%2Fwww.ajc.com%2Fnews%2Fnational%2Fspotify-pulls-white-supremacist-music-from-the-service%2FuSpBqkO6ImiMNzUVOZe9sL%2F

Chan, Sue (2003, September 29) Oregon Apologizes for Sterilizations. *CBS News*. Retrieved March 5, 2019 from https://www.cbsnews.com/news/oregon-apologizes-for-sterilizations/

Charles Powne. *Buzzfile*. Retrieved September 17, 2017 from http://www.buzzfile.com/business/Charles-Powne-503-281-4736

Chastagner, Claude (2012). Hate Music. *Translantica American Studies Journal*. Retrieved June 2, 2017 from https://journals.openedition.org/transatlantica/6075

Cifuetes, Lance Cpl. Michael S (2006, September 26). Former skinhead, Marine "StrHate Talks" Combat Center. *Headquarters Marine Corps*. Retrieved April 8, 2018 from https://www.hqmc.marines.mil/News/News-Article-Display/Article/552391/former-skinhead-marine-strhate-talks-combat-center/

City of Vienna (n.d.). Expulsion, Deportation and Murder—History of the Jews in Vienna. *Wien.gv.at*. Retrieved April 14, 2018 from https://www.wien.gv.at/english/culture/jewishvienna/history/nationalsocialism.html

Clark, Kevin L (2013, August 9). Das Racist: The 15 Most Racist Songs of All Time. *HipHopWired*. Retrieved March 21, 2018 from http://hiphopwired.com/249697/das-racist-the-15-most-racist-sosngs-of-all-time/16/

Clifton, Derrick (2014, August 6). 7 Things People With Disabilities Are Tired of Hearing. *mic.com*. Retrieved March 7, 2019 from https://mic.com/articles/94988/7-things-people-with-disabilities-are-tired-of-hearing

Coalition for Disabled Musicians, Inc (n.d.). *Coalition for Disabled Musicians, Inc*. Retrieved September 3, 2018 from http://www.disabled-musicians.org

Cohen, Ben (2017, July 16). Music Platform Drops Antisemitic Canadian Rapper as Montreal Police Launch Hate Crime Investigation. *Algemeiner.com*. Retrieved September 2, 2017 from https://www.algemeiner.com/2017/07/16/music-platforms-drop-antisemitic-canadian-rapper-as-montreal-police-launch-hate-crime-investigation/

Cohn, Mark. Ellis Island (lyrics). *Google*. Retrieved December 14, 2018 from https://www.google.com/search?source=hp&ei=Fe0bXMr

FF42w0PEP9Oq7qAM&q=Ellis+Island+lyrics+Marc+Cohn&b
tnK=Google+Search&oq=Ellis+Island+lyrics+Marc+Cohn&gs_
l=psy-ab.3..0.6724.16598..18817...0.0..0.58.1523.29......0....1..gws-
wiz.....0..0i131j0i22i30.2Vea-pxtbOk

Cook, Ian (2008, October 17). The Holocaust and Disabled People FAQ—frequently asked questions. *The BBC.* Retrieved Septembrer 3, 2018 from
http://www.bbc.co.uk/ouch/fact/the_holocaust_and_disabled_people_
faq_frequently_asked_questions.shtml

Country Music Project (n.d.) (no author). Let's Take a Journey Through Country
Music: 7 Songs That Show Progress Regarding Racism. Retrieved October 9, 2018 from http://sites.dwrl.utexas.edu/countrymusic/the-history/
lets-take-a-journey-through-country-music-7-songs-that-show-progress-
regarding-racism/

CQ Counter.com (n.d.). Get Some 88. Retrieved August 5, 2017 from http://
cqcounter.com/site/getsome88.com.html

Cropper, Carol Marie (1998, June 10) Black Man Fatally Dragged in a Possible Racial Killing. *New York Times.* Retrieved December 1, 2017 from
http://www.nytimes.com/1998/06/10/us/black-man-fatally-dragged-in-
a-possible-racial-killing.html

Cummins, Guylyn R (2000, November) MP3s and DVDs Spawn Novel First
Amendment Issues. *Journal of Internet Law*

Dahl, Melissa. If Gabby Giffords still struggles to speak, how can she sing?
(2014, January 9) *Today.* Retrieved from http://www.today.com/health/
if-gabby-giffords-still-struggles-speak-how-can-she-sing-2D11888324

Darby, Seyward (2018) The Secret Weapons of the Far Right. *Topic Magazine.*
Retrieved March 11, 2019 from https://www.topic.com/the-secret-weap-
ons-of-the-far-right

Darren, Matthew (n.d.). Against Music Censorship. Retrieved September 5,
2017 from http://matthewdarren.weebly.com/works-cited.htm.

Darrow, Alice-Ann (n.d.). Ableism and Social Justice: Rethinking Disability
in Music Education (abstract of book). *oxfordhandbooks.com.* Retrieved
March 7, 2019 from http://www.oxfordhandbooks.com/view/10.1093/
oxfordhb/9780199356157.001.0001/oxfordhb-9780199356157-e-54

Davidson, Kavitha A (2013, February 6). Wayne Simmonds Showered With
Racist 'Monkey' Chant By Czech Hockey Fans. *Huffington Post.* Retrieved
January 22, 2018 from https://www.huffingtonpost.com/2012/10/31/
wayne-simmonds-racist-chant-monkey-czech-fans_n_2045043.html

Davis, William B., Gfeller, Kate E., and Thaut, Michael H. An Introduction to Music Therapy Theory and Practice. Wm. C. Brown Publishers: Dubuque, Iowa (1992)

Davis, William B. Keeping the Dream Alive: Profiles of Three Early Twentieth Century Music Therapists. *Journal of Music Therapy*, Vol. XXX(1), Spring,1993, pp.34-45, the National Association for Music Therapy.

Davis, William. Personal emails from Davis, in his role as an historian at the national archives of the American Music Therapy Association, maintained at Colorado State University.

Degruy, Joy, Ph.D., Post Traumatic Slave Syndrome: America's Legacy Of Enduring Injury and Healing. *Joy Degruy Publications, Inc.*, Portland, Oregon, 2005 (originally published in hard cover by Uptone Press)

Democracy Now.org (n.d.). Meet the FBI Informant Who Organized Neo-Nazi Gathering Attended by Jo Cox Murder Suspect in 2000. Retrieved November 8, 2017 from https://www.democracynow.org/2016/6/22/meet_the_fbi_informant_who_organized

Democratic Underground.com (2012, August 6). Fuck you Label 56 (blog post by malaise). Retrieved (n.d.). from https://www.democraticunderground.com/10021082677

Department of Justice (n.d.). FBI Releases 2017 Hate Crime Statistics. Retrieved March 13, 2019 from https://www.justice.gov/hatecrimes/hate-crime-statistics

Diamond, Neil. America (Lyrics). *Google*, Retrieved December 12, 2018 from https://www.google.com/search?source=hp&ei=eOsbXLrqEIHQ9 AOAnbiIAQ&q=america+neil+diamond+lyrics&oq=america+neil+dia &gs_l=psy-ab.1.1.0l10.2164.5410..7876...0.0..0.57.801.16......0....1..gws-wiz .....0..0i131j0i10.0f5Exf8rPlI

Discogs (n.d.). Behold Barbarity. Retrieved February 15, 2018 from https://www.discogs.com/label/651853-Behold-Barbarity

Discogs (n.d.). Jew Slaughter. Retrieved April 14, 2018 from https://www.discogs.com/artist/3204986-Jew-Slaughter

Discogs (n.d.). Get Some 88 Records. Retrieved August 5, 2017 from https://www.discogs.com/label/588525-Get-Some-88-Records

Discogs (n.d.). Resistance Records. Retrieved February 12, 2019 from https://www.discogs.com/label/33630-Resistance-Records-3

Discogs (n.d.). Stormtroop 16. Retrieved August 23, 2018 from https://www.discogs.com/artist/24221627-Stormtroop-16

References   395

Discogs (n.d.). Stormtroop 16—The New Voice of Oi. Retrieved August 5, 2017 from https://www.discogs.com/Stormtroop-16-The-New-Voice-Of-Oi/release/6406203

DeNoon, Daniel J (n.d.). Gabrielle Giffords' Brain Injury: FAQ. *webmd.com*. Retrieved August 2, 2017, from http://www.webmd.com/brain/news/20110109/gabrielle-giffords-brain-injury-faq#1

Dobson, Carolyn (n.d.). Neurologic Music Therapy Group Helps People with Parkinson's Disease. *American Parkinson Disease Association*. Retrieved December 19, 2018 from https://www.apdaparkinson.org/what-is-parkinsons/treatment-medication/alternative-treatment/music-therapy/

Du, Susan (2017, August 16). One Minneapolis lawyer's neo-Nazi record label, and the fight to shut it down. City Pages. Retrieved August 19, 2017 from http://www.citypages.com/music/one-minneapolis-lawyers-neo-nazi-record-label-and-the-fight-to-shut-it-down/440595353

Duke University. Historic American Sheet Music. Visited at https://library.duke.edu/digitalcollections/hasm/

Dunn, Barbara; Hearns, Maureen; Jackert, Lisa; Rio, Robin, and Winnwalker, Jodi (2016). Daughters of Harriet Songbook. Self-published.

DW.com (January 2, 2018). Austria Freedom Party's Udo Landbauer resigns over Nazi song scandal. Retrieved April 14, 2018 from https://www.dw.com/en/austria-freedom-partys-udo-landbauer-resigns-over-nazi-song-scandal/a-42405730

Dyck, Kirsten. Reichsrock: The International Web of White-Power and Neo-Nazi Hate Music. *Rutgers University Press*: New Brunswick, New Jersey, and London, 2017.

Earle, Steve. City of Immigrants (lyrics). *Google*. Retrieved December 12, 2018 from https://www.google.com/search?source=hp&ei=2u0bXInNFeLs9APokqOICw&q=City+of+Immigrants+lyrics+steve+earle&btnK=Google+Search&oq=City+of+Immigrants+lyrics+steve+earle&gs_l=psy-ab.3..0i22i30.1133.7721..9951...0.0..0.176.2179.35j2......0....1..gws-wiz.....0..0j0j0i131.Nsc4b5iLtFE

East. Susie (2015, February 25). English Football Association probes chants mocking disabled. *CNN*. Retrieved February 11, 2018 from https://www.cnn.com/2015/02/25/football/kevin-kilbane-west-ham-football-fans-disabled-fa/index.html

Editorial Team (2018, July 24). Music Therapy: Sing Your Way Through Parkinson's. *Parkinson's Disease.net*. Retrieved December 19, 2018 from https://parkinsonsdisease.net/clinical/music-therapy-symptom-management/

Elliott, Debbie (2019, April 17). After Allegations Of Toxic Culture, Southern Poverty Law Center Tries to Move Forward, *National Public Radio* (heard on Morning Edition*).* Retrieved 1/8/2020 from https://www.npr.org/2019/04/17/713887174/after-allegations-of-toxic-culture-southern-poverty-law-center-tries-to-move-for

emPower Music & Arts. Retrieved August 11, 2017 from https://www.empowerma.com/

Encyclopedia Metallum (n.d.). Resistance Records. Retrieved November 8, 2017 from https://www.metal-archives.com/labels/Resistance_Records/642

Enoch, Nick (2012, June 27). 'Marijuana changed us from Nazis to peace-loving hippies': Twin sisters who sparked outrage with pop band named after gas used on Jews claim they've grown up. *Daily Mail.* Retrieved March 11, 2019 from https://www.dailymail.co.uk/news/article-2165342/Prussian-Blue-twins-Lynx-Lamb-Marijuana-changed-Nazis-peace-loving-hippies.html

Ernst, Aaron and Putzel, Christof (2015, October 9). The new face of white-power music. *America Tonight.* Retrieved March 20, 2018 from http://america.aljazeera.com/watch/shows/america-tonight/articles/2015/10/13/the-new-face-of-white-power-music.html

EUTimes (2007, November 7). Interview with rock band Stormtroop 16. Retrieved August 23, 2018 from http://www.eutimes.net/2007/11/interview-with-rock-band-stormtroop-16/

Falsone, Nick (2015, March 23). Skinheads, black separatists both operated out of Lehigh Valley in 2014, center says. *Lehigh Valley Live.* Retrieved May 10, 2018 from http://www.lehighvalleylive.com/breaking-news/index.ssf/2015/03/skinheads_black_separatists_bo.html

FANDOM (n.d.). Merle Haggard: The Immigrant Lyrics. *Wikia.* Retrieved 12/12/2018 from http://lyrics.wikia.com/wiki/Merle_Haggard:The_Immigrant

Farber, Jim (2012, August 6). Label 56 signed Wisconsin Sikh temple killer Wade Michael Page to recording contract. *New York Daily News.* Retrieved (n.d.). from http://www.nydailynews.com/news/national/label-56-signed-wisconsin-sikh-temple-killer-wade-michael-page-recording-contract-article-1.1130002

FBI.gov (n.d.). Hate Crimes. Retrieved 1/08/2020 from https://www.fbi.gov/investigate/civil-rights/hate-crimes

Federis, Marnette (2018, April 27). In the 1930s, an ethnomusicologist tried to preserve the history of immigration in California—and combat anti-immigrant feelings with song. *PRI's The World.* Retrieved November 26,

2018 from https://www.pri.org/stories/2018-04-27/1930s-ethnomusicol-
ogist-tried-preserve-history-immigration-california-and-combat

Fidelman, Lillie (2016, September 12). 6 Popular Songs That Are Disrespectful
to Women. *Odyssey*. Retrieved March 11, 2019 from https://www.theodys-
seyonline.com/6-popular-songs-disrespectful-women

Fingas, Jon (2013, December 2). German police may use a song recognition
app to fight neo-Nazi music. *engadget.com*. Retrieved September 10, 2017
from https://www.engadget.com/2013/12/02/german-police-may-use-
song-recognition-to-fight-neo-nazi-music/

First Amendment: An Overview (n.d.). *cornell.edu*. Retrieved March 7, 2017
from https://www.cornell.edu

Fitzthum, Elena and Gruber, Primavera. Give Them Music: Musiktherapie im
Exil am Beispiel von Vally Weigl. *Edition Praesens*: Vienna, Austria, 2003.

Flashnews.com. (2007, September 21). Singing Lawyer Writes Pop Song About
Immigration. Retrieved December 12, 2018 from http://www.flashnews.
com/news/wfn7070921J30011.htm

Flock, Elizabeth (2017, August 18) Spotify has removed white power music
from its platform. But it's still available on dozens of other sites. *PBS News-
hour*. Retrieved March 21, 2018 from https://www.pbs.org/newshour/arts/
spotify-removed-white-power-music-platform-still-available-dozens-sites

Florida Center for Instructional Technology *(n.d.)*. A Teacher's Guide to the
Holocaust: Music of the Holocaust. *University of South Florida*. Retrieved
November 10, 2018 from http://fcit.usf.edu/HOLOCAUST/arts/music.htm

Flynn, Meagan (2018, April 17). How thousands of songs composed in concentration camps are finding new life. *Washington Post*. Retrieved April
20, 2018 from https://www.washingtonpost.com/news/morning-mix/
wp/2018/04/17/how-thousands-of-songs-composed-in-concentration-
camps-are-finding-new-life/?utm_term=.8aa59fd108b1

Folami, Akilah N (2007) From Habermas to "Get Rich or Die Tryin": Hip Hop,
the Telecomunications Act of 1996, and the Black Public Sphere. *Michigan
Journal of Race and Law*, Vol. 12, pp. 234-303.

Folk-metal.nl (n.d.). Invoking full emotions. Retrieved June 26, 2017 from
https://www.folk-metal.nl

Forbes, Robert and Stampton, Eddie. The White Nationalist Skinhead Movement: UK and USA 1979-1993. *Feral House*: Fort Townsend, Washington,
2015.

Forman, Bill (2017, October 10). White Supremacists Face the Music. *Progressive.org*. Retrieved March 11, 2019 from https://progressive.org/dispatches/white-supremacists-face-the-music/

Fowler, Glenn (1989, October 10). Ira Hirschmann Is Dead at 88; Executive and Leading Nazi Foe. *New York Times*. Retrieved November 6, 2018 from https://www.nytimes.com/1989/10/10/obituaries/ira-hirschmann-is-dead-at-88-executive-and-leading-nazi-foe.html

France, Jasmine (2008, July 18). Top 5 online music stores. *C.net*. Retrieved (n.d.). from *C.net*.

Freedom of Expression at the National Endowment for the Arts (2005, July 4) *National Endowment for the Arts*. Retrieved September 6, 2017 from http://web.csulb.edu/~jvancamp/intro.html

Fries, Kenny (2017, September 13). The Nazis' First Victims Were the Disabled. *New York Times*. Retrieved September 3, 2018 from https://www.nytimes.com/2017/09/13/opinion/nazis-holocaust-disabled.html

Gabby Giffords: Finding Voice Through Music Therapy (n.d.). *ABC News*. Retrieved July 30, 2017 from http://abcnews.go.com/Health/w_MindbodyNews/gabby-giffords-finding-voice-music-therapy/story?id=14903987

Gale, David (2012, September 20). Disability and the media: music and song lyrics. *disabilityhorizons.com*. Retrieved February 11, 2018 from http://disabilityhorizons.com/2012/09/disability-and-the-media-music/

Genesis (n.d.). Illegal Alien (lyrics). *Google*. Retrieved December 12, 2018 from https://www.google.com/search?source=hp&ei=MZseXMaiEqHo9AONsYTQDQ&q=illegal+alien+lyrics&oq=Illegal+Alien&gs_l=psy-ab.1.3.0l9.1722.5059..8099...0.0..0.65.674.13......0....1..gws-wiz.....0..0i131j0i10.G8XaP93lRYc

Geiger, Jennifer. Personal email December 18, 2017, sending me her notes for the nomination of Deforia Lane for a Lifetime Achievement Award from the American Music Therapy Association

Gell, Aaron (2006, February 14). Minor Threat. *GQ.com*. Retrieved March 11, 2019 from https://www.gq.com/story/prussia-blue-hitler

German History Docs (n.d.). "Degenerate Music": Title Page of the Exhibition Guide (1938). Retrieved November 10, 2018 from http://germanhisotrydocs.ghi-dc.org/sub_image.cfm?image_id=2082

Gilchriest, Zach (2017, June 28) White Supremacist Conference Returns to State Park. *Nashville Scene*. Retrieved April 3, 2018 from https://www.amren.com/news/2017/07/white-supremacist-conference-returns-state-park/

Goldenberg, Anna (2018, February 22). Secretive Fraternities Are Feeding Anti-Semitism in Austria. *The Atlantic*. Retrieved April 14, 2018 from https://www.theatlantic.com/international/archive/2018/02/austria-fraternities-jews/552929/

Grasberg, Lynn (1976, July 28). Vally Weigl: Music's Renaissance Woman. *WomensWeek*. Pages 12 and 15.

Gross, Terry (2018, September 24). How a Rising Star of White Nationalism Broke Free From the Movement. *National Public Radio (NPR)*. Retrieved April 25, 2019 from https://www.npr.org/2018/09/24/651052970/how-a-rising-star-of-white-nationalism-broke-free-from-the-movement

Gruber, Primavera Driessen. e-mail-information February 2018 from Primavera Driessen Gruber, Forschungsdatenbank BioExil, in preparation of "Österreichisches Biographisches Handbuch der NS-verfolgten Musikschaffenden

Haggard, Merle (1978) The Immigrant, from the album I'm Always on a Mountain When I Fall. *Wikia*. Retrieved December 12, 2018 from http://lyrics.wikia.com/wiki/Merle_Haggard:The_Immigrant

Hall, Andre R (n.d.). Music Censorship. First Amendment Site. *Lehigh University*. Lehigh University, 2009. Web. 3 April 2013. Retrieved March 6, 2017

Halpern, Micah D (2014, March 19). Ugly Racist Chants at Soccer Game. *Huffington Post*. Retrieved November 27, 2017 from https://www.huffingtonpost.com/micah-d-halpern/ugly-racist-chants-soccer_b_4611760.html

Hankes, Keegan (2014, November 20). Music, Money & Hate. *Southern Poverty Law Center Intelligence Report*. Retrieved (n.d.). from https://www.splcenter.org/fighting-hate/intelligence-report/2014/music-money-hate-0

Harbert, Wilhelmina K. Opening Doors Through Music: A Practical Guide for Teachers, Therapists, Students, Parents. *Charles C. Thomas*: Springfield, Illinois, 1974.

Hardy, Spencer. Personal interview conducted April 6, 2019.

Harlan, Justin (2017, September 19). Introduction to Resistance Records. *Medium.com*. Retrieved February 12, 2019 from https://medium.com/know-your-enemy/introduction-to-resistance-records-7cbc7c7810f2

Hassan. Adeel (2019, November 12). Hate-Crime Violence Hits 16-Year High, FBI Reports. *New York Times*. Retrieved 1/8/2020 from https://www.nytimes.com/2019/11/12/us/hate-crimes-fbi-report.html

Hate Music (n.d.). *The Southern Poverty Law Center.* Retrieved March 8, 2017 and October 28, 2018 from https://www.splcenter.org/fighting-hate/extremist-files/ideology/hate-music

Hatewatch Staff (2017, March 7). Statement regarding Soleilmoon Recordings and Death in June. *Hatewatch, Southern Poverty Law Center.* Retrieved March 8, 2017 from https://www.splcenter.org/hatewatch/2017/03/07/statement-regarding-soleilmoon-recordings-and-death-june

Hatewatch Staff (2016, May 27). NYC OI! Fest Returns to New York City With New Kind of Hate. *Southern Poverty Law Center.* Retrieved June 23, 2017 from https://www.splcenter.org/hatewatch/2016/05/27/nyc-oi-fest-returns-new-york-city-new-kind-hate

Hatewatch Staff (2014, January 27). Court Records Provide Inside Look at the Tumultuous Family Life of a Violent Skinhead. *Southern Poverty Law Center.* Retrieved September 18, 1918 from https://www.splcenter.org/hatewatch/2014/01/27/court-records-provide-inside-look-tumultuous-family-life-violent-skinhead

Haynes, Tina. Personal interview January 19, 2018. Personal emails July 27, 2017; August 31, 2017; December 11, 2017; January 16, 2018; January 18, 2018; April 28, 2018; July 9, 2018; January 31, 2019

Hawkins, Derek (2017, September 11). Antifa, far-right protestors clash again in Portland, disrupting peaceful rallies. *Washington Post.* Retrieved July 1, 2018 from https://www.washingtonpost.com/news/morning-mix/wp/2017/09/11/antifa-far-right-protesters-clash-again-in-portland-disrupting-peaceful-rallies/?utm_term=.61f053edf65d

HC Streetwear. Retrieved May 17, 2017 from *Facebook.*

Heim, Joe; Barrett, Devlin; and Natanson, Hannah (2018, June 27). Man accused of driving into crowd at Charlottesville 'Unite the Right' rally charged with federal hate crimes. *Washington Post.* Retrieved July 2, 2018 from https://bangordailynews.com/2018/06/27/news/nation/man-accused-of-driving-into-crowd-at-charlottesville-rally-charged-with-federal-hate-crimes/

Heim, Joe (2012, August 7). Wade Michael Page was steeped in neo-Nazi 'hate music' movement. *Washington Post.* Retrieved March 20, 2018 from https://www.washingtonpost.com/lifestyle/style/wade-michael-page...e-dfe8-11e1-a19c-fcfa365396c8_story.htlm?utm_term=.8cda11d0118c6

Helm, Sarah. Ravensbrück. *Anchor Books,* New York, New York, 2015.

Heltzel, Ellen Emry (1979, March 20) Therapist communicates joy of music to special students. *The Oregonian.* Retrieved from The University of Oregon Libraries.

Hemmer, Nicole (2017, September 18). *Vox.* The women fighting for male supremacy. *Vox.* Retrieved March 11, 2019 from https://www.vox.com/the-big-idea/2017/9/18/16323686/women-alt-right-power-subservience-paradox-klan

Heritage Connection Band (2010, August 9) Blog website.

Heritage Connection (n.d.). *Metapedia.* Retrieved April 3, 2018 from http://en.metapedia.org/wiki/Heritage_Connection

Herron, Elise (2018, October 31). Here's What Happened the Night Mulugeta Seraw Was Murdered—and Afterward. *Willamette Week.* Retrieved March 2, 2019 from https://www.wweek.com/news/2018/10/31/heres-what-happened-the-night-mulugeta-seraw-was-murdered-and-afterward/

Hilliard, Russell. Personal interview November 17, 2018. Personal emails July 25, 2017; August 6, 2017; November 8, 2017; January 19, 2018; January 30, 2019. Russell sent additional materials.

Hinds, Deon (2016, October 1) Johnny Rebel, American country singer, Died at 77. *Deadobituary.com.* Retrieved August 30, 2017 from https://deadobituary.com/johnny-rebel-american-country-singer-died-at-77/

Hirsch, Lily (2014, December 30) The right to free speech includes rap. Misunderstanding it makes bad law. *The Guardian.* Retrieved October 8, 2018 from https://www.theguardian.com/commentisfree/2014/dec/30/free-speech-rap-music-bad-law

Hoehn, Laurel (2003/2004) First Amendment. *Journal of Juvenile Law.* Vol 24 Retrieved March 3, 2017 from https://litigation-essentials.lexisnexis.com/webcd/app?action=DocumentDisplay&crawlid=1&srctype=smi&srcid=3B15&doctype=cite&docid=24+J.+Juv.+L.+204&key=5a8de137befdd57715e72120a6438c37

Holten, Sandra. Personal interview November 13, 2018. Thirteen emails exchanged between August 22, 2017 and January 30, 2019. Sandra also provided a mini-bio

Hudson, David L., Jr (2018) Rap Music and the First Amendment. *Middle Tennessee State University.* Retrieved February 2, 2019 from https://mtsu.edu/first-amendment/article/1582/rap-music-and-the-first-amendment

Hudson, Jerome (2016, July 24) 9 Musicians Who Barred Donald Trump from Using Their Music. *Bretibart.* Retrieved July 30, 2017 from http://www.

breitbart.com/big-hollywood/2016/07/24/8-musicians-barred-donald-trump-using-music/

Hudson Valley Creative Arts Therapy Studio website. Visited January 23, 2018 at http://hvcats.org/

Huffington Post (2013, April 26). Ace of Base's Nazi Past Revealed in Disturbing Lyrics of Ulf Ekberg's Former Band (UPDATED). Huffington Post. Retrieved September 10, 2017 from https://www.huffingtonpost.com/2013/04/24/ace-of-base-nazi-past-lyrics_n_3148797.html

Hunter-Tilney, Ludovic (2018, August 17). The re-emergence of white supremacist pop. *Financial Times*. Retrieved December 1, 2018 from https://www.ft.com/content/68033ace-9732-11e8-b747-fb1e803ee64e

Iadarola, Alexander (2017, February 22) Civil Rights Organization Deems Oregon Industrial Label a Hate Group for Promoting Racist Music. *Thump*. Retrieved June 23, 1917 from https://thump.vice.com/en_us/article/d7j5xx/soleil-recordings-splc-hate-group

Ingber, Sasha (2019, April 11). 'Evil Acts': Son of Sheriff's Deputy Is Chief Suspect in Black Church Arson Cases. *NPR*. Retrieved April 29, 2019 from https://www.npr.org/2019/04/11/712173532/authorities-arrest-suspect-linked-to-3-burned-black-churches-in-louisiana

In Search of Coon Songs, Racial Stereotypes in American Popular Song, (2000, April). *The Parlor Songs Academy*. Retrieved March 7, 2017 from http://parlorsongs.com/insearch/coonsongs/coonsongs.php

Insel, Thomas (2011, January 11). Post by Former NIMH Director Thomas Insel: Understanding Severe Mental Illness. *National Institute for Mental Health*. Retrieved July 30, 2017, from https://www.nimh.nih.gov/about/directors/thomas-insel/blog/2011/understanding-severe-mental-illness.shtml

Intelligence Report (2001, August 29). Former Hate Music Promoter George Burdi Discusses His Experiences with Racism and the White Power Music Industry. *Southern Poverty Law Center*. Retrieved February 12, 2019 from https://www.splcenter.org/fighting-hate/intelligence-report/2001/former-hate-music-promoter-george-burdi-discusses-his-experiences-racism-and-white-power

Intelligence Report *(2018)* Hate and Extremism in 2017. *Southern Poverty Law Center*.

Intelligence Report (1998, March 15). Racist Label Resistance Records Isn't Slowing Down. *Southern Poverty Law Center*. Retrieved February 12, 2019 from https://www.splcenter.org/fighting-hate/intelligence-report/1998/racist-label-resistance-records-isn't-slowing-down

Intelligence Report (2000, March 15). Todd Blodgett Discusses Working For High-Profile Extremists. *Southern Poverty Law Center.* Retrieved November 8, 2017 from https://www.splcenter.org/fighting-hate/intelligence-report/2000/todd-blodgett-discusses-working-high-profile-extremists

Jaafari, Joseph Darius (2017, August 17). Neo-Nazi Music Is On The Rise. These Companies and People are Taking It On. *Nation Swell.* Retrieved October 30, 2017 from http://natonswell.com/white-supremacist-fashwave-music

Jackert, Lisa. Personal interview August 11, 2017. Lisa also sent emails July 2, 2017; August 3, 2017; August 7, 2017; August 11, 2017; October 22, 2017; November 5, 2017; January 19, 2018; March 12, 2018; March 14, 2018; January 31, 2019. Lisa also sent additional materials.

Jacobson, Louis (2017, September 25). A short history of the national anthem, protests and the NFL. *Politifact.* Retrieved March 11, 2018 from http://www.politifact.com/truth-o-meter/article/2017/sep/25/short-history-national-anthem-and-sports/

J.D. "Jay" Miller (2018, January 25) *Wikipedia.* Retrieved January 25, 2018 from https://en.wikipedia.org/wiki/J._D._%22Jay%22_Miller

Jewish Telegraphic Agency (2018, January 25). Austrian chancellor calls to punish author of anti-Semitic fraternity song. Retrieved April 14, 2018 from https://www.jta.org/2018/01/25/global/austrian-chancellor-calls-to-punish-author-of-anti-semitic-fraternity-song

Jewish Telegraphic Agency (2017, November 13). Number of anti-Semitic hate crimes edged up last year, FBI reports. Retrieved February 2, 2019 from https://www.jta.org/2017/11/13/united-states/number-of-anti-semitic-hate-crimes-edged-up-last-year-fbi-reports

Johns Hopkins University. The Lester S. Levy Sheet Music Collection. Visited at https://levysheetmusic.mse.jhu.edu

Johnny Rebel, American country singer, Died at 77, *Dead Obituary,* Retrieved August 30, 2017 from https://deadobituary.com/johnny-rebel-american-country-singer-died-at-77/

Johnny Rebel (singer), *Wikipedia,* Retrieved July 30, 2017 from https://en.wikipedia.org/wiki/Johnny_Rebel_(singer)

Johnny Rebel on Howard Stern Part 1 of 2, *YouTube,* Viewed September 16, 2017 on https://www.youtube.com/watch?v=uDw-IS8yXdk

Johnny Rebel on Howard Stern Part 2 of 2, *YouTube,* Viewed September 16, 2017 at https://www.youtube.com/watch?v=VSdh0FuEfS4

Johnson, Jason (2016, July 4). Star Spangled Bigotry: The Hidden Racist History of the National Anthem. *The Root*. Retrieved March 11, 2018 from https://www.theroot.com/star-spangled-bigotry-the-hidden-racist-history-of-the-1790855893

Joplin, Kendall and Dvorak, Abbey. A Survey Exploring the Current State of Censorship in Adult Psychiatric Music Therapy Practice. *Music Therapy Perspectives, 35(2), 2017, 199-208*

Julian, Hana Levi (2017, November 2). ADL Reports Anti-Semitism Skyrocketing in United States. *Jewish Press.com*. Retrieved February 2, 2018 from https://www.jewishpress.com/news/us-news/adl-reports-anti-Semitism-skyrocketing-in-united-states/2017/11/02/

JustSomeLyrics.com (n.d.). Lyrics for Stormtroop 16 songs. Retrieved August 21, 2018 from https://www.justsomelyrics.com/1994768/stormtroop-16-rank-upon-rank-lyrics.html and https://www.justsomelyrics.com/2005100/stormtroop-16-nationalism-lyrics.html

Kahn-Harris, Keith (2017, June 29). White power music and the changing face of extremism. *New Humanist*. Retrieved February 9, 2018 from https://newhumanist.org.uk/articles/5203/white-power-music-and-the-changing-face-of-extremism

Kaplan, Ronna (2015, May 10), ABC's David Muir Names Music Therapists 'Persons of the Week'. *Huffington Post*. Retrieved November 1, 2017 from https://www.huffingtonjpost.com/ronna-kaplan-ma/abcs-david-muir-names-mus_b_6835508.hrml

Keller, Larry (2010, September 3). Little Pulaski, Tenn., To Suffer Through Another Racist Event. *Southern Poverty Law Center*. Retrieved April 3, 2018 from https://www.splcenter.org/hatewatch/2010/09/03/little-pulaski-tenn-suffer-through-another-racist-event

Kelley, Brendan Joel (2017, October 9). The alt-right's new soundtrack of hate. Hatewatch. *The Southern Poverty Law Center*. Retrieved September, 2018 from https://www.splcenter.org/hatewatch/2017/10/09/alt-right's-new-soundtrack-hate

Kelly, Annie (2018, June 1). The Housewives of White Supremacy. *New York Times*. Retrieved March 11, 2019 from https://www.nytimes.com/2018/06/01/opinion/sunday/tradwives-women-alt-right.html

Kim, T.K (2006, April 19). A Look at White Power Music Today. *Southern Poverty Law Center*. Retrieved May 10, 2018 from https://www.splcenter.org/fighting-hate/intelligence-report/2006/look-white-power-music-today

Kimmel, Michael. Healing from Hate: How Young Men Get Into—And Out

Of—Violent Extremism. *University of California Press*: Oakland, California, 2018.

Kitchener, Caroline (2017, August 18). The Women Behind the Alt-Right. *The Atlantic*. Retrieved March 11, 2019 from https://www.theatlantic.com/politics/archive/2017/08/the-women-behind-the-alt-right/537168/

Kite, Kathryn (2016, April 14). 12 Musicians who refused to let politicians use their songs. *ontheaside.com*. Retrieved July 30, 2017 from http://ontheaside.com/music/12-musicians-who-refused-to-let-politicians-use-their-songs/

Knight, John (2010, June 16). Bob Kauflin's "Song for Those With Disabilities". *desiringgod.org*. Retrieved February 11, 2018 from https://www.desiring-god.org/articles/bob-kauflins-song-for-those-with-disabilities

Koberidze, Gubaz (2014, May 15). Murder Music: Free speech vs. hate speech. *nohatespeechmovement.org*. Retrieved October 8, 2018 from http://blog.nohatespeechmovement.org/murder-music-free-speech-vs-hate-speech/

Koehler, Daniel. Personal email received September 2, 2017.

Kornhaber, Spencer (2017, August 17). Getting Hate Speech Off Music-Streaming Services. *The Atlantic*. Retrieved October 8, 2018 from https://www.theatlantic.com/entertainment/archive/2017/08/spotify-and-other-music-services-kick-off-racist-bands/537213/

Kothari, Sunil and Kirschner, Kristi L Abandoning the Golden Rule: The Problem with "Putting Ourselves in the Patient's Place. *Topics in Stroke Rehabilitation*, Fall, 2006,13(4): 68-73

Label 56.com (n.d.). List of recordings for sale.

Lager, Justin "Thunder" (posted by), (2010, December 10) Johnny Rebel pulls the "I'm not racist but...card. *Chainbreaker*. Retrieved August 30, 2017 from http://thisischainbreaker.blogspot.com/2010/12/jouhnny-rebel-pulls-im-not-racist-but.html

Lane, Deforia with Wilkins, Rob. Music is Medicine. *Zondervan Publishing House*: Grand Rapids, Michigan, 1994

Lane, Deforia. Personal interview November 16, 2017. Personal emails July 24, 2017; November 12, 2017; November 29, 2017; November 19, 2018; February 2, 2019. Deforia also sent additional materials, including her notes from her acceptance speech for a Lifetime Achievement Award from the American Music Therapy Association at the AMTA conference in St. Louis, Missouri in 2017; and her notes from her keynote address at the AMTA national conference in Dallas, Texas in 2018.

Lee, Chris (2012, August 6). Inside the Creepy World of 'Hate Music'. *The Daily Beast*. Retrieved June 2, 2017 from https://www.thedailybeast.com/inside-the-creepy-world-of-hate-music

Lemons, Stephen (2010, June 2). Ray Stevens' Dumb, Anti-Immigrant Song "Come to the U.S.A. *Phoenix New Times*. Retrieved November 26, 2018 from https://www.phoenixnewtimes.com/news/ray-stevens-dumb-anti-immigrant-song-come-to-the-usa-6499371

Levin, Brian, J.D (2012, August 7). Exclusive: interview With Professor Who Extensively Studied Alleged Wisconsin Mass Killer. *Huffington Post*. Retrieved September 7, 2012 from https://www.huffingtonpost.com/brian-levin-jd/exclusive-interview-with_b_1751181.html

Levine, Jean (2001, November 20). Hatred's New Home. *The Trentonian*. Retrieved (n.d.). from http://www.trentonian.com/article/TT/20011120/TMP02/311209999

Levit, Donny (2017, February 15). Alleged Right-Wing Skinhead and White Power Bands Played Fundraiser in Brooklyn Last Weekend. *New Pulp City*. Retrieved May 17, 2018 from https://newpulpcity.com/2017/02/15/alleged-right-wing-skinhead-and-white-power-bands-played-fundraiser-in-brooklyn-last-weekend/

Levitin, Daniel J. This is Your Brain on Music. *Penguin Books Limited*: London, England, 2006.

Leyden, TJ with Cook, M. Bridget. Skinhead Confessions. *Sweetwater books*: Springville, Utah, 2008.

Library of Congress Historic Sheet Music Collection. Visited at https://www.loc.gov/collections/historic-sheet-music/about-this-collection/

Linked In, Deforia Lane Professional Profile. Retrieved September 18, 2017 from https://www.linkedin.com/in/deforia-lane-2a0a004

Life After Hate (n.d.). A brief history of Life After Hate. Retrieved March 17, 2020 from https://www.lifeafterhate.org/history

List or Manifest of Alien Passengers For The United States. SS President Roosevelt, April 15, 1938. Retrieved September 3, 2017.

Living My Social Work (2014, September 15). Musings on Music and Ableism (Inspired by Kanye West). *wordpress.com*. Retrieved February 11, 2018 from https://livingmysocialwork.wordpress.com/2014/09/15/musings-on-music-and-ableism-inspired-by-kanye-west/

Locke, Cathy (2016, January 25). Ask Sacto 911 crime Q&A: What happened to the man arrested following slaying of white supremacist in Citrus Heights? *The Sacramento Bee*. Retrieved August 23, 2018 from https://www.sacbee.com/news/local/crime/article56585618.html

Loder, Kurt (1986, September 11). You Can't Get It Right All the Time, in the *Rolling Stone* Special Collectors Edition Paul McCartney. Time Life Specials. October 19, 2017

Londberg, Max (2018, October 30). 'I don't want to be hated': After Pittsburgh synagogue shooting, Jewish girls bring song to Squirrel Hill. *USA Today Network*. Retrieved November 8, 2018 from https://www.usatoday.com/story/news/nation-now/2018/10/29/pittsburgh-synagogue-shooting-community-mourns-squirrel-hill/1814095002/

London, Paul. Ian Stuart: Nazi Rock Star. *Midgard Records AB*: Alingsas, Sweden, 2015.

Love, Nancy S. Trendy Fascism: White Power Music and the Future of Democracy. *State University of New York Press*: Albany, New York, 2016.

Lulic, Michelle (2016, January 26). 12 Songs That Are Actually Full of Super Misogynistic Lyrics. *Bustle*. Retrieved March 11, 2019 from https://www.bustle.com/articles/137558-12-songs-that-are-actually-full-of-super-misogynistic-lyrics

MacKenzie, Amy (2018, February 7). Bournemouth Symphony Orchestra launches professional disabled ensemble. *classic.fm*. Retrieved September 29, 2018 from https://www.classicfm.com/music-news/first-professional-disabled-ensemble/

Maddox, Kyra (2017, March 1). Report: Steady increase in hate groups nationwide; see list of 47 operating in NY. *NYUp.com*. Retrieved May 14, 2018 from http://www.newyorkupstate.com/news/2017/03/report_shows_steady_increase_in_hate_groups_see_where_47_groups_operate_in_ny.html

Manson, Jake (2011, August 1, updated 2018, October7). Prussian Blue. *The Weirdest Band in the World.com*. Retrieved March 11, 2019 from https://weirdestbandintheworld.com/2011/08/01/prussian-blue/

Marsden, James (n.d.). The Murder of Matthew Shephard. *WyoHistory.org*. Retrieved December 2, 2017 from https://www.wyohistory.org/encyclopedia/matthew-shephard

Martin, Douglas (2015, November 1). Willis Carto, Far-Right Figure and Holocaust Denier, Dies at 89. *New York Times*. Retrieved November 13, 2017 from https://www.nytimes.com/2015/11/02/us/willis-carto-far-right-figure-and-holocaust-denier-dies-at-89.html

Mathias, Christopher (2017, June 1). The White Terror Crisis in Portland. *Huffington Post.* Retrieved May 7, 2018 from https://www.huffingtonpost.com/entry/portland-oregon-white-terror_us_592ef9cbe4b09ec37c31055b

Mayerson, Arlene (1992). The History of the Americans with Disabilities Act. *Disability Rights Education & Defense Fund.* Retrieved March 5, 2019 from https://dredf.org/about-us/publications/the-history-of-the-ada/

Maza, Christina (2017, November 8). What to Do When You Accidentally Book a White-Supremacist Band. *Pacific Standard Magazine.* Retrieved May 17, 2018 from https://psmag.com/social-justice/fighting-white-supremacist-bands

McAleer, Tony. The Cure for Hate. *Arsenal Pulp Press*, Vancouver, British Columbia, 2019.

McGrath, Ciaran (2018, March 9). Why Germans are Banned from Singing First Two verses of the National Anthem. *Express.* Retrieved March 11, 2018 from https://www.express.co.uk/news/world/929504/germans-banned-national-anthem-nazi-adolf-hitler-third-reich

McLaren, Jodi (2016, October 20). Ableism: what it is and why it matters. *medium.com.* Retrieved March 7, 2019 from https://medium.com/@noteables/ableism-what-it-is-and-why-it-matters-ed6ee7e111dd

McRae, Elizabeth Gillespie (2018, February 2). The Women Behind White Power. *New York Times.* Retrieved March 2, 2019 from https://www.nytimes.com/2018/02/02/opinion/sunday/white-supremacy-forgot-women.html

McWhorter, John H (2003, Summer). How Hip-Hop Holds Blacks Back. *City Journal.* Retrieved October 8, 2018 from https://www.city-journal.org/html/how-hip-hop-holds-blacks-back-12442.html

Membis, Liane (n.d.). Southern Rap Song 'Wheelchair Shawty': Offensive or Not?. *clutchmag.online.* Retrieved February 11, 2018 from http://clutchmagonline.com/2019/11/southern-rap-song-wheelchair-shawty-offensive-or-not/

Memorial Hermann Rehabilitation Network (n.d.). Affiliated with TIRR Memorial Hermann (n.d.) Retrieved August 1, 2017 from http://www.mmeorialhermann.org/lifeyoulove/

Mental Health Myths and Facts (n.d.). *mentalhealth.gov.* Retrieved July 30, 2017 from https://www.mentalhealth.gov/basics/myths-facts/index.html

Mettler, Katie (2017, February 1). 'Give me your tired, your poor': The story of poet and refugee advocate Emma Lazarus. *Washington Post.* Retrieved

March 6, 2019 from https://www.washingtonpost.com/news/morning-mix/wp/2017/02/01/give-us-your-tired-your-poor-the-story-of-poet-and-refugee-advocate-emma-lazarus/?utm_term=.841bcb61eacf

Micetrap Distribution LLC, *Facebook,* Retrieved (n.d.). from https://www.facebook.com/search/top/?q=micetrap%20distribution

Micetrap Distribution LLC (n.d.). *Zoominfo,* Retrieved (n.d.). from https://www.zoominfo.com/c/micetrap-distribution-llc/345923643

Micetrap Distribution LLC (n.d.). website shut down.

Micetrap Records Gone (2017, August 22). *Racial Loyalty News.* Retrieved May 10, 2018 from https://crreativityalliance.com/forum/indes.php?topic=9899.0

Michaelis, Arno. My Life After Hate. *Authentic Presence Publications*: Milwaukee, Wisconsin, 2012.

Miles, Kathleen (2012, August 9). Wade Michael Page: Orange County Hate Music Scene Nurtured Alleged Mass Murderer (PHOTOS). *Huffington Post.* Retrieved September 10, 2017 from https://www.huffingtonpost.com/2012/08/09/wade-michael-page-orange-county-neo-nazi-hate-music-bands_n_1760817.html

Miller, Joshua Rhett (2009, February 26). Racist Music Just a Download Away on Mainstream Music Sites. *Fox News.* Retrieved June 19 2018 from https://www.foxnews.com/story/racist-music-just-a-download-away-on-mainstream-music-sites

Miller-Rosenberg, Doran (2013, October 16). The 15 Most Misogynist Lines In Rap History. *Elite Daily.* Retrieved April 3, 2019 from https://www.elitedaily.com/music/music-news/the-20-most-misogynist-lines-in-rap-history

Moisse, Katie and ABC News Medical Unit (2011, March 8). *ABC News.* Gabby Giffords Finding Voice Through Music Therapy. Retrieved July 20, 2017 from http://abcnews.go.com/Healht/w_MindBodyNews/gabby-giffords-finding-voice-music-therapy/story?id=14903987

Mokalla, Matteen (2017, February 27). I'm a former neo-Nazi. Don't ignore the threat of white extremism. *Vox.* Retrieved March 23, 2018 from https://www.vox.com/videos/2017/2/27/14738170/former-neo-nazi-don't-ignore-threat-of-white-extremism-picciolini

Molinet, Jason (2015, February 17). SEE IT: Gabby Giffords sings 'Annie' with Houston music therapist. *New York Daily News.* Retrieved July 30, 2017 from http://m.nydailynews.com/news/gabby-giffords-sings-annie-houston-music-therapist-article-1.2117827#bmb=1

Montemayor, Stephen (2017, August 19) Minnesota has seen its own rise in hate, clashes before Charlottesville. *Minneapolis Star Tribune*. Retrieved August 19, 2017 from http://www.startribune.com/minnesota-has-seen-its-own-rise-in-hate-clashes-before-charlottesville/441059473/

Moon, Mariella (2017, August 18). Google and Deezer promise to expunge racist music, too. *engadget.com*. Retrieved September 10, 2017 from https://www.engadget.com/2017/08/18/google-deezer-expunge-racist-music/

Morgan, Olivia (2017, March 7). The End of All Music to release EP benefiting Southern Poverty Law Center. *The Daily Mississippian*. Retrieved March 8, 2017 from https://thedmonline.com/end-all-music-benefit-record-splc/

Morrow, Maegan. Personal emails July 28, 2017; August 1, 2017; August 28, 2017; December 5, 2017; February 5, 2018; October 29, 2018; January 30, 2019

Morrison, Robert (2018, August 2). Neil Sedaka's 1975 song revived for anti-immigrant era. *The Conversation*. Retrieved November 26, 2018 from http://theconversation.com/neil-sedakas-1975-song-revived-for-anti-immigrant-era-100168

Mouledoux, John (1979, April 30). *California Institute of the Arts*. The Best Show I Have Ever Seen, Including Robin Hood. School of Theatre, California Institute of the Arts

Mount, Harry (2009, June 5). The human iPod: Derek Paravicini is blind and severely disabled yet can master any song after hearing it once…What is his secret? The *Daily Mail*. Retrieved February 11, 2018 from https://www.dailymail.co.uk/news/article-1191163/Derek-Paravicini-blind-severely-disabled-master-song-hearing--What-secret.html

Moyer, Justin Wm., (2017, October 13). After Charlottesville, some white power record labels disappeared. This one survives in Maryland. *Washington Post*. Retrieved March 23, 2018 from https://www.washingtonpost.com/local/after-charlottesville-some-white-power-labels-disappeared-this-one-survives-in-maryland/2017/10/13/baf06cfc-a23c-11e7-9335-16c8faedd676_story.html?utm_term=.b444ddbccd7d

Moore, Leroy (2016, September 6). Hip-Hop for Disability Justice Campaign. *Krip-Hop Nation*. Retrieved September 3, 2018 from http://kriphopnation.com/hip-hop-for-disability-justice-campaign/

Munkittrick, David (2010) Music as Speech: A First Amendment Category unto Itself. *Federal Communications Law Journal* Vol. 62: ISS3, Article 6. Retrieved March 6, 2017 from http://www.reositorylaw.indiana.edu/fdj/vol62/iss3/6

Music. *National Coalition Against Censorship*. Retrieved September 5, 2017 from http://ncac.org/issue/music

Musical Program To Be Given At Kohler Hall. (1951, March 29) *The Sheboygan Press*: Sheboygan, Wisconsin. Retrieved September 3, 2017 from Newspapers.com

Music therapist honored. No author, no date. Portland, Oregon. Copy of article apparently from an Emily School Newsletter.

Music Therapy (n.d.). *tirr.memorialhermann.org*. Retrieved August 1, 2017 from http://tirr.memorialhermann.org/programs-specialties/music-therapy/

Music Therapy & Congresswoman Giffords (2015, February 18) *American Music Therapy Association*. Retrieved July 30, 2017 from https://www.musictherapy.org/music/therapy/congresswoman/giffords/

Musicians Without Borders (web site) (2017, December 7-10) War Divides, Music Connects—Introduction. Retrieved July 29, 2017 from https://www.musicianswithoutborders.org

Mullins, Caroline. Christ Alone: Story and beautiful background song sung (n.d.), *caroline-mullins.tripod.com*. Retrieved September 3, 2017 from http://caroline-mullins.tripod.com/caroline/Christ-Alone.html

Murakami, Brea, MM, MT and Goldschmidt, Daniel, MT-BC. Music and Harm: What We Know and What We Need to Know. Presentation given at the national conference of the American Music Therapy Association, St. Louis, Missouri, November 19, 2017.

Naldony, Tricia L (2017, August 21). South Jersey seller of hate music says he is shutting down to find 'self peace', *The Inquirer*. Retrieved May 10, 2018 from http://www.philly.com/philly/news/politics/south-jersey-seller-of-hate-music-is-shutting-down-to-find-self-peace-20170821.html

Nasdaq.com (2017, August 18). Tech Giants Take Belated Stand Against Neo-Nazis *.rttnews.com*. Retrieved August 18. 2017 from https://www.rttnews.com/2806999/tech-giants-take-belated-stand-against-neo-nazis.aspx

Nasitir, Lonnie (2012, August 8). Hate with a Beat: White Power Music. *CNN*. Retrieved December 2, 2017 from https://www.cnn.com/2012/08/08/opinion/nasatir-white-power-bands/index.html

Nationalist Women's Front (n.d.). Featured interview with KT8. Retrieved April 3, 2019 from http://www.nationalistwomensfront.org/our-folk--our-music.html

Nazis Publish Blacklist of Jewish Composers (1935, November 25). *Jewish Telegraphic Agency*, Latest Cable Dispatches.

Needham Public Schools (n.d.). German Immigration: 1830-1860. Retrieved January 13, 2019 from http://www2.needham.k12.ma.us/nhs/cur/kane98/kane_p3_immig/German/germany.html

Negrin, Dotan (2016, April 21). Addiction to Music is as Real as Addiction to Drugs. *Piano Around*. Retrieved March 10, 2018 from http://www.piano-around.com/blog/addiction-to-music-is-as-real-as-addiction-to-drugs

Neiwert, David (2017, October 10). When white nationalists chant their weird slogans, what do they mean? *Hatewatch; Southern Poverty Law Center,* Retrieved June 14, 2018 from https://www.splcenter.org/hatewatch/2017/10/10/when-white-nationalists-chant-their-weird-slogans-what-do-they-mean

Nelson, Cody (2017, August 15). The state of hate in Minnesota. *News-Cut*. Retrieved August 19, 2017 from http://blogs.mprnews.org/news-cut.2017/08/the-state-of-hate=in-minnesota/

Nelson, Leah (2011, February 27). Jamaica's Anti-Gay 'Murder Music' Carries Violent Message. *Southern Poverty Law Center Intelligence Report*. Retrieved March 21, 2018 from https://www.splcenter.org/fighting-hate/intelligence-report/2015/jamaicas-anti-gay-murder-music-carries-violent-message

Nordoff, Paul and Robbins, Clive. Therapy in Music for Handicapped Children. *Victor Gjollancz Ltd.*: London, 1992, page 115

Neo-Nazi Hate Music: A Guide (n.d.). *Anti-Defamation League* (no longer available online).

New Tune (n.d.). 'Nazi' Duo Prussian Blue Now Liberal. *The Daily Beast*. Retrieved March 11, 2019 from https://www.thedailybeast.com/nazi-duo-prussian-blue-now-liberal

No Irish Need Apply, Written by John F. Poole, H. De Marsan, Publisher, 54 Chatham Street, New York. *Library of Congress*. Retrieved December 14, 2018 from https://www.loc.gov/resource/amss.as109473.0/?st=text

Nokes, Greg (2018, June 1) Chinese Massacre at Deep Creek. *Oregon Encyclopedia*. Retrieved March 4, 2019 from https://oregonencyclopedia.org/articles/chinese_massacre_at_deep_creek/

Nwoko, Uzochi P (2018, February 27). Alleviating the Effects of Misogyny in Rap and Hip Hop Music. *The Crimson*. Retrieved March 11, 2019 from https://www.thecrimson.com/column/where-rap-meets-race/article/2018/2/27/whererapmeetsrace-installment2/

Obituary for Clifford Joseph Trahan (n.d.). *obittree.com.* Retrieved February 5, 2018 from https://obittree.com/obituary/us/louisiana/crowley/duhon-funeral-home-of-crowley/clifford-trahan/2699945/

Obituary of Dr. John T. Wolmut (1953, April 23) *Chicago Tribune.* Retrieved September 3, 2017 from Newspapers.com

O'Brien, Luke: Liebelson, Dana; and Schulberg, Jessica (2017, September 29). Our Search For A Secret White Supremacist Meeting In A Tennessee Forest. *Huffington Post.* Retrieved January 20, 2018 from https://www.huffingtonpost.com/entry/white-supremacist-stormfront-tennessee_us_59ce6a59e4b09538b50802be

O'Neill, Helen (2011, November 1) A skinhead's journey from racism to redemption. *CBS News.* Retrieved August 27, 2018 from https://www.cbsnews.com/news/a-skinheads-journey-from-racism-to-redemption/

Oppenheim, Maya (2018, July 25). Misogyny is a key element of white supremacy, Anti-Defamation League report finds. *Independent.* Retrieved October 28, 2018 from https://www.independent.co.uk/news/world/americas/misogyny-white-supremacy-links-alt-right-antidefamation-league-report-incel-a8463611.html

Oregon Death Record. Felice Wolmut. Retrieved September 3, 2017.

Oregon State University Special Collections and Archives Research Center. Vally Weigl files from the Linus Pauling collections (correspondence and other documents shared between Ava Helen Pualing, Linus Pauling, and Vally Weigl)

Palladino, Christina (2017, August 16) Can you get fired for bigotry? KMSP, *Fox News.* Retrieved August 18, 2017 from http://www.fox9.com/news/can-you-get-fired-for-bigotry

Palmer, Brian (2008, October 29) White Supremacists by the Numbers. *Slate.com.* Retrieved September 18, 2017 from http://www.slate.com/articles/news_and_politics/explainer/2008/10/white_supremacists_by_the_numbers.html

Parente, Alice (n.d.). Personal resume, received via email

Parente, Alice and Parente, Joe. 20+ Personal emails between July 28, 2017 and March 17, 2019. Personal interview October 12, 2018 in Sacramento, California.

Parente, Joe (n.d.). Personal resume, received via email, March 19, 2019.

Parente, Joe (n.d.). Fatso, 1977-2019 and Fatso—A new Musical. *Google.*

Retrieved September 23, 2018 from https://drive.gooogle.com/drive/folders/0B0wmFPeq5NRFbkh6dU5PaGFjSm8

Parkinson's Disease Foundation (n.d.). Statistics on Parkinson's. Retrieved August 23, 2017 from http://www.pdf.org/parkinson_statistics

Parkinson's Foundation (n.d.). Feel the Rhythm: Music Therapy and Parkinson's Disease. Retrieved November 19, 2018 from https://parkinson.org/blog/research/Music-Therapy-Parkinsons-Disease-Feel-Rhythm

Parkinson's Foundation (n.d.). Stages of Parkinson's. Retrieved December 19, 2018 from https://www.parkinson.org/Understanding-Parkinsons/What-is-Parkinsons/Stages-of-Parkinsons?gclid=EAIaIQobChMI4tn9g_uO4AIVkxx9Ch31Twa8EAAYASAAEgIzBfD_BwE

Parknicollet.com (n.d.). Struthers Parkinson's Center—Our History. Retrieved August 19, 2018 from https://www.parknicollet.com/specialtycenters/struthers-parkinsons-center/our-history

Parknicollet.com (n.d.). Struthers Parkinson's Center—Our Services. Retrieved December 19, 2018 from https://www.parknicollet.com/specialtycenters/struthers-parkinsons-center/Our-Services

Patman, Jean. (2001) Free Speech and Music: A Teacher's Guide to Freedom sings. First Amemdment Center. Retrieved March 2, 2017 from http://www.newseuminstitute.org/wp-content/uploads/2016/10/freespeechandmusic.pdf

PBS News Hour (2015, December 31). How federal law draws a line between free speech and hate crimes. *PBS News Hour.* Retrieved November 28, 2017 from https://www.pbs.org/newshour/nation/how-feder-law-draws-a-line-between-free-speech-and-hate-crimes

Pegoda, Dr. Andrew Joseph (2017, April 9). Ableism and the Music Industry—A Few Thoughts. *andrewpegoda.com.* Retrieved September 17, 2017 from https://andrewpegoda.com/2017/04/09/ableism-and-the-music-industry-a-few-thoughts/

Peled, Shachar (2017, November 5). Ladies' Night at the Alt-right: Meet the Women Trying to Soften the White Nationalist Movement. *Haaretz.* Retrieved March 11, 2019 from https://www.haaretz.com/us-news/premium-meet-the-women-trying-to-soften-the-white-nationalist-movement-1.5462886

Perestroika (n.d.) *Wikipedia,* Retrieved September 13, 2017 from https://enwikipedia.org/wiki/Perestroika

Permissible Restrictions on Expression. *Encyclopedia Britannica.* Retrieved

March 13, 2017 from https://www.britannica.com/topic/First-Amendment/Permissible-restrictions-on-expression

Petridis, Alexis (2010, March 18). Misunderstood or hateful? Oi!'s rise and fall. *The Guardian.* Retrieved September 30, 2017 from https://www.theguardian.com/music/mar/18/oi-cockney-rejects-garry-bushell-interview

Petridis, Alexis (2004, December 10). Pride and prejudice. *The Guardian.* Retrieved April 10, 2019 from https://www.theguardian.com/music/2004/dec/10/gayrights.popandrock

Petrucci, Monica (2017, March 13). Let's Not Ignore the Misogyny In Country Music. *Odyssey.* Retrieved April 3, 2019 from https://www.theodysseyonline.com/lets-not-ignore-the-misogyny-country-music

Phillips, Amber (2015, June 24). What it's like to be a white supremacist. *Washington Post.* Retrieved November 8, 2017 from https://www.washingtonpost.com/news/the-fix/wp/2015/06/24/what-its-like-to-be-a-white-supremacist/?utm_term=.7888a472d31e

Phillips, Betsy (2018, February 27) In Tennessee, Hate Groups Are Nothing New. *Nashville Scene.* Retrieved April 3, 2018 from https://www.nashvillescene.com/news/pith-in-the-wind/article/20994213/in-tennessee-hate-groups-are-nothing-new

Picciolini, Christian. White American Youth: My Descent into America's Most Violent Hate Movement—and How I Got Out. *Hachette Books*: New York, New York, 2017.

Pieslak, Jonathan. Radicalism and Music: An Introduction to the Music Cultures of al-Qa'ida, Racist Skinheads, Christian-Affiliated Radicals, and Eco-Animal Rights Militants. *Weslyan University Press*: Middleton, Connecticut, 2015.

Pitofsky, Marina (2018, August 9). Are women changing 'Unite the Right' or just 'rebranding' the movement? *USA Today.* Retrieved March 11, 2019 from https://www.usatoday.com/story/news/2018/08/09/women-unite-right-rally-2018/874631002/

Poker Face (2005, October). *Stormfront.org.* Retrieved May 12, 2018 from https://www.stormfront.org/forum/t264632/

Rice, Boyd (2009, February 19). Revolt Against Penis Envy/ R.A.P.E. *Word Press.* Retrieved May 6, 2028 from https://idabby.wordpress.com/2009/02/19/43/

Pittman, Nick (2003, June 10) Johnny Rebel Speaks, *Best of New Orleans Gambit,* Retrieved August 30, 2017 from https://www.bestofneworleans.com/gambit/johnny-rebel-speaks/Content?oid=1241588

Places in Tennessee to Explore African American History. *Tennessee Vacation*. Retrieved April 3, 2018 from https://www.tnvacation.com/articles/places-tennessee-explore-african-american-history

Porter, Tom (2018, October 14). Antifa and Patriot Prayer Clash with Batons and Pepper Spray on the Streets of Portland. *Newsweek*. Retrieved November 11, 2018 from https://www.newsweek.com/far-right-patriot-prayer-and-antifa-clash-batons-and-pepper-spray-streets-1168798

Posi music (n.d.). *Wikipedia*. retrieved August 11, 2017 from https://en.wikipedia.org/wiki/Posi_music

Process Theatre, Inc *(n.d.)*. Process Theatre Welcome and Our Purpose. *Processtheater.org*. Retrieved September 23, 2018 from http://www.process-theatre.org/

Prodanovic, Darko and Abdool-Karim, Essa (2017, August 8). Hate laws put reasonable limits on freedom of speech. *Toronto Star*. Retrieved November 28, 2017 from https://www.thestar.com/opinion/commentary/2017/08/08/hate-laws-put-reasonable-limits-on-freedom-of-speech.html

RAC (n.d., no author) *last.fm*. Retrieved August 11, 2017 from https://www.last.fm/tag/rac

Ranker.com. The Best Rap Songs About Racism (n.d.). Retrieved October 8. 2018 from https://www.ranker.com/list/best-rap-songs-about-racism/ranker-hip-hop

rateyourmusic.com (n.d.). Resistance Records. Retrieved November 8, 2017 from https://rateyourmusic.com/label/resistance_records/

Render, Michael and Nielson, Erik (2016, February 18) Killer Mike: Free speech—unless it's rap? *Cnn.com*. Retrieved October 8, 2018 from https://www.cnn.com/2016/02/17/opinions/rap-first-amendment-supreme-court-render-nielson/index.html

Renegade, Gus T (2015, July 15). #WhiteGirlsDoItBetter: Why White Women Remain One of Racism's Most Slept On Weapons. *Atlantablackstar.com*. Retrieved March 2, 2019 from https://atlantablackstar.com/2015/07/15/whitegirlsdoitbetter-white-women-remain-one-racisms-slept-weapons/

Rettman, Tony (2012, August 20). Racist Rock: An Overview of White Supremacy in Punk and Metal. *NoiseCreep*. Retrieved October 28, 2018 from http://noisecreep.com/white-power-punk-hardcore/

Rhodes, Alvin (n.d.). Immigrant Song (parody lyrics). *amiright.com*. Retrieved December 12, 2018 from http://www.amiright.com/parody/70s/lwdzeppelin44.shtml

Rolling Stone (2017). Special Collectors Edition Paul McCartney. *Rolling Stone, LLC.*

Romero, Ernesto (2018, February 2). *KYMA.* Calipatria State Prison investigating inmate death as a Homicide. Retrieved August 23, 2018 from https://www.kyma.com/news/calipatria-state-prison-investigating-inmate-death-as-a-homicide/695672902

Roncero-Menendez, Sara (2017, February 17) Southern Poverty Law Center Identifies Four Hate Groups on Long Island. *Long Island Wins.* Retrieved May 13, 2018 from https://longislandwins.com/news/southern-poverty-law-center-identifies-four-hate-groups-long-island/

Rose, Peppermint (2014, June 1). Stray Observations from the Field at a Death in June Show. *Noisey.* Retrieved September 17, 2017 from https://noisey.vice.com/en_au/article/6ew3p6/death-in-june-austin-concert-review

Ross, Alex (2016, July 4). When Music is Violence. *The New Yorker.* Retrieved June 2, 2017 from https://www.newyorker.com/magazine/2016/07/04/when-music-is-violence

Roth, Sara (2017, May 28). Portland MAX attack: What we know. *KGW8.* Retrieved March 2, 2018 from https://www.kgw.com/article/news/local/portland-max-attack-what-we-know/283-444221342

Roy, Jody. M. Autobiography of a Recovering Skinhead: The Frank Meeink Story as told to Jody M. Roy, Ph.D, *Hawthorne Books and Literary Arts:* Portland, Oregon, 2009.

Rutledge-Borger, Meredith E (2012, August 23) Rock and Roll vs. Censorship. *Rock and Roll Hall of Fame.* Retrieved September 5, 2017 from https://www.rockhall.com/rock-and-roll-vs-censorship

RV Force. Diamond in the Dust: The Ian Stuart Biography. *RV Force,* 2001, reprinted 2010.

Samsanova-Jellison, Olga (2017, March 19, 2017) Immigration, Acculturation, and Music Therapy. Handouts from workshop at the joint WRAMTA/MWRAMTA conference in Denver, Colorado.

Samsonova-Jellison, Olga. Personal interviews August 31, 2017 and March 1, 2019. Twenty-seven personal emails between June 24, 2017 and January 31, 2019. Olga also sent additional materials.

Sanchez, Daniel (2017, August 23). Intellectual Property Lawyer by Day, Neo-Nazi Label Owner by Night. *Digital Music News.* Retrieved August 26, 2017 from https://www.digitalmusicnews.com/2017/08/23/patterson-thuente-aaron-w-davis-neo-nazi/

Satanism 101—Jared Loughner's Satanic Video (n.d.). *stop-obama-now.com*. Retrieved August 3, 2017, from https://stop-obama-now.net/laughners-satanic-video/

Saslow, Eli. Rising Out of Hatred: The Awakening of a Former White Nationalist. *Doubleday*: New York, 2018.

Satter, Marlene Y (2017, August 15). Can employers fire racists? Should they? *Benefitspro.com*. Retrieved August 29, 2017 from http://www.benefitspro.com/2017/08/15/can-employers-fire-racists-should-they

Schafer, Joseph (2017, January 29). Behold Barbarity Releases Brazen Anti-Semitic Tee Shirt. *invisibleoranges.com*. Retrieved February 5, 2018 from http://www.invisibleoranges.com/behold-barbarity-releases-brazen-anti-semitic-tee-shirt/

Schmid, Thacher (2017, February 21) A Northeast Portland Record Label Lands on a National Hate-Group Registry. *Willamette Weekly*. Retrieved March 8, 2017 from http://www.wweek.com/news/business/2017/02/21/a-northeast-portland-record-label-lands-on-a-national-hate-group-registry/

Schweitzer, Ally (2014, May 7). Band With Alleged Neo-Fascist Ties To Play D.C. Area This Weekend. *bandwith.wamu.org*. Retrieved August 17, 2017 from http://bandwidth.wamu.org/band-with-alleged-neo-fascist-ties-to-play-d-c-area-this-weekend/

Sciabarra, Chris Matthew (2001, May). The Subtle Racism of "Jazz". *Just Jazz Guitar*. Retrieved October 29, 2018 from http://www.nyu.edu/projects/sciabarra/essays/jazz.htm

Scutti, Susan (2017, August 8). Study casts doubt on music therapy for kids with autism. *CNN*. Retrieved March 10, 2018 from https://www.cnn.com/2017/08/08/health/autism-music-therapy-study/index.html

Sedaka, Neil. The Immigrant (lyrics). *Google*. Retrieved December 12, 2018 from https://www.google.com/search?source=hp&ei=U-EbX JLXKKTD0PEPz9qh6AQ&q=the+immigrant+by+neil+sedaka+ lyrics&oq=the+immigrant+by+neil+&gs_l=psy-ab.1.1.0l2j0i22i 30l2.2222.6212..8689...0.0..0.64.1121.22......0....1..gws-wiz.....0..0i131j0i1 0j0i22i10i30.Axyp8COyXtQ

Shapreau, Carla (2014, August). The Austrian Copyright Society and Black-listing During the Nazi Era. *The Orel Foundation*. Retrieved September 6, 2018 from http://orelfoundation.org/journal/journalArticle/the_austrian_copyright_society_and_blacklisting_during_the_nazi_era

Shepherd, Katie (2018, October 16). Portland Mayor Proposes Emergency Rules to Keep Warring Protest Groups from Beating People in the Streets.

Willamette Week. Retrieved November 11, 2018 from https://www.wweek. com/news/city/2018/10/15/portland-mayor-adopts-emergency-rules-to-keep-warring-protest-groups-from-beating-people-in-the-streets/

Sherwell, Phillip. Garbrielle Giffords: How music therapy is helping her recovery (2011, February 26). *telegraphj.co.uk.* Retrieved July 30, 2017 from http://www.telegraph.co.uk/news/worldnews/northamerica/usa/8349351/ Garielle-Giffords-How-music-therapy-is-helping-her-recovery.html

She's a Little Bit Classical, He's a Little Bit Rock & Roll, *Rainbow Bridge Music Studio,*Retrieved 8/31/17 from http://rainbowbridgestudio.com/who-we-are/

Shmoop.com (n.d.). Race in Country Music History. Retrieved October 9, 2018 from https://www.shmoop.com/country-music-history/race.html

Sikh temple shooting suspect Wade Michael Page was white supremacist (2012, August 6) (no author). CBS News. Retrieved October 28, 2018 from https:// www.cbsnews.com/news/sikh-temple-shooting-suspect-wade-michael-page-was-white-supremacist/

Simi, Pete and Futrell, Robert. American Swaztika: Inside the White Power Movement's Hidden Spaces of Hate. *Roman and Littlefield,* Lanham, Maryland, 2015

Sinders, Caroline (2017, September 27). There's an alt-right version of everything. *Quartz.* Retrieved September 28, 2017 from https://qz.com/1086797/ theres-an-alt-right-version-of-everything/

Skolnik, Jes (2017, March 6). A History of Anti-Fascist Punk Around the World in 9 Songs. *pitchfork.com.* Retrieved March 21, 2018 from https:// pitchfork.com/thepitch/1460-a-history-of-anti[fascist-punk-around-the-world-in-9-songs/

Skullbone Music Park *(n.d.).skullbonepark.com.* Retrieved April 16, 2018 from https://skullbonepark.com/

Smith, James L (2014, December 3). 'Klanbly Friendly' Tennessee: State Becomes Hate Tourist Mecca. *Southern Poverty Law Center.* Retrieved January 20, 2018 from https://www.splcenter.org/hatewatch/2014/12/03/ klanbly-friendly-tennessee-state-becomes-hate-tourist-mecca

Social Security Death Record. Felice Wolmut. Retrieved September 3, 2017.

Solomon, Alan L., Davis, William B., and Heller, George N. Historical Research in Music Therapy, 4th Edition. *The American Music Therapy Association*: Silver Spring, Maryland (2002)

Songs of the KKK (n.d.). Voices Across Time: American History Through Music. *voices.pitt.edu*. Retrieved September 22, 2018 from http://voices.pitt.edu/lessoplans/SongsoftheKKK.htm

Soprano Slated for Assembly (1961, May 7) *Statesman Journal* (Salem, Oregon). Retrieved September 3, 2017 from Newspapers.com

Soshensky, Rick. Personal interviews September 8, 2017 and January 23, 2018. Personal emails June 24, 2017; July 26, 2017; September 7, 2017; September 11, 2017; January 11, 2018; January 22, 2018; August 26, 2018; January 30, 2019. Rick also provided some additional materials.

Southern Poverty Law Center (2002, June 18). Music Manufacturer Boots Resistance Records. Intelligence Report. Retrieved June 23, 2017 from https://www.splcenter.org/fighting-hate/intelligence-report/2002/music-manufacturer-boots-resistance-records

Southern Poverty Law Center (n.d.). William Pierce. Extremist Files. Retrieved November 8, 2017 from https://www.splcenter.org/fighting-hate/extremist-files/individual/william-pierce

Southern Poverty Law Center (n.d.). April Gaede. Extremist Files. Retrieved March 23, 2019 from https://www.splcenter.org/fighting-hate/extremist-files/individual/april-gaede

Southern Poverty Law Center (2002, March 5). Author Kathleen Blee Discusses the Role of Women in White Supremacist Groups. *The Intelligence Report*. Retrieved March 2, 2019 from https://www.splcenter.org/fighting-hate/intelligence-report/2002/author-kathleen-blee-discusses-role-women-white-supremacist-groups

Southern Poverty Law Center (2011, November 15). Pop-Singing Gaede Twins Renounce Racism. The Intelligence Report. Retrieved March 11, 2019 from https://www.splcenter.org/fighting-hate/intelligence-report/2011/pop-singing-gaede-twins-renounce-racism

Southern Poverty Law Center (2011, June 17). Racist Skinhead Leader David Lynch Slain in California Home Invasion. The Intelligence Report. Retrieved August 5, 2017 from https://www.splcenter.org/fighting-hate/intelligence-report/2011/racist-skinhead-leader-david-lynch-slain-california-home-invasion

Southern Poverty Law Center (2013, August 21) The Blotter. Updates on Extremism and The Law. Retrieved August 23, 2018 from https://www.splcenter.org/intelligence-report/2018/holy-hate-far-right's-radicalization-religion?page=29

Southern Poverty Law Center (2014, February 25). Why They Join. The Intelligence Report. Retrieved March 25, 2018 from https://www.splcenter.org/fighting-hate/intelligence-report/2014/why-they-join

Southern Poverty Law Center (2015, March 9). iTunes Dumps Hate Music, But Spotify and Amazon Still Selling. Intelligence Report. Retrieved March 25, 2018 from https://www.splcenter.org/fighting-hate/intelligence-report/2015/itunes-dumps-hate-music-spotify-and-amazon-still-selling

Southern Poverty Law Center (2017). Ten Ways to Fight Hate: A Community Resource Guide. Retrieved August 17, 2018 from https://www.splcenter.org/20170814/ten-ways-fight-hate-community-response-guide?gclid=EAIaIQobChMI8MH36-714QIVFtVkCh1TfgYDEAAYAS-AAEgL_yfD_BwE

Stanglin, Doug and Ingersoll, Stephanie (2017, October 29). White nationalists rally in 2 Tenn. cities. USA Today. Page 1B.

Stern, Alexandra Minna (2016, January 7). That Time The United States Sterilized 60,000 Of Its Citizens. Huffington Post. Retrieved March 5, 2019 from https://www.huffingtonpost.com/entry/sterilization-united-states_us_568f35f2e4b0c8beacf68713

Steven (no last name) (2006, November 19). Death in June: a Nazi band?—Midwest Unrest. Libcom.org. Retrieved September 17, 2017 from https://libcom.org/library/death-in-june-a-nazi-band

Stephenkuusisto.com (2017, November 12). Why I can't forgive John Lennon. Retrieved February 11, 2018 from https://stephenkuusisto.com/category/music/

Stevens, Ray (n.d.). Come to the U.S.A (lyrics). letssingit.com. Retrieved December 12, 2018 from https://www.letssingit.com/ray-stevens-lyrics-come-to-the-u.s.a.-8n4h32v

Stewart, Scott (n.d.). 'Ignore Them:' Pulaski Has Legacy of Success Dealing with Unwanted Groups. Giles News. Retrieved April 3, 2018 from https://gilesnews.com/news/ignore-them-pulaski-has-legacy-of-success-dealing-with-unwanted-groups/

Strauss, Neil (2001, May 30). Concerts Rock the Tiny Kingdom of Skullbonia; A Music Park in Rural Tennessee Draws the Stars, Liquor, and White Supremacists. New York Times. Retrieved April 3, 2018 from https://www.nytimes.com/2001/05/30/arts/concerts-rock-tiny-kingdom-skullbonia-music-park-rural-tennessee-draws-stars.html

Storey, Kate (2017, January 10). Inside the Lives of White Supremacist Women. marieclaire.com. Retrieved March 2, 2019 from https://www.marieclaire.com/politics/a24163/white-supremacist-women/

Stormfront.org (2014,May 15). Get Some 88 question. Retrieved n.d. from https://www.stormfront.org/forum/t1041518/

Stormfront.org (n.d.). George Burdi, are you here?. Retrieved February 12, 2019 from https://www.stormfront.org/forum/t1263797/

Stormfront.org (2009, February 25). Racist Music Just a Download Away on Mainstream Music Sites. Retrieved June 23, 2017 from https://www.stormfront.org/forum/t575577/

Swash, Rosie (2007, June 14). Beenie Man, Sizzla and Capleton renounce homophobia. *The Guardian.* Retrieved April 13, 2019 from https://www.theguardian.com/music/2007/jun/14/news.roseieswash

2011 Tucson shooting (n.d.). *Wikipedia.* Retrieved July 30, 2017, from https://en.wikipedia.org/wiki/2011_Tucson_shooting

2017 AMTA Member Survey and Workforce Analysis: A Descriptive, Statistical Profile of the AMTA Membership and the Music Therapy Community. *American Music Therapy Association*, Silver Spring, Maryland

Taylor, Dave (2016, January 5). Is Hate Speech by Rappers a Protected Right? *Lifezette.com.* Retrieved October 8, 2018 from https://www.lifezette.com/2016/01/is-hate-speech-by-rappers-a protected-right/

Tempey, Nathan (2017, February 13). Right-Wing Skinheads Attack Grad Students At LES Bar Over Antifascist Cellphone Sticker. *Gothamist.* Retrieved June 23, 2017 from http://gothamist.com/2017/02/13/nazis_punch_back.php

The Alan Short Center-Arts for the Handicapped (n.d.). Program for Fatso. The Alan Short Center-Arts for the Handicapped: Stockton, California.

The Central Archive for the History of the Jewish People, Jerusalem. Microfilm of CV Archives, *Center for the Preservation of Historical Documentary Collection* (OSOBI), Moscow. Fond. 721, File 47.

The First Amendment. *PBS Culture Shock.* Retrieved March 13, 2017 from https://www.pbs.org/wgbh/cultureshock/whodecides/firstamendment.html

The Forgiveness Project (n.d.). Matthew Boger and Tim Zaal. *The Forgiveness Project.* Retrieved March 11, 2020 from https://www.theforgivenessproject.com/matthew-boger-and-tim-zaal

The Great Lecture Library. Dr. Deforia Lane. *Chautauqua Institution.* Retrieved September 18, 2017 from http://www.thegreatlecturelibrary.com/index.php?select=speaker&data=508

The Local de (2017, July 17). 6,000-strong neo-Nazi music festival sparks call for ban on far-right gigs. *The Local.* Retrieved October 30, 2017 from https://www.thelocal.de/20170717/6000-strong-neo-nazi-music-festival-sparks-call-for-ban-on-far-right-gigs

The man from...Soleilmoon! Charles Powne. *Muslimgauze.org.* Retrieved October 30, 2017 from http://www.muslimgauze.org/people.html

The Museum of International Propaganda (n.d.). brochure. Visited October 18, 2018

The Real Johnny Rebel Story—Part 1—The Rock N Roll Years. *YouTube.* Viewed September 16, 2017 at https://www.youtube.com/watch?v=OoM_OO4KN_4

The Real Johnny Rebel Story—Part 2—Hillbilly & Viking Years. *YouTube.* Viewed September 16, 2017 at https://www.youtube.com/watch?v=w3dYaqUlJuE

The Vandals (n.d.). The Vandals Lyrics. *plyrics.com.* Retrieved September 17, 2017 from http://www.plyrics.com/lyrics/vandals/crippledandblind.html

The World Staff (2018, December 26). A formerly anti-gay reggae star returns to Jamaica. This lesbian poet calls it 'complicated'. *PRI's The World.* Retrieved April 13, 2019 from https://www.pri.org/stories/2018-12-26/formerly-anti-gay-reggae-star-returns-jamaica-lesbian-poet-calls-it-complicated

Time, Place, and Manner Restrictions (n.d.). *The Free Dictionary.* Retrieved October 19, 2017 from http://legal-dictionary.thefreedictionary.com Time%2C+and+Manner+Restrictions

Todeskino, Marie (2013, May 31). The hateful side of Wagner's musical genius. *dw.com.* Retrieved September 25, 2018 from https://www.dw.com/en/the-hateful-side-of-wagners-musical-genius/a-16850818

Topic is Music Therapy (no author) (1972, October 21) *Statesman Journal* (Salem, Oregon). Retrieved September 3, 2017 from Newspapers.com

Travel Circuit (1957, September 18) *The Amarillo Globe-Times,* Retrieved September 3, 2017 from Newspapers.com

Tribune, Tn (2017, July 27). Community Groups Respond to the Presence of Extremist White Supremacist Conference in Tennessee Park. Retrieved January 20, 2018 from http://tntribune.com/community/community-groups-respond-presence-extremist-white-supremacist-conference-tennessee-state-park/

Tumblr.com (2013, January 14). Women Who Have Made a Difference Through Leadership and Service: Deforia Lane Biography. Retrieved Septem-

ber 18, 2017 from http://womenwhohavemadeadifference.tumblr.com/
post/40502500255

Tune Core (2013, May 1). Terms and Conditions. Received as attachment to
email, June 23, 2017.

Turn it Down (2011, December 15). *Nationalismofsound.wordpress.com.*
Retrieved October 7, 2018 from https://nationalismofsound.wordpress.
com/2011/12/15/turn-it-down/

UCLA Sheet Music Consortium. Visited at http://digital2.library.ucla.edu/
sheetmusic/

Ugwu, Reggie (2016, December 13). How Electronic Music Made by Neo-Nazis
Soundtracks the Alt-Right. *Buzzfeed News.* Retrieved September 28, 2017
from https://www.buzzfeednews.com/article/reggieugwu/fashwave

umwblogs.org (n.d.). The History of Music and Art Therapy. umwblogs.org.
Retrieved July 29, 2017 from http://musicandarttherapy.umwblogs.org/
music-therapy/music-therapy-during-the-great-depression/

United Riot Records (n.d). Visited June 23, 2017 at https://unitedriotrecords.
net/shop?olsPage=products.

United Riot Records (n.d.). Visited May 17, 2018 at http://unitedriotrecords.
blogspot.com/2017/09/united-riot-records.html

United States Holocaust Memorial Museum (n.d.). Music of the Holocaust,
Retrieved February 2, 2018 from https://www.ushmm.org/collections/
the-museums-collections/collections-highlights/music-of-the-holocaust-
highlights-from-the-collection/music-of-the-holocaust

United States Naturalization Citizenship Certificate. Felice Gertrude Wolmut.
Retrieved September 3, 2017.

University Hospitals Health System—Rainbow Babies and Children's Hospital
(n.d.) Music as Medicine: Deforia Lane, Ph.D., MT-BC. *musicamedicine.
com.* Retrieved September 18, 2017 from http://www.musicasmedicine.
com/staff/deforialane.cfm

University of Oregon. The Historic Sheet Music Collection. Visited at https://
library.uoregon.edu/music/sheet

US Constitution—5th and 14th Amendments. *FindUSLaw.* Retrieved August 10,
2017 from https://finduslaw.com/us-constitution-5th-14th-amendments

Valdinoci (2013, September 16). Why we don't like Death in June. New York
City Antifa, *World Press.* Retrieved September 17, 2017 from https://

nycantifa.wordpress.com/2013/09/16/why-we-dont-like-death-in-june/

Valdinoci (2016, December 21). Alt-Right Bonus Dox: New York's Racist Heathens. *NYC Antifa*. Retrieved May 4, 2018 from https://nycantifa. wordpress.com/2016/12/21/new-yorks-racist-heathens/

Vanac, Mary (2009, June 19). Deforia Lane: Inspiring patients through music. *MedCity News*. Retrieved September 18,2017 from http://medcitynews. com/2009/06/deforia-lane-inspiring-patients-through-music/

Very Special Arts of California (n.d.) Fact sheet (Document emailed by Alice Parente).

Vieru, Tudor (2011, January 22). Addiction to Music Has Biochemical Basis. *Softpedia News*. Retrieved March 10, 2018 from http://news.softpedia. com/news/Addiction-to-Music-Has-biochemical-Basis-179952.shtml

Voice Teacher Studies Mexico's Music, Dance (1956, September 3). *The Amarillo Globe-Times*. Retrieved September 3, 2017 from newspapers.com

vsa,weebly.com (n.d.). I Can Do That! (fact sheet). Retrieved September 23, 2018 from http://icandodthat-vsa.weebly.com/

Wallace, Hunter (2013, July 27). Why Women Reject White Nationalism. *Occidental Dissent*. Retrieved March 6, 2019 from http://www.occidentaldis-sent.com/2013/07/27/why-women-reject-white-nationalism-movement/

Washington Post Staff (2017, August 18) Deconstructing the symbols and slogans spotted in Charlottesville. *Washington Post*. Retrieved October 26, 2017 from https://www.washingtonpost.com/graphics/2017/local/charlottesville-videos/?utm_term=.2c6f13e133fb

Weinstein, Adam (2012, August 6). The Sikh Temple Shooter's Racist Tattoos, Deciphered. *Mother Jones*. Retrieved June 23, 2017 from https://www.motherjones.com/crime-justice/2012/08/wade-michael-page-tattoos-sikh-temple-shooting/

Weiss, Jessica (2017, August 16). Why do white supremacists hate (white) jews so much? *Univision*. Retrieved February 2, 2018 from https://www.univision.com/univision-news/united-states/why-do-white-supremacists-hate-white-jews-so-much

Welcome to the City of Kingston, NY. *Kingston-NY.gov,* Retrieved June 15, 2018 from https://www.kingston-ny.gov/11648/11089/11091/default.aspx

West, Aaron (2016, November 15). Ref stops La Liga game due to fans' racist chants at Athletic Bilbao's Inaki Williams. *Fox Sports*. Retrieved January 22, 2018 from https://www.foxsports.com/soccer/story/ref-stops-la-liga-game-due-to-fans-racist-chants-at-athletic-bilbaos-inaki-williams-082116

Westfall, Sandra Sobieraj (2015, February 24). Gabby Giffords Says Music Therapy Has Helped Her Recovery. *People*. Retrieved July 30, 2017 from http://people.com/crime/gabby-giffords-says-music-therapy-has-helped-her-recover/

Whelan, Brian (2013, September 24). Ian Stuart Donaldson and a Legacy of Hate. *Channel 4 News*. Retrieved January 28, 2019 from https://www.channel4.com/news/ian-stuart-donaldson-a-legacy-of-hate

White Pride Blog by Micetrap Distribution, LLC (n.d.) (no author) web site no longer available.

Wikipedia. African Americans in Tennessee. Retrieved April 3, 2018 from https://enwikipedia.org/wiki/African_Americans_in_Tennessee

Wikipedia. Aktion T4. Retrieved March 5, 2019 from https://en.wikipedia.org/wiki/Aktion_T4

Wikipedia. American Front. Retrieved August 5, 2017 from https://en.wikipedia.org/wiki/American_Front

Wikipedia. Anaheim, California. Retrieved August 14, 2017 from https://en.wikipedia.org/wiki/Anaheim_California

Wikipedia. Anti-Irish sentiment. Retrieved December 20, 2018 from https://en.wikipedia.org/wiki/Anti-Irish_sentiment

Wikipedia. Billy Taylor. Retrieved October 19, 2018 from https://en.wikipedia.org/wiki/Billy_Taylor

Wikipedia. Boyd Rice. Retrieved September 17, 2017 from https://en.wikipedia.org/wiki/Boyd_Rice

Wikipedia. Charles Mingus. Retrieved October 29, 2018 from https://en.wikipedia.org/wiki/Charles_Mingus

Wikipedia. Death in June. Retrieved September 17, 2017 from https://en.wikipedia.org/wiki/Death_in_June

Wikipedia. Disability Hate Crime. Retrieved September 17, 2017 from https://en.wikipedia.org/wiki/Disability_hate_crime

Wikipedia. Dixie (song). Retrieved July 2, 2018 from https://en.wikipedia.org/wiki/Dixie_(song)

Wikipedia. Douglas P. Retrieved September 17, 2017 from https://en.wikipedia.org/wiki/Douglas_P.

Wikipedia. George Burdi. Retrieved November 8, 2017 from https://en.wikipedia. org/wiki/George_Burdi

Wikipedia. Ian Stuart Donaldson. Retrieved January 28. 2019 from https:// en,wikipedia.org/wiki/Ian_Stuart_Donaldson

Wikipedia. Intimidation One. Retrieved April 14, 2018 from https://translate. google.com/translate?hl=en&sl=de&u=https://de.wikipedia.org/wiki/ Intimidation_One&prev=search

Wikipedia. Jim Crow (character). Retrieved September 21, 2018 from https:// en/wikipedia.org/wiki/Jim_Crow_(character)

Wikipedia. Life After Hate. Retrieved March 17, 2020 from https://en.wikipedia. org/wiki/Life_After_Hate

Wikipedia. List of neo-Nazi bands. Retrieved October 30, 2017 from https:// en.wikipedia.org/wiki/List_of_neo-Nazi_bands\

Wikipedia. Misogyny in rap music. Retrieved October 8, 2018 from https:// enwikipedia.org/wiki/Misogyny_in_rap_music

Wikipedia. Music and Politics. Retrieved September 10, 2017 from http://www. wow.com/wiki/Muic_and_politics

Wikipedia. Oi!. Retrieved October 10, 2017 from https://en.wikipedia.org/ wiki/Oi!

Wikipedia. Parents Music Resource Center. Retrieved April 1, 2018 from https:// en.wikipedia.org/wiki/Parents_Music_Resource_Center

Wikipedia. Reichsmusikkammer. Retrieved November 10, 2018 from https:// en.wikipedia.org/wiki/Reichsmusikkammer

Wikipedia. Posi Music. Retrieved August 11, 2017 from https://en.wikipedia. org/wiki/Posi_music

Wikipedia. Prussian Blue (duo). Retrieved March 11, 2019 from https:// en.wikipedia.org/wiki/Prussian_Blue_(duo)

Wikipedia. Resistance Records. Retrieved November 8, 2017 from https:// en.wikipedia.org/wiki/Resistance_Records

Wikipedia. Rock Against Racism. Retrieved October 30, 2017 from https:// en.wikipedia.org/wiki/Rock_Against_Racism

Wikipedia. San Rafael, California. Retrieved November 1, 2018 from https:// en.wikipedia.org/wiki/San_Rafael_California

Wikipedia. Stop Murder Music. Retrieved April 10, 2019 from https://en.wikipedia.org/wiki/Stop_Murder_Music

Wikipedia. Strange Fruit. Retrieved October 29, 2018 from https://en.wikipedia.org/wiki/Strange_Fruit

Wikipedia. Tennessee. Retrieved April 3, 2018 from https://en.wikipedia.org/wiki/Tennessee

Wikipedia. White Power Music. Retrieved October 28, 2018 from https://en.wikipedia.org/wiki/White_power_music

Wikipedia. White Power Music. Retrieved September 10, 2017 from http://www.wow.com/wiki/Segregation_music

Wikipedia. Willis Carto. Retrieved November 8, 2017 from https://en.wikipedia.org/wiki/Willis_Carto

Wikipedia. Yekaterinburg, retrieved 8/31/17 from https://en.wikipedia.org/wiki/Yekaterinburg

Williams, Don (1956, February 13). Former Opera Singer Praises Voices of Amarillo's Youth. The Amarillo Globe-Times, Retrieved September 3, 2017 from Newspapers.com

Williams, Jennifer; Ward, Alex,; Kirby, Jen; and Sakuma Amanda (2019, March 18). Christchurch mosque shooting: what we know so far. *Vox.* Retrieved April 16, 2019 from https://www.vox.com/world/2019/3/14/18266624/christchurch-mosque-shooting-new-zealand-gunman-what-we-know

Wilson, Cassie and Laurent, Lu (2016, September 7). Accessibility in the Music Scene: An Introduction to Ableism. *kryptonitemusic.com.* Retrieved February 11, 2018 from https://kryptonitemusic.com/2016/07/13/accessibility-in-the-music-scene-an-introduction-to-ableism/

Winnwalker, Jodi. Personal interviews October 26, 2017 and January 31, 2018. Personal emails July 26, 2017; July 27, 2017; August 29, 2017; October 31, 2017; January 23, 2018; May 7, 2018; January 30, 2019. Jodi also sent additional materials.

Wynberg, Simon (2011, December). Music, Conscience, Accountability, and the Third Reich. *The Orel Foundation.* Retrieved September 6, 2018 from http://orelfoundation.org/journal/journalArticle/music_conscience_accountability_and_the_third_reich

Yaccino, Steven; Schwirtz, Miachael; and Santora, Marc (2012, August 5). Gunman Kills 6 at a Sikh Temple Near Milwaukee. *New York Times.*

Retrieved March 23, 2018 from https://www.nytimes.com/2012/08/06/us/shooting-reported-at-temple-in-wisconsin.html

Yahoo! Answers (n.d.). What are some jazz songs on racism? *Answers.yahoo.com*. Retrieved October 29, 2018 from https://answers.yahoo.com/question/index?qid=20090815233602AAVfeqD&guccounter=1

Youngland (n.d.). Fight to the End (lyrics). *Mojim.com*. Retrieved December 12, 2018 from https://mojim.com/usy192111x1x1.htm

Zaitchik, Alexander (2007, January 16). Former Hate Rocker Anthony Pieront Targets Old Colleagues in New Project. *The Intelligence Report, Southern Poverty Law Center*. Retrieved March 14, 2018 from https://www.splcenter.org/fighting-hate/intelligence-report/2007/former-hate-rocker-anthony-pierpont-targets-old-colleagues-new-project

ABOUT THE AUTHOR

Ted Ficken, PhD, CPHQ, MT-BC/L
Contact the Author at:
Email: tedficken@tedfickenmusic.org
Linkedin: Ted Ficken
Website: tedfickenmusic.org

Ted Ficken is an author, speaker, professor, and consultant. He has been a credentialed music therapist since 1974, with bachelor's and master's degrees in music therapy from the University of Kansas. He completed his Ph.D. in Public Health at Oregon State University in 2003. Between volunteer work, internship, and employment Ted has worked at ten different healthcare facilities in five states: California, Kansas, Oregon, Minnesota, and Arizona.

As a Music Therapist-Board Certified/Licensed (MT-BC/L) he has been an active member of NAMT and AMTA. Ted has served as the Vice President of the Great Lakes Region, and President of the Western Region. He served on the original Certification Board for Music Therapists. He has written articles and book reviews for music therapy journals and contributed a chapter to the book *Music Therapy and Addictions* (Jessica Kingsley, London, 2010). In 2004, Ted received the Professional Practice Award from AMTA.

Ted has taught at Oregon State University and Marylhurst University. Ted became a Certified Professional in Healthcare Quality (CPHQ) in 1988 and currently teaches "Quality Improvement in Healthcare" in the online Master of Healthcare Administration program at George Washington University in Washington, DC.

Made in the USA
Middletown, DE
12 March 2021